BULSA SUNSUELIMA

EDITED BY RÜDIGER SCHOTT

FORSCHUNGEN ZU SPRACHEN UND KULTUREN AFRIKAS
RESEARCHES ON AFRICAN LANGUAGES AND CULTURES
RECHERCHES SUR LES LANGUES ET CULTURES AFRICAINES

HERAUSGEGEBEN VON / EDITED BY / PUBLIÉES PAR

RÜDIGER SCHOTT

BAND/VOLUME 2

LIT

BULSA SUNSUELIMA

FOLKTALES OF THE BULSA IN NORTHERN GHANA

EDITED BY RÜDIGER SCHOTT

SERIES S: FOLKTALES OF THE SUPERNATURAL

VOLUME 1: TALES OF THE SKY-GOD *(WEN, NAAWEN)*

PART I

LIT

Gedruckt mit Unterstützung der Deutschen Forschungsgemeinschaft

Gedruckt auf chlor- und säurefreiem Werkdruckpapier

Cip-Kurztitelaufnahme der Deutschen Bibliothek
Bulsa Sunsuelima
: Folktales of the Bulsa in Northern Ghana / Schott, Rüdiger. –
Münster ; Hamburg : Lit 1993
(Forschungen zu Sprachen und Kulturen Afrikas; Bd. 2.)
ISBN 3-89473-616-x

NE: GT

Dieckstr. 56 4400 Münster 0 251 / 23 50 91
Hallerplatz 5 2000 Hamburg 13 0 40 / 446 446

TO THE MEMORY OF

ALIM AFOKO

Front side: Mr. Ayieta Azantinlow, Sandem-naab and Paramount Chief of the Bulsa, teller of mythological tale No. 01.01. (p. 38-41). Photograph by R. Schott, October 1966.

THE EDITOR'S INTRODUCTION TO THE SERIES 'RESEARCH ON AFRICAN LANGUAGES AND CULTURES'

The present series presents the cultures of African peoples by publishing source materials in their own languages. This series brings linguists and ethnographers together in the common endeavour to publish oral traditions of African peoples: not only their 'oral history' but also their stories and fairy tales, legends and myths, proverbs, riddles and other texts in African languages, all with annotated translations and learned comments. Dictionaries are also to be published in this series, documenting not only African languages, but also the cultural heritage of the particular peoples. The aim of the series 'Research in African Languages and Cultures' is to contribute to the recording of Africa's spiritual wealth.

The editor of this series is delighted to present as the inaugural publication Dr. Franz Kröger's 'Buli-English Dictionary', a monumental work of erudition, dedicated to the language and culture of the Bulsa, an ethnic group in the North of Ghana. The Bulsa have been the object of the editor's ethnographic and linguistic research since September 1966. This undertaking has been supported by many Ghanaian and German collaborators working at the Seminar für Völkerkunde (Ethnological Institute) of the University of Münster in Westphalia, Germany.

Dr. Kröger's dictionary forms the foundation-stone for further volumes in this series, the next being the publication of Bulsa folktales. Altogether more than 1,200 stories were collected, transcribed and translated by the series' editor and his many Bulsa and German co-workers. These stories, as well as the Buli-English dictionary, bear witness to the astounding creativity of the Bulsa people, one of the many African peoples whose verbal art is a treasure that must be recorded and preserved for their children and children's children. The editor and his collaborators hope they have made a small contribution to the immense work that remains for anybody ready to help in preserving the oral traditions of African peoples before these riches vanish forever.

Contributions to the series can be submitted by anyone wishing to publish text materials in African languages together with translations in major European languages. All too numerous are the publications of African folktales in European languages only, frequently purged and adulterated for the use of children and ignorant adults. The present series shall only publish African texts and annotated translations together with commentaries that meet strict scientific standards. The editor is of the opinion that African oral traditions deserve to be treated with the same respect and dedication that research on any of the world's important cultural heritages commands.

Münster in Westphalia, Spring 1992 Rüdiger Schott

CONTENTS OF

VOLUME 1: TALES OF THE SKY GOD (*WEN, NAAWEN*)

CONTENTS OF THE PRESENT VOLUME

NUMERICAL INDEX

PREFACE AND ACKNOWLEDGMENTS

The publication of Bulsa folktales from northern Ghana testifies to the success of a long-term German-Ghanaian joint effort in the recording and preservation of African folklore.

When I first visited the Bulsa, an ethnic group of farmers and cattle holders in the dry savannah of Northern Ghana numbering about 70,000 people, very little was known of their culture and traditions in general, and next to nothing of the immense wealth of their oral history and tales, riddles, proverbs and other expressions of oral art.

The Paramount Chief of the Bulsa and Chief of Sandema (*Sandem-naab*), Mr. Ayieta Azantinlow, received me kindly in September 1966 and introduced me to his nation's oral history, which shall be published in this series at a later date. I wish to thank him warmly for the support he has given my research and that of my collaborators ever since. The first story published in this volume was told by Mr. Azantinlow in March 1967, shortly before my return to Germany.

During my first stay among the Bulsa, from the end of September, 1966 to the beginning of April, 1967, I began to collect Bulsa stories in a rather haphazard way, assisted by my interpreter, Mr. Godfrey Achaw of Sandema-Kalijiisa, who was keenly interested in the folktales of his people and a good storyteller himself. He wrote down some of the stories as they were told to him by other people in Buluk, the country of the Bulsa, in Buli, the language of the Bulsa. Most of the stories, however, he transcribed from the tape recordings in Buli which we had recorded together. He also added an English translation to each of the stories. Mr. Achaw's untiring assistance in conducting this work is gratefully acknowledged.

During and following my second stay among the Bulsa, from the end of September, 1974 to the end of March, 1975, I received invaluable help from Rev. James Agalic, also from Sandema-Kalijiisa, and at that time District Pastor of the Presbyterian Church in Sandema. After my return to Germany, in 1976, Mr. Agalic worked with me for almost nine months at the Seminar für Völkerkunde (Institute of Ethnology) at the University of Münster in West Germany. He transcribed and translated many stories which I had collected and tape recorded during my previous stays among the Bulsa. Mr.

Agalic himself had recorded quite a number of stories on tape, which he added to my collection.

I have developed close ties with Mr. Agalic and other Bulsa collaborators, all of us sharing a common interest in preserving as much of the cultural heritage of the Bulsa people as possible in this age of rapid cultural and social change - for the benefit of future Bulsa generations as well as for the African and international public in general.

Further immeasurable help in translating the Bulsa stories and in preparing their publication was rendered by Mrs. Margaret Lariba Arnheim. A native of Gbedem, located in the centre of Bulsa territory, she came to Germany in 1979, intending to complete her training as a nurse. Ever since her arrival, as far as time has permitted, she has untiringly assisted me and my former student and present colleague, Dr. Franz Kröger. His Buli-English Dictionary[1)] has been published as Volume 1 of this series of Research on African Languages and Cultures. Without the constant help of Mrs. Margaret L. Arnheim we would not have succeeded in our endeavours on the language and culture of the Bulsa.

During a further stay among the Bulsa from September 1988 until March 1989, I recorded the bulk of the Bulsa stories which are to be published in the present series. With the help of Mr. James Agalic, who was granted leave of absence from his position as Research Officer at the Institute of African Studies, University of Ghana, Legon, Accra, more than 1,000 Bulsa stories were tape recorded from tellers in many Bulsa towns and villages. I would like to express my gratitude to Prof. Kwame Arhin, Director of the above-mentioned institute, for granting Mr. James Agalic permission to engage in fieldwork with me.

From January to March 1989, Dr. Sabine Dinslage took part in our ethnographic fieldwork among the Bulsa; in a relatively short period of time, she recorded more than 200 Bulsa stories and songs in Sandema-Kalijiisa and in Sandema-Kobdem. We were both assisted by many Bulsa helpers, among them Mrs. Melanie Akankyalabey, Headmistress of St. Martin's Junior Secondary School in Wiaga, Mr. George Akanligpare of Wiaga-Yisobsa, a student of linguistics at Legon University, Mr. Isaac Apaabe of Sandema-Kalijiisa, Mr. Akamara Atogtemi of Sandema-Longsa, who

1) From here on abbreviated as: Kröger BED. - The orthography of Buli words and texts used her conforms to Kröger's Buli-English Dictionary. See the Introduction to it, p.10-13, for explanations.

(1) Mr. Mouth died and they said that Mr. Leg (or Foot)[7] should come and take [him] and bury [him]. (2) Mr. Leg said that he would not take Mr. Mouth and bury [him]. (3) [Whenever] he used to take Mr. Mouth any place, he [Mr. Mouth] sat down and said whatever he liked.

(4) They said that Mr. Hands (or Arms) should take [Mr. Mouth] away and bury [him]; Mr. Hands said that he would not take Mr. Mouth and bury [him] because when he used to go and take [something] with his hands and took a thing of Mr. Mouth's [belonging to Mr. Mouth], Mr. Mouth grabbed it and took it away so that he came away empty-handed (lit. he was left).

(5) They said that Mr. Ear should take [him] away and bury [him]. (6) Mr. Ear said that he would not take Mr. Mouth and bury [him]. (7) Mr. Ear said: 'Mr. Mouth's doings were very evil. (8) When he [Mr. Ear] used to hear anything and wanted to talk, Mr. Mouth said that he should leave [it to him] and he would talk.' (9) This is the reason why he would not take Mr. Mouth and bury [him].

(10) They said that Mr. Eye should take [him] away and bury [him]. (11) Mr. Eye said: Not a bit of it! When he and Mr. Mouth went together and he saw something and wanted to take this (lit. his) thing, Mr. Mouth beat him to it, saying: (12) 'Look at my thing!' (13) Why then should he take Mr. Mouth and bury [him]?

(14) They said that Mr. Nose should take and bury [him]; Mr. Nose said: (15) 'Yes!'[8], he would not take Mr. Mouth and bury [him] because whenever he went and smelled (lit. 'heard' a smell) [something] somewhere (lit. at this place) and went to find out just saying: 'What is it that smells like that?', Mr. Mouth would quickly cut in saying: (16) 'What is it that smells like that?' (17) Therefore he would not take Mr. Mouth and bury [him].

(18) They said that if that were the case, Mr. Penis should take and bury [him]. (19) Mr. Penis said: 'Alright!' - he would bury Mr. Mouth; when they used to go to a girl's room, he lay in his nest (or sleeping place) whilst Mr. Mouth talked and talked and talked until he got tired, - when they climbed up to the *gbong* [platform roof of a room used for retiring at night during the hot season], Mr. Mouth offered (lit. took) him to take over; therefore he would take Mr. Mouth and bury [him].

(20) Mr. Testes said that although he could not have fun together [with Mr. Penis] (lit. help [him] to eat), while Mr. Mouth used to talk, he also came and stood at the entrance and peeped and watched - [therefore] he would help Mr. Penis dig the grave (lit. the hole). (21) And Mr. Penis and Mr. Testes helped each other, took Mr. Mouth and buried [him].

(22) This is the reason (lit. origin) [for the fact that] if you go to see a woman, Mr. Mouth will begin [to talk] and Mr. Penis all of a sudden gets up and stands. (23) This is [also] the reason [for the fact] that if a man dies, he will not [be left] to rot; when this happens [i.e. when he dies], he will [always] find someone (lit. a man) and will be buried (lit. so that they bury him).

---

7) Alternative translations of polysemantic lexemes are put in round brackets, short additions to the text and emendations not contained in the Buli text are put in square brackets. More detailed explanations are put in footnotes.

8) This must be a mistake; it should be 'No!'

Some of the technical details of the treatment a story like this receives in our research project shall now be discussed: The data pertaining to each story are filed according to a Data Scheme (see Appendices II and III, p. 258-261) which lists (01.) the address of the institute which prepared the file, (02.) the date it was last worked on and (03.) the collaborators who worked on it[9)].

Each story receives (04.) a code number and (05.) a title. Since most African stories are not given titles or headlines by their tellers, we try to render the essentials of the story in as short a form as possible, for example in the present case: Penis accepts to bury Mouth. We then provide (06.) the original African language in which the story was told and (07.) its linguistic affiliation, in the present case: Buli, the language of the Bulsa, a Gur language of the More-Dagbani family. We then indicate (08.) the translation(s) in which the story is available, i.e. in this case English. Then we give (09.) the source of the story, i.e. the publication(s) where it has appeared in print, or, if not yet printed, where the manuscript can be found. If the story has been published elsewhere, (10.) the bibliographic reference is quoted. We further note (11.) the place and (12.) date of the recording and (13.) who recorded it and (14.) whether it was taped (with the number of the tape) or handwritten.

After these more technical data there follows an entry with remarks on (15.) the telling conditions and the 'biology' of the tale[10)]; in the present case the tale was told in the presence of several men (no women were present), and Mr. Agalic noted: 'The atmosphere was cordial - all were relaxed.' Concerning the performance of the telling of this tale, one notes from the tape recording much laughter among the audience.

In the Buli texts and in the English translations, every sentence has been given a number, which facilitates the comparison between the two versions. Peculiar to the storytelling of the Bulsa is the custom that every sentence told by the teller will be repeated, one after another, by someone from the audience, designated henceforth as the 'repeater'. If, in rare cases, the repeater (b) diverges from what the teller (a) has said, this will be marked correspondingly after the sentence number.

---

9) These 'internal' data are not published in the Appendix III.

10) Cf. Linda Degh: Article on 'Biologie des Erzählguts' [The biology of tales] in Enzyklopädie des Märchens, vol. 2, Berlin 1979, col. 386-406.

The (16.1) name and the (16.2) social status, the (16.3) profession and (16.4) the education of the (literate or illiterate) teller, his or her (17.) age and (18.) sex, (19.) the place of birth and (19.2) residence(s), as well as his or her (20.) ethnic and (21.-22.) linguistic affiliation are also indicated.

The tale is then classified according to (23.1.1) its theme(s) following our 'internal classification', which has been developed for the particular corpora of Bulsa and Lyela tales (see Appendix I). This classification is based primarily on the principal actors in the tales, but it also considers genres. The main categories of our thematic classification are:

(A) Animal Tales.
(B) Tales about (Parts of) the Body.
(F) Formula Tales.
(H) Humorous Tales, Jokes and Anecdotes.
(L) Legends.
(M) Men and Their Social Relations.
(P) Tales about Plants.
(R) Riddles.
(S) Tales of the Supernatural.
(W) Tales of the Wise and the Foolish.
(Y) Mythological Tales.

Most of these principal categories are further subdivided, e.g. the story quoted is classified under (BS) Tales about Sex. Likewise, it is classified under (H) Humorous Tales and (WM) Tales of Wisdom and Morals. As most of the stories cannot be classified unequivocally, they have to be classified under several categories of themes accordingly.

For those folktales which have been recorded in several versions or variants we have tried to formulate (23.1.2) descriptors of types of the respective folktales in the sense of Annti Aarne's and Stith Thompson's 'The Types of the Folktale' (Aarne and Thompson 1961), that is, stories in which the episodes and/or motifs follow one another in more or less the same sequence are considered to belong to one 'type' of Bulsa folktales. This point, however, has not been analysed systematically; all respective entries must be considered as being provisional. These Bulsa tale-types are classified exclusively according to motifs and episodes inherent in Bulsa tales without any regard to comparative data from other African or non-African traditions.

Many problems arise from the classification of Bulsa tales according to (23.3) the type indices elaborated to classify Indo-European tales, such as the aforementioned tale-type index of Antti Aarne and Stith Thompson (AaTh). In principle, this tale-type index is not applicable to African tales. Nonetheless, we have also tried to classify our African stories according to comparable tales of the Indo-European folklore tradition. The nearest analogue to our story 'Penis accepts to bury Mouth' would seem to be AaTh 293 'Debate of Belly and Members'. A list of the nearest equivalents of our Bulsa tales to the Aarne-Thompson 'Tale-Types' is given in Appendix VI (p. 402-404).

As one aim of our research project has been to establish a tale-type index for African tales comparable to the Aarne-Thompson type index, we have also noted similar tales and variants of the tale (23.3.1) from the same and (23.3.2) from other ethnic groups[11)]. In the present case, there exists a similar variant among the Wala in NW-Ghana, which was published by Mona Fikry-Atallah (1972): 'Oral Traditions of the Wala of Wa' under the heading: 'Penis accepts to bury Mouth'.

We are not only interested in the contents of the stories, but also in their structure. Under a further entry we have tried, therefore, to establish (23.4) the structural type to which the story in question belongs. For this purpose we have attempted to adopt and modify the structural-type index developed by Lee Haring in his 'Malagasy Tale Index' (FFC 231, Helsinki 1982). The story of 'Penis accepts to bury Mouth' belongs to Lee Haring's structural type no. 1. 'Tales in ascending structure', sub-type 1.2. 'Liquidation of social lack'. The keywords (24.1) marking the structural components of the story are designated after (26.) the summary or abstract of the story has been made according to its episodes. The structural keywords read in our case: INITIAL SITUATION / LACK / LACK LIQUIDATED / HELPER, COMPLICITY / EQUILIBRIUM / TERMINAL MARKER.

The editor of the present volume admits that the structural analysis of the Bulsa stories attempted here is a weak point of our work and open to critique. There have

11) Variants of the same tale-type recorded from other ethnic groups have only be mentioned if known to us. No systematic research has been done; this is an urgent desideratum of Africanist folklore research.

been debates in our team on whether to complete structural analyses at all in the form attempted here. The structural categories developed by Denise Paulme[12)] and by Lee Haring proved to be either rather inapplicable, or somewhat insufficient for the structural analysis of the Bulsa stories. We were forced to introduce new concepts, but these are often too close to the contents of the story as to reflect its *structure*. It made even less sense to introduce too many new concepts which would have made the comparison of the structure of stories impossible. Moreover, the subjective element became evident when two or more collaborators, undertaking structural analyses of Bulsa stories independently of one another, arrived at quite different 'structures' of one and the same story. The editor confesses to be highly sceptical of structural analyses, but he is ready to learn from his critics if they are able show him how to improve on this method. He is equally ready to dispense with the structural analyses in further volumes.

Point (23.5) indicates the gender categories; it is differentiated according to (23.5.1) 'emic' categories of the people themselves and (23.5.2) 'etic' or scientific categories. In many instances both kinds of terms only fit the genre of the story in question very approximately. The Bulsa have very few 'emic' categories for their narratives: *sunsueli*, pl. *sunsuelima*, a term which Franz Kröger in his Buli-English Dictionary (Kröger BED) translates as 'story, narration, tale, fable'; it is frequently accompanied by a song, the refrain of which is sung by the audience. This term is contrasted with *wa-magsi*, pl. *wa-magsima* '1. story (usually without songs, and with a problem or question at the end), parable, riddle [...] 2. proverb [...]' (Kröger BED). Even these two very broad categories are not exclusive, i.e. tellers are often uncertain which of these two concepts they should attribute to a certain story. There is a third category, *wa-togi*, pl. *wa-togma*, referring to a 'story without songs' (Kröger BED) which, however, is infrequently used. Our categories of 'fairy tales', 'Märchen' etc. are only approximations of what the Bulsa understand under the above mentioned concepts.

---

12) Morphologie du Conte Africain. In: Cahiers d'études africaines, vol. 12, p. 131-163, reprinted in: Denise Paulme: La mère dévorante: essai sur la morphologie des contes africains, Paris: Éditions Gallimard, 1976, p. 19-50.

The next point in our data scheme is (24.2) keywords or catchwords denoting all essential points of the contents of the story. These keywords are listed alphabetically[13)]. For the present story, the first entries read:

BUL-E0435 **Bury,** members of the body refuse to b. Mouth, only Penis accepts to bury him;

BUL-E0435 **Cooperation** between Mouth and Penis when they go to a girl;

BUL-E0435 **Die,** if a man d.s he will always find s.o. to bury him;

BUL-E0435 **Die,** Mouth d.s.; bodily members refuse to bury him;

BUL-E0435 **Ear** refuses to bury Mouth; etc.

The keywords for each story have been filed by the electronic data-processing technique to form an alphabetic index. In the present volume the keyword indices of the stories published here have been combined to form one common index in Appendix IV. The keyword and motif indices of the single volumes are to be registered in cumulative indices for each major theme and, at a later date, for the whole corpus of Bulsa folktales. This cumulative index may, in fact, be extended to comprise any other corpus of keywords referring to tales of other African ethnic groups.

We also classified (25.) the motifs contained in our African tales according to Stith Thompson's Motif-Index[14)]. This index, although criticized for various reasons by almost everybody using it, continues to be the only motif-index internationally recognized. With our work we hope to contribute to a general motif index of (West-) African

---

13) Originally, we tried to list the keywords and motifs with a modified d-base 3plus data processing program on our Personal Computers. This was later abandoned, as it proved difficult to integrate this into the text written with a WordPerfect program. The sorting function of the latter program seems to be quite sufficient for our purposes.

14) Stith Thompson: Motif-Index of Folk-Literature, Revised and enlarged edition, 6 vols., Bloomington and Indianapolis: Indiana University Press 1955-1958. - Due to the technical specifications of the computerized sorting program, all motif numbers had to be extended to four digits by prefixing one or more zeros to figures of less than four digits; after the point, a zero had to be added if no further number followed.

tales. This task, if undertaken on a larger scale, could only be accomplished in a long term project and with the international cooperation of many scholars. For any sound comparative work on certain motifs and topics in African tales, a motif index, whether by keywords or by a systematically ordered arrangement, is indispensable.

What are the risks and rewards of a motif and keyword analysis like the one attempted here? As the motif analysis of African tales was one of the main objectives of this pilot project financed by the DFG (see above p.5), I would like to elucidate in some detail a number of the problems we faced in analyzing the Bulsa and Lyela tales according to Stith Thompson's 'Motif-Index of Folk-Literature' and according to our freely formulated keywords:

1. The following difficulties are encountered when analysing the **motifs** of African tales:

1.1 The **motifs** listed in Stith Thompson's Motif Index are **too specific:**

For example, in trying to classify the motifs of Bulsa stories belonging to the African tale-type 'Girl marries snake', Stith Thompson's Motif-Index provides the motif K1911.3.6 'Snake adopts true bride thrown into well (India)', but not: 'Snake takes his bride into a forest'. I also found Mot. B103.4.2.2 'Snake vomits jewels', but not: 'Snake vomits his mother-in-law'.

1.2 The **motifs** listed in Stith Thompson's Motif Index are **not specific enough:**

This applies particularly to motifs listed in the sections P. Society and T. Sex, which are totally inadequate for African stories in which social relations play a prominent role. Thus, I had to list many motifs of the tales belonging to the type 'Girl marries snake' under the unspecified Mot. numbers P210+ 'Husband and Wife', P230+ 'Parents and children', P232+ 'Mother and daughter', P262+ 'Mother-in-law' etc. The same applies to the unspecified motifs listed under T. 'Sex', such as e.g. Mot T50+ 'Wooing', T200+ 'Married life' etc. In an African context, it seems absurd to list 'Married life' under the heading 'Sex', but this is only one of the many inadequacies of Stith Thompson's classification of motifs.

1.3 Many **motifs** listed in Stith Thompson's Motif Index are **inadequate** for the analysis of African tales:

As Stith Thompson indexed only a few African tales according to their motifs, the specification given in his index does not correspond to the specific attributes of the motifs in our African tales and therefore, in many instances, it proved difficult to classify the motifs we find in our Bulsa and Lyela stories according to that index. Following a suggestion made by Stith Thompson himself, we marked many, in fact the bulk, of our motifs with a + sign and a qualifying remark following the word ' ...; here:', as for example the story rendered above under Mot. A1350 'Origin of sex functions'; this entry in Stith Thompson's Index is qualified by us: A1350+ '... here: Origin of Penis' erection', or Thompson's motif no. D1610.5 'Speaking head', is qualified by us: D1610.5+ ' ... here: Speaking Leg', or Thompson's Mot. F547.3 'Extraordinary penis' is qualified by the addition: F547.3+ 'Penis accepts to bury mouth' etc.

1.4 Relatively few motifs resist any attempt at classification according to Stith Thompson's Motif-Index. Regarding the present story, we did not find in that index any entry that would allow us to classify the motifs 'Death of a bodily member' or 'Burial of a bodily member'. These **unclassified motifs** are listed at the beginning of the list of motifs under the abbreviation 'uncl.0000'.

In spite of these and some other difficulties and reservations concerning the analysis of African tales according to Stith Thompson's Motif Index, I would still insist that such a classification is useful and necessary. With all its oddities and inadequacies, Thompson's Index has at least two qualities which still make it an indispensable tool for tale analysis: It does not rely on abstract logical terms, but on concrete realities. Secondly, it is still the only internationally recognized motif index which allows a comparison of motifs on a world-wide basis. As every cultural anthropologist and ethnologist knows, any 'cross cultural' comparison is beset by a host of methodological problems and difficulties; the 'cross cultural' analysis of motifs in folktales is no exception. Yet, if we see any value in 'cross cultural' comparisons at all, we have no other choice but to use a 'meta-language'. In the present case this is formulated by Stith Thompson in his monumental 'Motif-Index of Folk-Literature'. *Faute de mieux* we have no alternative but to continue working with this Motif Index.

To overcome some of the problems of the motif analysis of our African tales, we have added, as shown above, an independent **keyword analysis**. This keyword analysis allows us to formulate motifs without having any restraints placed upon us by the pre-formulated motifs of Stith Thompson's Index. The single-sentence explanations attached to each keyword enable the user of the index to recognize related motifs in different tales and to discriminate between unrelated motifs appearing accidentally under one keyword. The user interested in ethnographically relevant motifs and/or themes may find the registration of motifs according to keywords to be more profitable than the registration according to Stith Thompson's Motif-Index. Under the keywords we can formulate motifs without regard to any preconceived categories that may force typical African concepts and ideas into an alien mould.

As we have tried to formulate one sentence for every keyword and a keyword for every important item coming up in our stories, our keyword index should ideally reflect the contents of our African stories in their entirety in a phraseology adequate to these stories. However, this is the ideal. In reality, the keyword analysis is also beset with many problems.

2. The following difficulties are encountered when **analysing keywords** in African tales:

2.1 The keywords are listed **alphabetically** and **not according to a hierarchical system.** It would seem desirable to establish such a system based pragmatically on a hierarchy of concepts.

2.2 The **phrasing of the sentences** explaining the keywords is left to individual arbitrariness, e.g. under the keyword 'Swallow' (= eat, devour) we find in one case the explanatory sentences: ' ... snake swallows his wife's mother' as well as ' ... snake-husband swallows his mother-in-law'. The semantic content of the two sentences is exactly the same, but it has been phrased differently. In an alphabetic catalogue, the two sentences appear at different spots. The entries need to be standardized, which makes for tedious work.

2.3 What shall we do with **synonyms**? Shall we list the quoted episode 'Snake swallows his mother-in-law' under the keyword 'swallow', or 'eat', or 'devour', or possibly under other lexemes such as 'gulp down', 'bolt' etc.? In some such cases we established **cross references.** But in the original language words may be synonyms which are not synonyms in the English translation. Thus, the Buli word *lie* means 'daughter' and 'girl', or *biik* may be translated as 'son', 'boy' or 'child'. In these cases we had to make an arbitrary decision under which keyword we would list the relevant motifs. 'Cry', with the meaning 'to weep', we have indexed under 'Weep', but 'Cry for help' has been listed under the keyword 'Cry'. In some cases, we had no other choice but to list synonyms twice or even three times.

2.4 **Homonyms** may also pose problems. The word 'swallow' as a noun means a kind of bird, as a verb it means 'to devour'. 'Arms' may mean 'weapons' or certain 'limbs'. In such cases we added the explanatory word in square brackets. The computer can then put the word in the right alphabetic order without confusion as to its semantic content.

2.5 **Complex terms** cause far more difficulties. The Buli word *kuli* means 'to go home' - should this be listed under the word 'go' or under the word 'home'? The word *ngmoruk* means in Buli 'rain', but also 'tempest', 'thunder', 'lightning', i.e. the celestial phenomena accompanying the tropical 'rain'. If we list the complex concept of *ngmoruk* under the sole term 'rain', we miss its semantic richness. Similarly, the word *nong* means 'friend of different sex', i.e. 'boy-friend' or 'girl-friend', but it may also be translated as 'lover' or even 'concubine'.

2.6 Other problems are caused by **compound words.** In the Buli text of tale no. E0265:100 it reads: '*Ni kan tiri n ba-zuisanga*!' which means: 'Do not touch my pubic hair!' The Buli word *ba-zuisa* is a compound of the root *ba-* which also appears in the word *badiak*, 'vagina, vulva' and the plural form *zuisa* of sing. *zuik*, 'hair'. Thus a more literal translation of the said sentence reads: 'Do not touch the hair of my vagina!' In this case I have made three entries under 'Hair', 'Pubic hair' and 'Vagina'.

2.7 Further complications are caused by **vernacular terms** that are difficult to translate or are untranslatable. Wherever possible we have listed the entries under the English term with approximately the same semantic content. Thus, motifs to be classified under the Buli word *daam* have been listed under the English words **millet beer**, or entries under the Buli word *saab* have been listed under the English term **millet porridge**, although the latter phrase is a very inadequate translation.

In other cases, there are simply no equivalents whatsoever in the English language, as for instance the word *bogta*, which I have listed under '***Bogta*-soup**', a kind of slimy soup or sauce prepared from the leaves of a Hibiscus species. The sliminess of this 'soup' or 'sauce' is its essential characteristic, rendering entries under the words 'Soup' or 'Sauce' inadequate.

Some of the vernacular terms designating fundamental concepts and/or frequently used Buli words in need of explanation have been incorporated into a **glossary** in Appendix VII for reference purposes.

2.8 In principle we have only indexed keywords which actually occur in the texts. Occasionally, however, we have also listed **abstract concepts** which do not appear expressis verbis in the texts. We have, for example, listed the word '**Jealous**, mother is j. of her co-wife because she has received gifts from her daughter's snake-husband', although the word 'jealous' does not appear in the text. The same applies to words denoting abstract concepts like 'Advice', 'Capabilities', 'Disguise', 'Disobedience', 'Envy', 'Hospitality' etc.

2.9 Another dilemma with which we were constantly faced was: How **detailed** should the keyword analysis be? Of course, all essential actors and actions, objects and places are considered and listed under keywords. But what is an 'essential' actor or action? How detailed should the explanatory sentences to each keyword be? Even a basic three-word sentence such as 'Girl marries snake' would demand at least three different entries. We have tried to avoid sentences in the passive mood. Thus, in the present case, the phrasing would be: '**Snake,** girl marries s.' and not 'Snake is married by girl'.

2.10 Subjective evaluations cannot be avoided when distinguishing between **important and unimportant items** in a story, i.e. what deserves an entry under a keyword and what does not? In Bulsa tale BUL-E0265 the father of the girl is referred to in sentence no. 4 only once; he is never mentioned again in this version of the tale 'Girl marries snake'. Yet in other versions of this tale-type the father plays a prominent role, and therefore I have also listed the unimportant father of the story BUL-E0265. The word 'Vagina' is mentioned incidentally in two stories of this tale-type, and even in these stories the vagina is of no importance at all to the course of events. Yet anyone interested in vaginas will be able to find them in these tales by consulting our keyword index. Things that may be unimportant in one tale may be of central importance in others, even in tales of the same tale-type. *In dubio pro verbo*: if in doubt whether to register a keyword or not, we have usually decided to do so. From the point of view of the user of the index it is very frustrating if he or she notices that the index is incomplete and as a consequence, he or she has to thumb through all the stories again.

2.11 Despite our concerted effort to register keywords as thoroughly as possible, a certain **arbitrariness of selection** is unavoidable. A subjective element plays a role when selecting and phrasing keywords. In order to mitigate the negative effects of subjectivity somewhat, the keywords listed for each Bulsa tale by one collaborator were checked and supplemented by at least one other collaborator.

I have spoken about the 'risks' of a motif and keyword analysis of African tales. What are the 'rewards' of this procedure? Does the pedantic listing and sorting of motifs and keywords constitute more than a kind of butterfly collection? I am convinced it does. By sifting the motifs and keywords carefully, we can see exactly what the central concepts of a tale-type are, and what, on the other hand, are minor details of secondary importance. Furthermore, we can provide answers to some of the central questions of African folklore research: Are we justified in speaking of 'Tale-types' which are characteristic of African oral traditions? What liberties do the tellers take in reciting these stories? An investigation of the minor details will shed light upon the kind and degree of variation which occurs in the telling of these stories. In an 'impressionistic' way we sense that there is such variation, but a careful analysis of motifs and concepts is required in order to ascertain its nature and extent.

Furthermore, if we wish to systematically compare the motifs of tales from various African ethnic groups with each other or the motifs of African tales with tales from other continents, a motif analysis is indispensable. As the Motif-Index of Stith Thompson is not adequate for such an analysis it must, at the very least, be supplemented by a keyword analysis.

Appendix III provides (26.) a summary of each story. This may be useful for those wishing to inform themselves about the contents of the stories without going into every detail of the text itself. These summaries served as the basis for our structural analysis of each story. The (24.1) 'structural keywords' are written in capital letters between each episode. Here again, a certain subjective element in analysing the 'structure' of a tale seemed unavoidable. Other problems of such a structural analysis were mentioned above.

In a further point of our data scheme we try to establish (27.) the 'messages' which the tales convey to the people listening to them. We distinguished between (27.1) 'explicit messages' and (27.2) 'implicit messages'. The former are formulated expressis verbis by the teller himself or herself and are usually added to the story at the end. In our story 'Penis Accepts to Bury Mouth' the teller concludes it with two explicit messages: (1.) He gives an etiological explanation of the different roles of a man's mouth and penis in seducing a woman and of the origin of the *penis erectus*, and (2.) the story proclaims that 'if a man dies, he will not be left to rot; when he dies, he will [always] find someone who will bury him.'

This latter sentence hints at (27.2) the 'implicit message', which is not expressed directly. Here, as in many other tales, the message is intended to drive home a certain moral tenet to the audience, which in our case may be phrased as follows: However selfish you are, there will always be someone who remembers something good you have done to him and who, by the maxim of reciprocity, will see to it that at least after death your body will not be neglected, but will be properly buried. The story may, however, also imply that unless you have helped at least someone during your lifetime, you cannot count upon being buried. Should you be a thoroughly anti-social being, such as a witch or a wizard (Buli: *sakpak*), eating the 'souls' of other human beings, your body will not be buried in the earth, but thrown into the bush to rot and be devoured by wild beasts.

Thus, the story 'Penis accepts to bury Mouth', on the surface an obscene merry tale of juicy humour, expresses a most serious message concerning a fundamental social norm, which even has religious connotations: the Earth, one of the mightiest religious powers according to the creeds of the Bulsa, accepts no one who has sinned against the fundamental precepts of social life. One of the most interesting, and at the same time most delicate tasks, seems to me to be the elucidation of the 'hidden' meanings of African tales. It can be said with almost total certainty that none of these tales can be understood 'unidimensionally'.

If, however, we want to investigate concepts of the body as expressed in African tales, we would need a broader comparative basis. With our data processing technique, for example, we could search for the word 'body' or certain parts of the body throughout our stories or use the keyword or motif indices accordingly. We might also wish to examine the contexts in which these words occur. The editor has applied this method in searching for the word 'God' throughout the corpus of Bulsa tales. Some of the findings of this search are published in the following Introduction to Vol. 1 of the Series S (Tales of the Supernatural): Tales of the Sky-god (*wen*, *Naawen*)[15]. I have shown there that the somewhat diffuse ideas of the Bulsa referring to a distant Sky-god called *Naawen* are much more distinct in their tales than in explications of informants who hesitate to express abstract views on his attributes and qualities which, on the other hand, the tales of the Bulsa referring to God formulate much more clearly.

Thus, in our opinion, the documentation of African tales and their analysis into keywords and motifs is not an end in itself. These works provide the necessary basis for using these tales as comparative ethnographic sources.

The first volumes of this series will be dedicated to Bulsa tales of the Sky-God, called *wen*[16] or *Naawen* by the Bulsa. These volumes will introduce the series S: 'Tales of the Supernatural', also containing stories about Earth-shrines (*tanggbana*, sing.

---

15) A German version of this was published under the title 'Gott in Erzählungen der Bulsa (Nord-Ghana)' in the Festschrift for Eike Haberland in Paideuma, vol. 35, 1989, p. 257-272 (Schott 1989c).

16) See glossary.

tanggbain[17]) and other 'supernatural' beings, about Death and the Dead, ghosts, ogres etc. A further series, M, will be a collection of Bulsa stories dealing with 'Men and Their Social Relations', such as stories about Marriage, Husband and Wife, Parents and their Children, Twins and Orphans, Chiefs and Handicapped People etc. In another series, A, many of the Animal Tales of the Bulsa are to be published. (See also Appendix I for a list of themes of Bulsa stories).

The present volume, to be published in at least three parts, contains *all* the stories of our corpus of Bulsa folktales referring to the theme 'God'. It seemed important to me to demonstrate the immense wealth of the oral tradition of the Bulsa by publishing the *variants* and *types* of tales treating the same *theme*. I have also printed some incomplete and distorted stories to illustrate the range of storytelling quality exhibited by the narrators. In rendering the stories as near to the version recorded on tape as is sensible, I also hope to transmit something of the atmosphere of the 'performance' of storytelling[18], although I am aware of the fact that unavoidably much is lost in transposing the spoken and acted word into written form.

On the other hand, I am of the opinion that the 'oral literature' of a people has the same value and dignity as the writings of literate persons. The testimonies of 'oral traditions' should, therefore, be treated with at least the same care and scientific scrutiny as literary products. African folktales have often been published as fairy tales for children ('Kindermärchen'). In fact, many of the Bulsa stories published here were addressed to this audience, and undoubtedly the pedagogic purpose of these stories is most important. But it would be foolish to consider these folktales only as 'childish' fables. Many of them contain insights into human nature, into the relations of man to the spheres of nature and the supernatural, and into social conflicts that far transcend the perspective of children. They reflect the world view of the adult Bulsa and in some cases they express truths that pertain to humanity as a whole.

---

17) See glossary.

18) Concerning this topic, I would like to refer the reader to the article by Agalic 1978, p.261-278.

INTRODUCTION TO VOL. 1:
TALES OF THE SKY-GOD (*WEN, NAAWEN*)

God (*wen*, *Naawen* or *wen-naab*) does not play a conspicuous role in the everyday life of the Bulsa in Northern Ghana. He receives neither sacrifices nor any other kind of veneration. It is true that one does often hear the pious wish: *Naawen le maari fu*! 'May God help you!' (or: 'God will help you!') or simply: *Naawen le maari*! - 'God will (may) help!' But it is hard to obtain any details from Bulsa informants concerning this helpful God.

If someone's life is in utmost danger, such as when a sick person is in a critical condition, this God will be invoked. From certain other customs and verbal utterances we may also conclude that the Bulsa regard God as the Lord reigning over life and death. If someone has died in a compound, his or her mat will be carried by two naked men into the cattle yard. The eldest son of the dead person, standing near the entrance to the compound, then asks the dead person, represented by the mat: 'Who has caused your death: your own children, one of your neighbours, the ancestors or any other supernatural power?' If any of these questions is answered in the affirmative, the mat, carried by the two men, will move forward towards the entrance; if it is answered negatively, it moves backward. If all questions concerning possible culprits have been answered in the negative, the mat oracle ends by the son asking the question: 'Was it the work of God (*Naawen tuima*) which has caused the death?' If this question is answered in the affirmative, the dead person has died a 'natural death' according to our secular concepts, but according to the beliefs of the Bulsa, he was called by God.

The Bulsa voice various opinions concerning the fate of the dead. Some informants say that their 'souls' (*chiisa*, sing. *chiik*) go to a certain realm of the dead (*kpilung*) which, in most cases, is thought to be situated beneath the surface of the earth, at a well or in a certain tree; every clan (*buuri*) has its own locality to which the dead go and where they remain (unless or until they return to be reborn). Other informants, however, believe that the dead go to God (*Naawen*) and some even told me that the dead are regarded as mediators between God and their descendants living on earth. However, I have not discovered what the ancestors actually do as mediators between God and men.

Dr Franz Kröger, my former student and present colleague has attempted to clarify the meanings of the words *wen* and *Naawen* in Buli, the language of the Bulsa. The word *wen* is translated by the Bulsa with the English word 'god'. Dr. Kröger has defined *wen* 'as being the force determining a person's fate. It always resides outside the person's body. Every *wen* is related to a definite person. After having descended from the sky, the *wen* receives sacrificial offerings of food [and beverage, RS]. The *wena* of dead persons receive their sacrificial offerings from the male descendants of the dead person.' (Kröger 1978:392[19]). Kröger has also interpreted the concept of *wen* as a 'religious concept denoting the "alter ego" or "personal god" of an individual.' (Kröger BED). This personal *wen* is also called *tintueta wen*, 'saliva *wen*', because the person receiving his or her *wen* in a particular ceremony has to spit on the stone representing this *wen*; a man three times, a woman four times. According to some informants, this personal *wen* comes from God (*Naawen*) or from the sky (*wen*).

Wen means not only the sky or heaven, but also the sun, and finally God, i.e. the High God residing in Heaven. In the latter sense, the Bulsa mostly speak of *Naawen*, the word being composed of *nààb*, 'chief', and *wen*, 'sky' or 'heaven', which thus may be rendered as 'Lord of the Sky or the Heaven'. (All Christian missionaries of all denominations have come to use the word *Naawen* for 'God'.)

Naawen is Lord over Life and Death. This is also made clear by the fact that if the personal *wena* (pl. of *wen*) of a man and his wife - as an informant said - 'do not agree, they will never have a child; if however, their *wena* agree, none of their children will die.' The informant continued: 'If your wife does not conceive, you may hold your (personal) *wen* and your ancestors responsible for that, because it is their duty to help your wife to conceive. If she does not conceive, you may know that this has been imposed on you by God (*Naawen*); you cannot help it.'

Many Bulsa names also express this belief in God's power over life and death, such as: *Awenate* or *Awanate* (God gives), *Akanvariwen* (One cannot force God), *Awenbiik* (Child of God). The latter name may be given to a child born in wedlock, but

---

19) Translation mine.

it may also be bestowed on one conceived by a woman out of marriage; in this case the child may also be named *Awentiirim* (Gift of God).

All this ethnographic information on the beliefs of the Bulsa concerning God is of a rather general and unspecific nature. Let us see if their stories, *sunsuelima* and *wa-magsima*, can teach us something more concrete about who or what God is and what he does according to the creed of the Bulsa.

I. GOD WAS NEAR TO MAN AND GAVE HIMSELF AS FOOD TO HIM

In one of the tales of the Bulsa (BUL-E1698, 01.01)[20] it is said that in the beginning of this world God was near to the earth and to man living on it. Man did not have to work for his livelihood because God gave himself to him as food. Whenever human beings were hungry, they would cut off a piece of him and eat it, i.e. his flesh. However, God imposed a taboo on mixing his meat with a certain spice; an old woman violated this taboo and that transgression brought the original, paradisical state of man to an end.

There are many parallel stories known from other West African peoples. They all proclaim one or several of the following messages:

1. In the beginning man had everything necessary for his livelihood without having to work for it. This corresponds to the Biblical message (Genesis 1, 29-30; 2, 8-9, 15-17; 3, 17-19).

2. According to some versions of the African myth, as in the one quoted from the Bulsa, God gave himself as food to man living on earth; in most versions, however, it is only said that God gave food to man in abundance and without his having to work for it.

3. As in the Biblical myth (Gen. 2, 17; 3, 1-19) one of the human beings infringes God's prohibition concerning the eating of a certain fruit, or, as in the case of the Bulsa myth, the use of a certain spice.

---

20) The first of the two numbers refers to the number under which the story has been registered, the second pair of numbers to the chapter and the number under which it is published in this volume, which will be divided into three sub-volumes.

4. As a consequence of this disobedience God - or the sky identified with him - withdraws from man on Earth. Many African tales contain this motif of the separation of Heaven or Sky (=God) and the Earth, and of God's retreat from the Earth. Man, living remote from God, is forced to suffer henceforth.

5. In the Bulsa myth quoted, this is attributed to an old woman who infringed a command of God. In an African society such as the Bulsa, old women past the age of childbearing may either gain high respect or are despised as being 'useless' or even pernicious to the younger generation. In a patrilinear virilocal society like that of the Bulsa, the women who have married into the clan of their husbands remain strangers there to a certain extent for the rest of their lives.

6. Man has had to work for his livelihood ever since his 'fall'; this work is considered as a punishment of God.

II. GOD HEALS INFIRMITIES

Although humans insulted God, causing his withdrawal from them, he is not considered a *deus otiosus*. Several tales of the Bulsa make it clear that on special occasions he actively intervenes in the lives of men. This, as a rule, he does not do himself, but sends one of his 'children' (*biik*, pl. *bisa*) or juniors, or, maybe, a bird, as for example in story BUL-E0510 (see Chapter 04.02) where God sends a bird which leaves a 'medicine' to cure a blind man from his blindness and a leper from his leprosy. The bird imposes certain taboos on the use of his 'medicine'. The blind man may not drink cow's milk and the leper may not laugh and clap his hands. Both break these taboos and return to their miserable states.

From this story we learn the following 'messages':

7. God can heal infirmities.

8. God punishes man for the violation of even seemingly trivial prohibitions.

9. God does not impose anything unreasonable on man. It is, therefore, man's own fault that he has to suffer the consequences of his transgressions if he does not obey the commandments of God.

III. GOD HAS POWER OVER LIFE AND DEATH

Several stories of the Bulsa express the message which confirms what we have heard from informants already:

10. God has power over life and death; God can resuscitate the dead.

In one Bulsa tale (BUL-E0455, Chapter 08.01), which my Ghanaian collaborator, Mr. James Agalic, recorded in Sandema-Kalijiisa from a young man, God sends a messenger to resuscitate a dead boy. Both he and his girlfriend, who tried to save him from the fire, were burnt to ashes. The boy's parents did not dare to go near the fire to save their son from it. Other stories of this type also end with the 'moral': the love of a friend is stronger than that of parents or brothers. More stories containing the motif of resuscitation of a dead person by God or his helpers are to be published in Chapter 08.

These stories and those in Chapter 03. also convey the following message:

11. God forces human beings to marry, i.e. to accept their social roles as a man or a woman.

In one such story (BUL-E0503, 03.03) a man refuses to marry any woman at all. God makes him marry his daughter, who transforms herself from dry wood into a half-woman. Later, she resuscitates the boy from the fire into which he is thrown by a jealous chief. In this tale it is God's daughter, and in the previous one it is a 'child' or 'son' of God, i.e. a member of God's family, who acts as a life-saver; in both cases God's love proves to be stronger than the love of the parents to their son.

In another tale (BUL-E0514, 03.04), a daughter of a chief refuses to marry any of her suitors. A leper comes to her house and she is forced to marry him. She maltreats him, but upon the death of her father, he retransforms himself into God and revives him. God gives the woman's father a tail with which he may revive dead people, but he must not take this tail into a house. A woman gets hold of the tail; it is put into the rafters of a house and its 'medicine' is spoilt. Ever since then, dead people have not been able to be revived.

From this tale we can infer several statements about God:

12. God may come to man in the shape of a despised leper or beggar.

This belief is meant to determine the behaviour of the Bulsa towards people who beg for alms as lepers, insane persons, beggars or unknown strangers: whoever turns them away may be turning away God. Regarding this, James Agalic (1978: 267) writes: 'Prominent among the ethics of the Bulsa people is the demand that one should take a positive attitude towards people like orphans, strangers and the handicapped [...] A man should not maltreat such people as he cannot be sure whether he is not in fact facing an ancestor or some other supernatural being who is appearing in that form to test him [...].'

13. God does not take revenge for unjust behaviour or rejection he has experienced from man. Rather, he gives his gifts irrespective of a person's merits. God is above retaliating misdeeds he experienced at the hands of human beings who are far below him.

We may also learn from the stories quoted that the Bulsa conceive bad luck, suffering and death not as the consequence of a personal 'guilt' or a 'sin' in a moral sense, but as a 'automatic' consequence of transgressions or violations of God's commandments, even if they seem to be morally irrelevant. We have seen before that the violation of a taboo, such as the spicing of God's flesh with *kaam*, the drinking of milk, the clapping of hands, and the keeping of a tail in the rafters of a house, has grave consequences. Again we may formulate the following message:

14. Man has to observe God's commandments even if he does not understand their meaning.

IV. GOD GIVES AND DESTROYS RICHES; HE HUMILIATES THE PROUD ONES

In one Bulsa tale (BUL-E0531, Chapter 06.02) it is said of a rich man: 'Because he was rich, he used to insult people. [...] He used to say that he did not know anything called 'God'. [He was asking himself:] Is he not able to farm, is he not able to rear animals [without the help of God]?' His superciliousness and arrogance was punished by God who miraculously transported him to a rock in a river from which he could not escape. We conclude from the beginning of this story:

16. Riches seduce man to act contemptuously and insult fellow human beings as well as God. In the present case the rich man even denies the existence of God; in a sinful manner he boasts of his own powers and abilities in the face of God.

17. God punishes the hybris of man by placing him in a hopeless dilemma.

In one tale (BUL-E0424, Chapter 12.01), to be discussed in the next section, God sends a horde of monkeys into the field of a rich man and lets them destroy it, apparently without any particular reason. God, asked by Mr. Toad why he had done so, gives no answer. From that episode we may infer:

18. God is not accountable to man for his deeds.

19. God acts in an arbitrary manner, but always in such a way that the proud are humiliated and the humiliated are exalted[21)].

This idea is apparent in a story (BUL-E0676, Chapter 05.01) about three brothers; one of them is an orphan. Their father gives them hens and goats; those of the orphan multiply, whereas the animals of his elder brothers do not or only sire male specimens. All three marry, and '[...] the senior son's wife gave birth to a baby girl; the intermediate son's wife became pregnant but miscarried. [However] the orphan's wife gave birth to twin boys', i.e. once again the orphan has good luck; the Bulsa prefer boys to girls. When the elder brothers attribute their bad luck to their father, he says 'that every man's *wen* is his *wen*[22)].' The story ends with the words: 'That is why it is said: 'Your *wen* [is] your *wen*; we do not share [our] *wena*[23)]. Even if you are an orphan, if your *wen* says that you [shall] arrive at a certain place [in life], you will certainly arrive there.'

---

21) Cf. 1. Samuelis 2, 4-8; Ps. 75, 7.

22) According to the beliefs of the Bulsa, every person has his own *wen*, which may be defined as a 'religious concept denoting the 'alter ego' or 'personal god' of an individual ... as this personal *wen* is also responsible for the person's destiny on earth, *wen* can also be translated by: destiny, fortune, luck.' (Kröger BED). See also the glossary.

23) I.e. every person has his own *wen*, and consequently his own destiny, his own bad or good luck.

The word *wen* is used here in the sense of the 'personal *wen*' mentioned at the beginning. Nevertheless, it may not be out of place to assume that this 'personal *wen*' stands in a certain relation to *wen* in the sense of *Naawen*, the High God.

V. NOTHING HAPPENS AGAINST THE WILL OF GOD; GOD IS THE ULTIMATE CAUSE OF EVERYTHING

The credo: Nothing happens against the will of God; that God is the ultimate cause of everything is proclaimed in several Bulsa stories, perhaps most clearly in the story BUL-E0427 (see Chapter 07.01) which begins with the words: 'There was a boy who said that if God does not permit it, a chief will never kill him.' The chief tries to kill him by many ruses and by leading the boy into temptation, but he does not succeed. Instead, the chief kills his own son in the end. This story proclaims at the end: 'This is the reason why if you want to do a certain work, and God does not permit it, if you don't call God's name in addition, but if you say that you will do this work all by yourself, you will not be able [to do this]. It is God who permits everything.'

We deduce from this tale:

20. Nothing happens without or even against the will of God; God is the ultimate cause (*causa prima*) of everything that happens.

21. Before God even the most powerful men on earth are powerless. God helps the poor and the helpless.

In the preceding story the connection between *wen*, in the sense of 'personal fate', and 'God' (*Naawen*) becomes quite clear: that which man thinks to be chance or accidental is in truth to be attributed to the will and working of God as the ultimate cause of all that happens. This idea is also expressed in some so-called chain-stories of the Bulsa, as in the following story (BUL-E0424, Chapter 12.01) mentioned above, which humourously treats the grave problem of why the almighty and loving God, the *summum bonum*, allows evil in his world, i.e. the problem of theodicy. I shall give a shortened version of this story here, leaving out the repetition of all the 'chain-links':

Mr. Toad had married his wife, who went by the name of Atatirigalii; she used to bring him food and water in his bush-field[24].

One day Mrs. Toad did not come to Mr. Toad in the bush; he almost died of hunger and thirst. When going home, he found Mrs. Toad lying on the road. He asked her: 'Why are you lying there?' Mrs. Toad answered: 'Look, it was the flat-headed Bush cow who danced and trampled on my waist and broke it - so I am lying here!'

Mr. Toad went to the flat-headed Bush cow and asked her why she had done this. Mrs. Bush cow answered: 'Look, a child was sitting in a tree, playing a flute, and it was so nice that I, the flat-headed Bush cow, danced, trampling on Atatirigalii's waist and breaking it, so that today she did not bring you water.'

Mr. Toad went to the boy who had sat in the tree playing a flute and asked him why he had done this[25]. The boy said: 'Look, black-eyed girls were standing in a river, laughing and shouting, so that I sat in a baobab-tree and played the flute and it was so nice that the flat-headed Bush cow danced and trampled on Atatirigalii's waist and broke it, so that today she did not take water to the bush for you.'

Mr. Toad asked the girls why they had been laughing and shouting. They told him that little mice had made them laugh because the little testicles of their children were dangling to and fro.

Mr. Toad asked the little mice why their childrens' testicles were dangling to and fro. The mice replied: The owner of a bushfield had burnt it, and therefore the little mice had placed their children in safety.

Mr. Toad went to the owner of the bushfield; he told him that a horde of monkeys had destroyed his bushfield, and therefore he had set fire to the field.

Mr. Toad asked the monkeys why they had done this. The monkeys said: 'Look, it was God who let us loose, telling us to go and destroy the field-owner's riches[26] and the field-owner set fire [to his bush-field][27], so that the *kantelisa*-mice took [their] children with dangling testicles; black-eyed girls standing in a river saw this and laughed and shouted and a boy sitting in a tree blew his flute so nicely that the flat-headed Bush cow danced and trampled on Atatirigalii's waist and broke it, so that today she did not bring water into the bush for you.'

Mr. Toad went to God who said: 'It was me who let the monkeys loose so that they should spoil the field-owner's riches and the field-owner set fire to his field ...' etc.

---

24) The Bulsa work their fields (*duk*, pl. *duksa*) in front of (*doning*) and behind (*nan-gaang*) their compounds (*yeri*, pl. *yie*) as well as fields on clearings in the bush (*talim*, pl. *talinta*); the latter may be situated at a far distance from the villages.

25) In the original version, the storyteller repeats all the 'chain links' of the story, trying to repeat them as quickly as possible in the right order - to the amusement of the audience.

26) *nganta*, lit. 'things'; see glossary under the entry *jaab*.

27) This refers to the common practice of clearing the bush by means of burning a plot (slash-and-burn cultivation).

As I have already pointed out, God did not give the toad any justification for his doings; instead he saw to it that Mr. Toad was taken back to earth on a rope.

From this we can draw the final conclusions:

22. God is also the primary cause of the most trivial occurrences; he always stands at the beginning and the end of all causal chains[28].

23. God even pays attention to such an insignificant and despised creature as a toad - which possibly, in this story, symbolizes the average Bulsa farmer and his wife.

VI. SUMMARY: ATTEMPT AT A PHENOMENOLOGY OF THE CONCEPTS OF THE BULSA CONCERNING GOD ON THE BASIS OF THEIR STORIES

Naawen, the High God of the Bulsa, is not a tribal or ethnic god like *Jahweh*, the Lord of the people of Israel. The God of the Bulsa is not a god who has revealed himself to his people, who leads his chosen people through history and who is infuriated by the sins of his people - a 'zealous' god. Neither is the God of the Bulsa a loving God of the New Testament, who sends his son to Earth as the saviour of mankind, or who founds a universal religion of charity. Nor is he the almighty God of the Muslims who has revealed his will through Mohamed, his prophet, in a Holy Book, the Koran.

According to the testimony of most of the stories quoted, *Naawen*, the God of the Bulsa, is above the trivial affairs of men in their everyday lives. At an early date he withdrew from man when one of his commandments was not heeded; he is above mankind, just as the sky is above the earth - often he is identified with the sky or heaven (*wen*). Being above human beings, he is not accountable to them for his deeds. On the other hand, human beings do not turn to him with their daily sorrows and needs, rather they appeal to the *wena* of their ancestors. Some informants regard them as mediators between God and man. As an elevated God he is above taking revenge on humans for their misdeeds, and is by no means a narrow-minded pedant who keeps tabs on the merits and sins of human beings who after their death punishes them for their sins by sending them to hell to be tormented by satan. These sadistic ideas, difficult to reconcile with the idea of a loving God, are utterly foreign to the concepts of God held traditionally by the Bulsa.

---

[28] This also comes out in another chain-story of the Bulsa (BUL-E0127).

The God of the Bulsa is above the trivial affairs of men, just as an elder (*kpagi*) among the Bulsa is above the foolish thoughts and doings of his 'children'. However, it must not be overlooked that in some stories the Bulsa god behaves like a human being. Thus, in one story (BUL-E0533, Chapter 08.04), God is depicted as the 'owner' or head of a compound (*yeri-nyono*): he has several wives, one of whom poses a difficult task to children who visit him from the earth. God himself retains their cows, which have gone astray, in his own herd. A cat who is grateful to the children shows them their own cows in God's herd. If they had not been able to pick out their own cows, which look exactly like God's own cows, from his herd, the children would have been killed. As, with the help of the cat, they succeeded in finding their own cows, God gives them one hundred cows from his own herd in addition to their cows. This may be seen as proof of God's magnanimity. However, God does not do anything miraculous in this story and in another version of it (BUL-E0407), it is not God, but a chief (*nààb*) who lets the children find their cows in his herd, with a cat helping them. The message of the story loses nothing of its validity when God is replaced by the figure of a chief.

In another Bulsa story (BUL-E0438, Chapter 01.04) fabulous and grotesque traits are intermingled with mythological statements: a child, born by ten women at the same time, wrestles with a water monster and conquers it. Son-of-Ten-Women and the monster (*kikiruk*) go hunting together. They leave the meat of the animals they have killed on a rock to dry. God sends his bull from the sky; he stealthily takes the meat from the rock and carries it to the sky. The Son-of-Ten-Women finally challenges God's bull. They wrestle; neither is victorious. In the end God pulls both of them to the sky on ropes. There, their dispute is to be settled; God himself shall act as judge. However, he is not in a hurry to settle the dispute in favour of one or the other. So, whenever Son-of-Ten-Women and God's bull meet one another in the sky, they wrestle. The sounds they make when wrestling are heard on earth as rain and thunder.

God has withdrawn to the sky; therefore, he is a distant God. That does not mean, however, that he is a *deus otiosus* who does not care at all about the doings of human beings. According to several stories, he himself rarely descends in order to effect something among them - except in the story where God changes into a leper in order to force the chief's daughter to marry.

As a rule, he sends one of his 'children' - a 'son' or a 'boy'; for all of these concepts the Bulsa use the word *bíík* (pl. *bisa*). This has nothing to do with the

Christian concept of God's son. In one story, a daughter of God forces her human husband to die and resuscitates him, and later on she saves him from the flames and brings him back to life again. In another tale it is a 'son' of God who, with the help of a magic tail, resurrects a child who was burnt to death. The same motif of the life-giving tail reappears in the tale of God who changed into a leper. God is Lord over life and death - this is the unequivocal message of these stories.

Moreover, the God of the Bulsa is a helpful God. In the beginning, he offered himself to man as sustenance so that he need not work for his livelihood. God can heal infirmities, as is demonstrated by the story of the blind man and the leper. God's helpfulness is also evident in the stories of the resuscitation of the dead. God and his helpers may use 'magic' means in performing their charitable acts.

It is man's fault that he forfeits the good things he receives from God as gifts. Man has not observed God's commandments. God issued commandments, but for the Bulsa these are not rigid laws like the Ten Commandments in the Bible, but rather trivial directions on how to act and what to avoid in certain situations or with regard to certain objects. God does not impose any unreasonable demands on man. If, however, man is foolish enough not to respect God's commandments, the consequences of his misbehaviour - his foolishness or his carelessness - rest with him.

These consequences are momentous: God withdraws from man forever and condemns him to work because he has used a certain spice together with the meat from God's 'body' against his will. God allows man to die irrevocably because one person did not observe his commandment not to take the life-giving tail of a cow or a horse into a room.

It seems doubtful whether one may speak of God's 'punishments' in these cases. As God is above the doings of man, it would be beneath God's dignity to punish him for relatively minor misdeeds. Whenever man violates God's rulings, the disastrous consequences result 'automatically', without any further interference from God.

This, however, does not mean that God is morally indifferent. Whoever does not comply to the fundamental orders of social life will be forced by God to take the right path. Nobody, boy or girl, is permitted to lead a life as a bachelor. Those who reject all suitors, being unwilling to bear the yoke of marriage, are sought out by God's daughter or God himself in a repulsive shape, as a half-woman or as a leper, who then forces him or her into marriage.

From several stories we learn that other kinds of self-conceit, arrogance and obstinacy are also punished by God. He withdraws from mankind when an old woman persists in using a certain spice against his will to make his 'meat' more tasty. God puts a man, who speaks in a blasphemous way about him and even doubts his existence, on a rock in a river and thereby in a hopeless situation. God, on the other hand, even talks to despised, insignificant creatures like a toad. The proud are humilitated, the humiliated are exalted.

The story of the boy who trusts in God and says: 'If God does not permit it, a chief will never kill him', most clearly conveys the message that before God even the most powerful men are impotent. God helps the poor and the helpless. And nothing happens against the will of God; God is the ultimate cause of everything.

I have divided the Bulsa tales of the Sky-God into twelve chapters: In Chapter 01. I have collected various stories with mythological motives. Chapter 02. contains ten variants of the tale type 'Girl(s) must not be killed', because God or some celestial being sent by God saves a girl or girls from being sacrificed. The next Chapter (03.) contains stories on the theme 'God makes Men and Women Marry'.

The theme 'God and the Fate of Man' is dealt with in the stories appearing in Chapters 04. ('God and the Handicapped') and 05. ('Three Sons and Their *Wena*'). Chapter 06. includes stories with the message: 'God is Omniscient - He Punishes Evil and Arrogant Behaviour'. In the following chapter (07.) there are stories proclaiming: 'God is Lord over Life and Death', comprising three variants of the above mentioned story 'God cannot kill a boy (or a man) against his will' and three variants of the story 'Friends promise to die together', but the surviving friend is prevented from committing suicide.

The last four Chapters (09.-12.) appear under the heading 'God and Animals' and contain stories about (09.) how the animals went to God, (10.) how a bird challenges God as to who can cry louder and (11.) chain stories beginning with 'A bird laid an egg into a mortar ...', and (12.) the aforementioned stories about God and the toad.

01. GOD IN MYTHOLOGICAL TALES OF THE BULSA

01. GOD IN MYTHOLOGICAL TALES OF THE BULSA

In this chapter, six folktales are presented which contain mythological motifs referring to the Sky-God *Naawen*. These stories are not 'myths' in the sense of sacred narratives about the origin of the world, man or natural phenomena. Rather, most of them could be classified under the genre 'merry tale' (German: 'Schwank') or 'Jokes and Anecdotes'[29]. In Aarne-Thompson's 'The Types of the Folktale' they could, however, also be classified under 'II. B. Religious Tales' (Aarne and Thompson 1981: 254-284) because although most of them are definitely funny, their messages proclaim religious truths of great import.

Thus, the first story (01.01) tells how in the beginning, man did not have to toil for his livelihood because God gave himself to man as food. However, God forbade the mixing of his flesh with a certain spice. An obstinate old woman did this; God (= the Sky) became angry and withdrew from man. Ever since then, man has had to work for his food.

The second story (01.02) is well known all over Africa[30]. It opens: '[At] the beginning of the earth ... God let Man die and come back, whereas Moon died and remained dead.' Dog failed to give God the message in time that Man wanted to go on in this way. While Dog dawdled, Goat went to God but told him that Man had said: 'Moon should die and come back whereas Man should die and remain dead'. God acted accordingly, and when Dog came to him with the right message later on, God was not willing to alter his decision.

The next story (01.03) shows that God is not only Lord over Life and Death of Man, but also over the forces of nature. A river argues that it could exist just as well without God. But when God withholds the rain and the river's children (the fish) all die, the river understands that it 'owed its very existence to God'.

In story 01.04 ten women give birth jointly to a son who names himself Common-Son-of-Ten-Women. He goes to fight with a monster in a river; after he has

29) This forms one of the major sections of Aarne and Thompson's classification of tales (Aarne and Thompson 1981: 374-521).

30) Cf. Baumann, Hermann 1936: 268-279.

overwhelmed it, the two of them go hunting. God sends his bull from the sky; it takes the meat away which the two have hunted. Common-Son-of-Ten-Women wrestles with God's bull; neither of them can fling the other one down. After four days, God pulls both of them up to the sky where they expect that God will proclaim the winner of their contest of strength. God withholds his decision, so they continue to fight. The noise they make causes the rumbling of thunder.

In story 01.05 Hare woos a chief's daughter. The girl's mother is prepared to give her away in marriage to Hare if he promises to let himself be buried when she, his mother-in-law, dies. Hare gives his word and takes the chief's daughter home. Shortly afterwards, his mother-in-law is said to have died. Hare cries; a being from the sky advises him to go in front of the chief's house and call God to give him a hoe, agricultural produce and the young of an animal so that he, Hare, may take it with him into the grave. When God gives the things to Hare, the people become afraid of being left destitute of all things they need for their sustenance. The chief's wife appears and says that she only feigned death in order to test Hare's honesty.

Chickens play a decisive role in the final story (01.06) of this chapter. God created man and woman, hen and cock. The human couple remains childless, not knowing how to copulate. The cock shows man how to do it, and the woman, desiring to have children, takes the initiative with the man. He, however, curses the chickens who then become the first animals to be slaughtered by man as a sacrifice. The story explains the origin of sacrifices.

Except in the first tale, which explains the origin of man's plight on earth, animals play a decisive role in all other stories: Dog and Goat for man's mortality, Fish in the argument between God and the River, God's bull fighting with Common-Son-of-Ten-Women as the cause of thunder, Hare as retainer of man's agricultural implements and produce and Chickens as man's teachers of sexual intercourse.

BUL-E1698 (BULI TEXT)

(1) [1] Ate [2] Naawen [3] jam [4] basi [5] nurba [6] la, [7] wa [8] jam [9] yueni [10] kama [11] ain [12] ba [13] kan [14] tom [15] tuini; [16] be [17] baa [18] de [19] ngandiinta: [20] wa-dek [21] ale [22] moata [23] teng [24] ate [25] ba [26] gebi [27] wa-dek [28] a [29] chim [30] ngandiinta. (2) [31] Wai-wai [32] kan [33] ngab, [34] wai-wai [35] kan [36] cheng [37] talim [38] a [39] de [40] a [41] boro. (3) [42] Ate [43] ba [44] yaa [45] nye [46] dila [47] de [48] boro [49] la, [50] wuu [51] ate [52] ku [53] ga [54] paa [55] ning [56] ate [57] wa [58] yueni [59] ain:

01. GOD IN MYTHOLOGICAL TALES OF THE BULSA

01.01 God as the Giver of Food and the Fall of Man

BUL-E1698 (ENGLISH WORD-FOR-WORD TRANSLATION)[31)]

(1) [1] when, before [2] Naawen (God, Sky-god[32)]) [3] came {also used for denoting narrative past tense, n.p.t.} [4] left[33)] [5] men [6] {marking end of subordinate clause, e.s.c.}, [7] he [8] {n.p.t.} [9] said [10] indeed {affirmative particle, a.p.} [11] that [12] they [13] not {negative particle, n.p.} [14] work {verb} [15] work {noun}; [16] should[34)] [17] they {+ particle denoting iterative or habitual tense, p.i.t.} [18] eat [19] food: [20] himself [21] will be {particle denoting future tense, p.f.t.} [22] near [23] earth [24] so that {consecutive conjunction, c.c.} [25] they [26] cut [with a knife] [27] himself [28] {p.i.t.} [29] become, turn into [30] food. (2) [31] nobody [32] not {n.p.} [33] grind [millet], [34] nobody [35] not {n.p.} [36] go [37] [to his] field, bush farm [38] {p.i.t.} [39] eat [40] {p.i.t.} [41] live, exist. (3) [42] so {c.c.} [43] they [44] then {particle denoting perfective narrative past, p.n.p.} [45] did, acted [46] this, like that [47] eat [48] live [49] {e.s.c.}, [50] every, all [51] then {c.c.} [52] it[53] went [54] arrived at, reached, came to

---

31) Abbreviations for grammatical concepts:

a.p.	affirmative particle
c.c.	consecutive conjunction
e.s.c.	particle marking end of subordinate clause
n.p.	negative particle
n.p.t.	narrative past tense
p.f.t.	particle denoting future tense
p.i.t.	particle denoting iterative or habitual tense
p.n.p.	particle denoting perfective narrative past

32) See glossary, entry *Naawen*, for further explanations.

33) I.e. 'was about to leave men on earth'.

34) The word *be* '1. introduces a polite order or request; [...] untranslated or translated by "then" [...] 2. imperative in indirect speech, often translated by "should" [...] 3. particle of emphasis [...]' (Kröger BED)

(4) [60] fi [61] dan [62] geb [63] lantanga, [64] fi [65] kan [66] pa [67] kaam [68] nyoro. (5) [69] Ate [70] nipok-nisom [71] kpak [72] a [73] yaa [74] zeri [75] a [76] ga [77] geb [78] lamu [79] a [80] dig [81] a [82] pa [83] kaam [84] nyoro. (6) [85] Ate [86] wen [87] sui [88] yaa [89] puuri - [90] te [91] weni [92] a [93] yaa [94] yiti, [95] a [96] yaa [97] a [98] jue [99] ngmain. (7) [100] Alege [101] yueni [102] to: (8) [103] nur' [104] miena [105] a [106] yaa [107] a [108] nam-oa [109] de [110] yogla. (9) [111] Wa [112] te [113] ba [114] siuk [115] ain [116] baa [117] de [118] ngandiinta [119] ate [120] ba [121] kisuk [122] ain [123] baa [124] kisi [125] ate [126] nipok-nisom [127] kpaka [128] a [129] zeri [130] ale [131] pa [132] kaam [133] nyo [134] lantanga [135] po [136] la. (10) [137] Dila [138] nying [139] ba [140] [nurba] [141] miena, [142] miena [143] yaa [144] tom [145] a [146] de [147] ngandiinta.

BUL-E1698 (FREE TRANSLATION)

(1) When God left the humans, he told them that they should not do [any] work; they should eat food: he himself would be near the earth and they should cut [off pieces of] him [which] became food. (2) No one should grind [millet], no one should go and farm in order to eat [to get food]. (3) And when they were behaving in this way, after a while he said: (4) 'If you cut off meat, you should not add [the spice] *kaam*'. (5) And a very old woman refused [to obey God's command] and went to cut off the meat,

[55] far, further on [56] that {c.c.} [57] he [God] [58] said [59] that: (4) [60] 'you [61] if [62] cut [with a knife] [63] meat [64] you [65] [should] not {n.p.} [66] take [67] kaam [a spice[35)]] [68] add, in addition.' (5) [69] And, but [70] an old woman [71] old [72] {p.i.t.} [73] then {p.n.p.} [74] refuse [75] {p.i.t.} [76] went [77] cut [78] the meat [79] {p.i.t.} [80] cooked [81] {p.i.t.} [82] took [83] kaam [84] added. (6) [85] And [86] the Sky, God [87] mind, mood, temper [88] then {p.n.p.} [89] overflowed, became angry[36)] - [90] and [91] the Sky, God [92] {p.i.t.} [93] then {p.n.p.} [94] arose [95] {p.i.t.} [96] then {p.n.t.} [97] {p.n.p.} [98] climbed [99] went away. (7) [100] And [101] said [102] well: (8) [103] men [104] all, every [105] {p.i.t.} [106] then {p.n.p.} [107] {p.i.t.} [108] suffer [109] eat [110] now. (9) [111] He [112] gave [113] them [114] way, permission [115] that [116] they {p.i.t.} [117] eat [118] food [119] and, but [120] their [121] taboo [122] that [123] they [124] [were] forbidden [125] but [126] an old woman [127] old [128] {p.i.t.} [129] refused [130] and [131] took [132] *kaam* [133] added to [134] meat [135] in, on [136] {e.s.c.}. (10) [137] This [138] on, because [139] they [140] [men] [141] all, every [142] all, every [143] then {p.n.p.} [144] to work [145] {p.i.t.} [146] eat [147] food.

---

cooked it, took *kaam* and added it [to the meat]. (6) And God [= the sky] then became angry - and God [= the sky] got up and rose (lit. climbed) upwards. (7) And he said: (8) Every man should suffer to eat [to obtain food] from then on. (9) He gave [had given] them permission to eat food and he gave [had given] them a taboo, but they did [had done] something forbidden (= violated a taboo) when a very old woman [had] refused [to obey his orders] and took [had token] *kaam* and added it to the meat.

(10) That is the reason why every man has to work in order to eat food [get food].

---

35) See glossary.

36) The verb *puuri* means '1. to abound, to be abundant, to overflow [...] 2. *sui puuri* [...] to be angry, annoyed, sad, scornful [...]' (Kröger BED).

BUL-E0402 (BULI TEXT)

(1) Tengka piilimka... (2) Wen a basi ate nur-biik kpi a jam abe chiik kpi a war'. (3) Ate biak a ga paa doa, ga paa nya ba bo a dig ngandiinta. (4) Ate biak doa a limsi ngandiintanga. (5) Kan tom tuim-tom-kai ate nur-biik tom ka la, ate bu-duk yaa chal ga paa wieni Naawen ain nur-biik a wieni ain wee: (6) 'Chiik a kpi a jam abe nur-biik a kpi a war'.' (7) Ate Naawen a wom bu-duku ale wieni dii la a ngman pilim jam. (8) Ate biaka ngman pilim jaa paari. (9) Ate biaka yaa ngman pilim wieni ngaang-nying ain: (10) 'Nur-biik wieni ain wee chiik kpi a war' abe nur-biik kpi a jam'. (11) Ate Naawen wieni ain wee di wom ka buuku le jam wien dii la. (12) Din ngmaa wom ngaang-noaini.

(13) Ka dila ale soa ate chiik a kpi a jam alege te nur-biik a kpi a war' du. (14) Ate nur-biik yaa wien wee biaka abe a nye ate wa kasim [kasi-yam] bo kum po taam wuu. (15) Dila la wan [wa yaali ain] wa pa biak chim ka lam a ngob. (16) Dan kan daa di nur-biik tin jaa ngob biak-a.

01.02 The Confounded Message: the Origin of Death

BUL-E0402 (ENGLISH TRANSLATION)

(1) [At] the beginning of the earth...[37] (2) God let man[38] die and come [back][39], whereas Moon died and remained [dead]. (3) And a dog went, arrived and lay down, went, arrived and saw that they[40] were cooking food. (4) And [the] dog lay down and waited for the food[41]. (5) As it did not do the work[42] man wanted him to do, a he-goat ran and went to tell God that man had said: (6) 'Moon [Soul] should die and come back whereas man should die and remain [dead]'. (7) And God heard what the he-goat had said and [God] came back again. (8) And the dog again [=also] came and arrived [with God]. (9) And the dog again said [coming] later on[43]: (10) 'Man said: 'Moon should die and remain [dead], whereas man should die and come [back].'' (11) And God said that he had heard what the goat had come to tell [him]. (12) He did not hear the latter message.

(13) That is why Moon dies and returns, whereas man dies and remains there [remains dead]. (14) And man said: It was the dog who made him remain dead[44] forever. (15) Because of that he [man] will take Dog and make meat [of it] and eat it. (16) If not because of that[45], man would not eat Dog.

---

37) After beginning this phrase, the teller was interrupted.

38) *nur-biik*, n. lit. 'child, son of man', 'human being, human (n.), mankind' (Kröger BED); in the present context, Man in the sense of primeval man.

39) In the sense of: 'return from death'.

40) Some people (undefined).

41) Therefore, he was slow in delivering the right message to God.

42) I.e. deliver Man's message to God.

43) I.e. the dog was later than the goat which had confused Man's message.

44) Lit.: '... that he would continue to be in death pass entirely.'

45) I.e., if Dog had not made this mistake.

BUL-E1856 (BULI TEXT)

(1) Kaa, mogi ale wen ale nag nampaga. (2) Weni yuen ain waa: (3) Ain: Di ale soa ate wa boro! (4) Mogni ain waa: (5) Daa wa nyinga; wa ta wa nyiamu kama. (6) Wa dan poom kan karo-a, nyiamu boro kama ate wa bisanga a vuugi. (7) Weni ain waa, wa be kul-a, ate wa gaa nyu-a, ate ba nya ba wai dek a lin wa paa wa choa la. (8) Amogi ain waa, wan wa paa ka wa. (9) Ba kuli ya.

01.03 God and a River Argue as to Who depends on Whom

BUL-E1856 (ENGLISH TRANSLATION)

(1) Once a river and sky (God)[46] had an argument[47]. (2) Sky (God) said: (3) He said: He [the river] owed[48] its very existence[49] to him [the sky (God)]. (4) The river said: (5) It wasn't because of him [the sky (God) that he existed]; he [the river] had [always] had his water. (6) [He said that] even if he [Sky (God)] did not exist, the water would still be there, so that his children[50] [could] live[51]. (7) The sky (God) said that [if that was the case, then] he [the river] should go home and go on drinking [his water], and they would see which of them would [in future] come to [see] the other one [to ask for help]. (8) River[52] said that he [the river] would not come to [see] him [the sky (God)]. (9) They went home.

---

46) The word *wen* means '1. sky, heaven', and also '5. God (the high God in heaven [...]' (Kröger BED), see glossary.

47) *nag nampaga*, 'to have an argument, to argue, to quarrel, to dispute or discuss something in a polemic way' (Kröger BED).

48) *soa*, v. '1. to own, to possess, to claim ownership of, to hold, to be in possession of [...] 2. to rule, to be in charge of, to have power over, to hold sway over, to control [...] 3. to be responsible for [...]' (Kröger BED). In the present context the meaning of the word *soa* is that the sky (God) is the necessary prerequisite of the river's existence, but at the same time, the verb expresses the idea that the sky (God) has power over, holds sway over, rules over or controls the river.

49) *boro*, v. '1. to exist, to live, to dwell, to inhabit [...] 2. to be alive [...] 3. to be, to be present, to be there, to be in [...]' (Kröger BED).

50) The teller does not say who the river's children are. It may be that he is referring to the fish and other animals living in the water of the river.

51) *vuugi*, v. 'to live, to be alive, to survive' (Kröger BED).

52) Here, and in the song following, the teller uses the personalized form *Amogi* for the name of the river; otherwise he speaks of *mogi*, def. *mogni*, '(the) river'.

(10) Ku ben, nyiamu kan ni. (11) Mogni a kpie, wen kan ni. (12) A kpie kpier-a, ale tali bakta nyiini, bisanga a kpi. (13) Wa nye kpier-a, a tom wa biika kanyi ain wa ga wieni Naawen ain waa, waa saalim wa, wa nye nyiam a te wa. (14) Biika yiri a cheng, a ga yin: 'Ngaang-nga, ngaang-nga!' (15) Ba sina, gaa paai ning-a, biika siag:

(16) Ni siag Amogi yeri wiik-a!
(17) Ni siag Amogi yeri wiik-a!
(18) Amogi yeri wiik-a!
(19) Ni siag Amogi yeri wiik-a!
(20) Ni siag Amogi yeri wiik-a!
(21) Amogi yeri wiik-a!

(22) Wa kuli ya, ba kan jam, bisa diem a kpi. (23) Wa ngmaa tom wa choa. (24) Wa gaa nye: 'Ngaang-nga!' (25) Weni wieni ain wa bisanga siag. (26) Waa piilim:

[Song repeated]

(27) Wa me kul; ba limsi kpie. (28) Wa dek nye kpie, yiri a cheng a ga yin: 'Ngaang-nga! Ngaang-nga!' (29) Ba sina, wa pilim yin: 'Ngaang-nga!' (30) Weni ain waa, ba siag. (31) Waa zaan:

(10) For a long time, the water [rain] did not pour down[53]. (11) The river dried up, [yet] the sky (God) did not [let it] rain. (12) He [the river] dried up so much that only silt remained and the [river's] children died. (13) He [the river] despaired and sent one of his children to go and tell God [the sky] that he was begging him to produce some water and give it to him. (14) The child got up, went [to the house of God] and said: 'Hallo, hallo[54]!' (15) They [the people in God's house] did not answer the greetings, [so] after some time, the [river's] child sang:

(16) Answer the call from River's house!
(17) Answer the call from River's house!
(18) The call from River's house!
(19) Answer the call from River's house!
(20) Answer the call from River's house!
(21) The call from River's house!

(22) He [the child] went back home, [because] they [the people in God's house] never came [to find out what the call was about] and the [river's] children continued to die. (23) He sent another [child]. (24) He [also] went and said: 'Hallo!' (25) The sky (God) told his children to answer [the call of the river's child]. (26) He [the river's child] began [to sing]:

[Song repeated]

(27) He [the river's other child] also returned home; they waited [for the rain?] in vain. (28) He [the river] himself despaired, got up and went [to God's house] and said: 'Hallo! Hallo!' (29) They did not answer the greetings, [so] he [the river] again said:

---

53) *ni*, v. 'to rain, to pour down, to fall (rain)' (Kröger BED).

54) *ngaanga*, interj. 'Hallo! Hey! (lit. behind, back, in the meaning 'Is there anybody behind?' interj. only used for calling somebody when approaching a compound as a stranger or neighbour' (Kröger BED). It is customary to call '*ngaanga*!' when approaching a compound as a stranger, otherwise one may be suspected to be a thief.

[Song repeated]

(32) Weni dek yaa nyini, a yueni mogni ain waa: (33) Nur an bag a nag nampaga ale wa. (34) Wa daam laa wieni wa ate wa a zeri la, wa wieni ain ka wa a lin wa paa wa la, daa wa ale ngman jam kal a saalim wa nna. (35) Wa din zeri nna, wa bisanga miena ate kan kpi ya? (36) Ain wa daam ze, abe waa saalim. (37) Ain wa yig wa ta kul ya wa basi ate wa paa yeri? (38) Ain wa yig wa ta kul. (39) Wa din ga nyin siuku ning-a, weni din ko, nag 'giri-giri-giri'. (40) A din jam daa ni, din sue mogni.

(41) Di le soa ate ba kan nag nampaga ale wen ya.

(42) Mi sunsuelini miena kpegtalegi.

'Hallo!' (30) The sky (God) said they should respond to the call. (31) He [the river] stood [and began to sing]:

[Song repeated]

(32) The sky (God) himself then came out and told the river: (33) There was no one who could argue[55] with him. (34) [God said] that when he had told him this, he [the river] had disagreed, saying that it was rather he [the sky (God)] who would come to him [the river], but now it is, in fact, he [the river] who has come to him, sitting [before him] and begging to him. (35) If he [the sky (God)] were to refuse [to help him], wouldn't all his children die? (36) He [the river] said that he had been ignorant and that he was begging him [to forgive him]. (37) He [the sky (God)] asked him whether he should accompany him home or should he allow him to get home first[56]? (38) He [River] said that he should accompany him home. (39) As he came out onto the road, the sky blackened [clouded] and sounded *'giri-giri-giri!'*[57]. (40) It [the rain] came and poured down and filled the river.

(41) That is why [it is said] that one cannot argue with God.

(42) That is my story.

---

55) *nag nampaga*, see footnote 47.

56) The question means: Should the Sky (God) send the rain while River is still on his way home or should he allow him to get home before the rain starts?

57) Imitation of the sound of thunder.

BUL-E0438 (BULI TEXT)

(1) Ka-a nipooba pi; ba miena ta puusa. (2) Ba miena maa chaab ba puusanga; nipooba pika miena a biag bi-yeng dek-i. (3) 'te biik-a a yiri la-a, kan din beni du. (4) 'te naab yaa beg nipooma ain waa: (5) 'Nama biika dek, 'te ni din biag nna, ka yue be tin le boa?' (6) Biika ain ka yue le Anipooba-Maa-Chaab-Pi-Biik.

(7) Biika din ga vaa yir-a, a yaalim; nyiem yiri cheng sagi, wa dan ga nya piung jaalung le ku doa, wa din ko wa lantanga, din dani du alege yiti yig beli a sing gaa pongti nyiamu. (8) Atieng-Lig-Mogi ain waa: (9) 'Ka wan laa pongti nyiamu?' (10) Wa yin ka wa, Anipooba-Maa-Chaab-Pi-Biik! (11) Ain: 'Fi ka Nipooba-Maa-Chaab-Pi-Biik,

01.04 God's Bull, 'Strong Boy' and the Origin of Thunder

BUL-E0438 (ENGLISH TRANSLATION)

(1) Once there lived ten women; they were all pregnant[58]. (2) All of them were pregnant together[59]; all the ten women gave birth [together] to one and the same child. (3) And the child (boy) got up before long[60]. (4) Then the chief asked the women: (5) 'Your child that you delivered, what should be his name?' (6) The child [himself] answered that his name was Common-Son-Of-Ten-Women[61].

(7) As soon as the boy had grown up, he took to hunting; he used to go to the bush and when he found a flat rock, he killed his meat [game], spread and dried[62] it there, before setting off for a river; he went down [to the river] and splashed the water about. (8) Then Beard-Covers-River[63] said: (9) 'Who is that splashing the water about?' (10) He said that it was he, Common-Son-Of-Ten-Women. (11) He [Beard-

---

58) Lit.: 'they all had bellies'.

59) Lit.: 'All of them helped one another with their pregnancies [lit. bellies] [...]'. The verb *maari*, short form *maa* means '1. to help, to support, to assist, to aid [...] 2. to take part (in), to participate, to join [...] 6. *maa chaab* (transl.) common - *Ti maa chaab biik ale nna*. This is our common child (said e.g. by the parents).' (Kröger BED).

60) If, in Bulsa folktales, a child is able to walk soon after his or her birth, it is a sign of his or her supernatural faculties. The child is considered to be a *kikiruk* (see glossary).

61) The Buli name *Anipooba-Maa-Chaab-Pi-Biik* means literally 'Women-Help-One another-Ten-Child', is here translated 'Common-Son-of-Ten-Women'. The abnormal faculty of the boy to speak immediately after he has been born (Mot. T585.2) and the circumstance that he names himself are further signs that he is a *kikiruk*, i.e. a monster or ogre (see glossary).

62) *dani*, 'v. to spread (e.g. sheanuts, millet, groundnuts etc.) on a clean place (e.g. courtyard or flat roof) for drying, to dry (by spreading)' (Kröger BED).

63) The name *Atieng-Lig-Beli* means 'Beard-Covers-River', i.e. his beard is so big that he could spread it to cover a whole river. Like the Common-Son-Of-Ten-Women, he is also a *kikiruk* or superhuman being.

be ngman pongti nyiamu saa buye!' (12) Wa ain wa pongti ya! (13) Wa daa jue', zu-guri tek, Anipooba-Maa-Chaab-Pi-Biik an ben' du, wa din kpa-a lu. (14) Wa yin waa: (15) 'Be dan ka dila, n be va fi ngaang te fi yaalim te taa de?' (16) Baa nyiem, ba ko lanta dani piungku zuk.

(17) Naawen lalik - ka num yeng, ka nang kanyi, ka bogi dinyi - yaa nyin wen jam zi. (18) Wa le jaa paari la, Anipooba-Maa-Chaab-Pi-Biik le wa vaanchoawa cheng goani la-a, wa yin: (19) 'N pai nna ne!' (20) Wa pai nbula ne. (21) 'N pai nbula ne!' (22) Wa pai bula ne. (23) 'Bui le doa n siuku po la-a!' (24) Wa pai bula ne. (25) Wa yig wen a jue.'

Covers-River] said: 'If you are indeed the Common-Son-Of-Ten-Women,then splash the water a second time!' (12) He [Common-Son-Of-Ten-Women] said that he had splashed [the water once again]. (13) He [Beard-Covers-River] climbed [came] out [of the water] and they began to wrestle by rubbing their foreheads against each other[64] - bang! -, and Common-Son-Of-Ten-Women wasted no time: he threw [Beard-Covers-River] down. (14) Then he [Beard-Covers-River] said: (15) 'If that is so[65], then I will follow you and you will hunt and we shall eat [together]!' (16) They roamed [the bush], killed some 'meat' [bush animals] and spread [the meat] on the rock to dry.

(17) Then God's[66] bull - it had one eye, it had one hind leg, it had one foreleg - came out of the sky [or: down from God[67]], and landed [by the rock where the game was being dried]. (18) When he [the bull[68]] came and Common-Son-Of-Ten-Women and his companion had gone to the bush, he [the bull] said: (19) 'Let me take this [piece of meat] and swallow [it]!' (20) And he took another [piece of meat] and swallowed [it]. (21) 'Let me take the other [piece of meat] and swallow [it]!' (22) He took it and swallowed it. (23) 'The one [the piece of meat] which is lying in my way there!' (24) He took [that piece of meat also] and swallowed [it]. (25) He [God's bull] again set off for the sky.

---

64) *zu-guri*, cmpd. v., to wrestle in such a way that both wrestlers put their foreheads against each other in the manner of cows or goats.

65) I.e. 'if you can subjugate me'.

66) James Agalic translates: 'There was a bull belonging to God' (*Naawen*). Cf. the word *Naawen* in the glossary. In the present context, the name refers to God as the 'Chief of the Sky' in its original sense.

67) In the present context the word *wen* is ambiguous: it may mean the 'sky' or 'God'. Pauline Akankyalabey: 'Since for the Bulsa, *wen*, the Sky and God are synonymous, anything that comes from the Sky also comes from God. One can therefore translate this sentence to mean either that a bull came from the Sky or from God'.

68) The teller personifies the bull by using the personal pronoun *wa* of the first class instead of the pronoun *ka* of the third class for *lalik*, the bull.

(26) Wa jam ain wa chiim lanta, lanta yariba. (27) Wa yin: (28) 'Hmmm', boan la nye wa lantanga nna? (29) Vara dila, vara dila. (30) Wa wieni ain Atieng-Lig-Mogi be kanla a nya lantanga, te ja-buui le jaa paai la, fi le wa nye te ti nya! (31) Atieng-Lig-Mogi kal-a; Naawen basi di lalik, 'te ka jam sing. (32) Wa jam pai lantanga daa ne, jam pai lantanga daa ne, Atieng-Lig-Mogi ga ain wa wien la, wa ga tab wa fer, le yig Naawen yeri a jueli. (33) Nipooba-Maa-Chaab-Pi-Biik jaa paar-a, wa yin: (34) 'Atieng-Lig-Mogi, ku tin soa ka se te lantanga daa nye dila?' (35) Wa yin wa nya ku ka nyeka. (36) Wa nya ka Naawen le basi lalik 'te ka jaa pai lantanga. (37) Ain: (38) 'Kal-a tin soa ka se?' (39) Ain wa cheng be wa ge 'te wa dek war'.

(40) Wentueng din moag-a, lalik din nyini wen jam zi, din ga laar-a pai lam, pilim gaa pai bu choa. (41) Wa yin: (42) 'Ja-buloruku nna, kan te lam ngman jue fi noai-a!' (43) Wa din chiem nya Anipooba-Pi-Biik mum jogsi. (44) Wa din ga laar-a pai wa lam.

(26) When he [Common-Son-Of-Ten-Women] came and counted the [pieces of] meat, there were fewer [than before][69]. (27) He said: (28) 'Hmmm!', what [thing] has done this to his meat? (29) This happened day after day. (30) Then he [Common-Son-Of-Ten-Women] told Beard-Covers-River to sit down and watch over the meat so that when the beast[70] came [again], you[71] and he will do [something] so that we shall see [who is the strongest]. (31) Beard-Covers-River sat [and watched]; God released his bull and it descended. (32) He[72] [the bull] came, took the meat and was swallowing [it], came, took the meat and was swallowing [it], when Beard-Covers-River told him [not to take the meat and swallow it]; [then] he [the bull] went and trampled on him, [trying to] drive him into the ground and [then the bull] went up to God's house [again]. (33) When Common-Son-Of-Ten-Women returned, he asked: (34) 'Beard-Covers-River, what exactly happened to the meat?' (35) He [Beard-Covers-River] said that it was impossible [for him to prevent the meat from being taken]. (36) [Beard-Covers-River said] he should realize that it was God who sent a bull to come down and take the meat. (37) [Common-Son-Of-Ten-Women] asked: (38) 'How big is it [the bull]?' (39) He [Common-Son-Of-Ten-Women] told him [Beard-Covers-River] to go [hunting] and leave him [Common-Son-Of-Ten-Women] to stay behind [and watch].

(40) When the sun shone brightly[73], the bull came down from the sky and landed [on the ground]; it went and reached out for [a piece of] meat, went again and reached out for another one. (41) He [Common-Son-Of-Ten-Women] said: (42) 'You ugly thing, don't let any more meat go up to your mouth!' (43) He [the bull] turned and took a sneering look at Son-Of-Ten-Women[74]. (44) Then he [the bull] went [again], reached

---

69) Lit.: '[pieces of] meat were missing'.

70) *ja-buui*, (< *jaab*) 'dreadful, wild beast or creature (unspecified, unknown; may e.g. be used to frighten a child)' (Kröger BED).

71) Here the teller switches partly into direct speech. The Bulsa storytellers usually prefer the reported speech, but sometimes direct and reported speech are mixed up, as in this sentence.

72) Here the teller again switches from the *ka*-class to the *wa*-class, cf. footnote 68.

73) Lit.: 'when the hottest time of the day was near', i.e. in the early afternoon.

74) *mum jogsi*: to close one's eyes arrogantly as an insulting gesture.

(45) Anipooba-Maa-Chaab-Pi-Biik din chien le wa kuta doari-a, din jam wien lalik ngoa nya. (46) Lalik le Anipooba-Maa-Chaab-Pi-Biik din ga jo-a, baa je, baa je, wenzuk munung, ba gai kal-a vuusi, kal-a vuusi. (47) Ba yiri ga jo ya, baa je, ba wai an yig wa choa lonsi ya - daa ngata.

(48) Da-dii la saari nganaansi-wa la-a, Naawen kali nya-a, Anipooba-Maa-Chaab-Pi-Biik wa pagra. (49) Ate wa pai miik a lonsi Anipooba-Maa-Chaab-Pi-Biik ngiri, pai nka a lonsi naamu ngiri, a dari ta yig wen a jueli. (50) Ba jue gan [= ga ain] ba de saaria-a, Naawa wieni ain nya kude-e, wan [=wa ain] wa dueni kama, be wa biisi ka mag-maga.

(51) Dila le soa, Achaab-Pi-Biik le lalika dan ga zig chaab-a, dila le soa ate weni nyiem a kum dila giri-giri-giri-giri wa la, bala le bo-a je.

(52) Mi sunsuelini miena le la.

out and took [another piece of] his meat. (45) Common-Son-Of-Ten-Women then came along with his iron stick and hit the bull with all his strength[75]. (46) The bull and Common-Son-Of-Ten-Women got hold of each other; they wrestled and wrestled till sunset, then they stopped and sat down to rest, sat down to rest. (47) They got up and got hold of each other again; they wrestled and wrestled, but neither of them could put down the other one - [this lasted for] three days.

(48) At the end of the fourth day, God sat and saw that Common-Son-Of-Ten-Women was strong. (49) So he took a rope and dropped it around the neck of Common-Son-Of-Ten-Women and took another [rope] and dropped it around the neck of the cow [bull] and pulled them up into the sky. (50) When they got up there and they wanted their case to be judged[76], the Chief (=God[77]) said that he had noted this [case], [but] he said that he would suspend the case, and then judge it very slowly and carefully.

(51) Whenever Common-Son-Of-Ten-Women and the bull come across each other, they wrestle [up there] and that is the reason why the sky always cries like this: *giri, giri, giri*[78].

(52) That is all my story.

---

75) [...] *ngoa nya*, lit. 'take [and] see!', idiomatic expression in the sense that the bull should receive a beating and watch its effects.

76) *saaria*, n. (lw. Hausa), def. *saariawa*, pl. *saariaba* 'judgment, [...] trial (with judgment) [...] *de saaria* (lit. to eat judgment) to judge a case, to hear a case.' (Kröger BED). - Pauline Akankyalabey: 'This is not a Buli word. Most likely it is a corruption of the Arabic word *sharia* which also means '(coranic) law' or 'judgement'.'

77) *Naawen* means literally 'Chief of the Sky'; see glossary.

78) *giri-giri* '(onom.) adv. imitates a low rumbling noise (e.g. of thunder).' (Kröger BED).

BUL-E1328 (BULI TEXT)

(1) Ka naab ale boro. (2) Wa le wa pok yo-o, poom ka pooba. (3) Wanyiwa yaa ta lie ate Asuom a cheng a yaa. (4) Wa nongku mawa a yaa yin waa, wa tog le pa liewa ate wa alege wa dan ga wom ain wa kpi, wa jam ate ba maa pa wa a gu. (5) Asuom ain wa wom dila, wa be siag ya. (6) Wa za a pa liewa a te wa.

(7) Ba le pa te wa la, ku an bo la paa daa ngaye ba yin nganuwa kpi. (8) Asuom yiti kum a jue goai, a ga kal goaini sunsung a nye wa yiili[79]:

(9) Ku nyini, nyini, nyini ka nang gbaaling de!
(10) Ku nyini, nyini, nyini ka nang gbaaling de!
(11) Wari a kperi biik ga ka nang gbaaling de!
(12) Ku nyini, nyini, nyini ka nang gbaaling de!
(13) Ku nyini, nyini, nyini ka nang gbaaling de!

---

79) The transcription and translation of the song given here were made by Mr. Anankpieng from Sandema-Kobdem. Ms. Pauline Akankyalabey, on the other hand, transcribed this song from the tape as follows:

(09) Ku ngana, ngana, ngana kanang gbang le boa,
(10) ku ngana, ngana, ngana kanang gbang le boa,
(11) wari kperi biik ga kanang gbang le boa.
(12) Ku ngana, ngana, ngana kanang gbang le boa,
(13) ku ngana, ngana, ngana kanang gbang le boa,
(14) wari kperi biik ga kanang gbang le boa.
(15) Ku ngana, ngana, ngana kanang gbang le boa,
(16) ku ngana, ngana, ngana kanang gbang le boa,
(17) wari kperi biik ga kanang gbang le boa.
(18) Ku ngana, ngana, ngana kanang gbang le boa,
(19) ku ngana, ngana, ngana kanang gbang le boa,
(20) wari kperi biik ga kanang gbang le boa.

She did not give a translation as she found this song to be incomprehensible. This is an example of the difficulties even Buli speakers have in transcribing and understanding songs in their own language.

01.05 Hare and His Mother-in-Law and the Origin of Agriculture

BUL-E1328 (ENGLISH TRANSLATION)

(1) There lived a chief. (2) He lived with his wife, indeed [many] wives. (3) One of them had a daughter, and Hare went and wooed [her]. (4) His girlfriend's mother said to him she would give the girl to him on the condition that when he heard she [the mother] had died, he would come and they would bury him as well. (5) Hare said he had understood this and agreed. (6) Then she gave him the [her] daughter.

(7) After [the girl] had been given to him, it did not take two days[80], when it was said that the mother-in-law had died. (8) Hare got up and headed for the bush crying[81]; he went and sat down in the middle of the bush and started singing:

(9) Come out, out, out, there is a weak[82] leg here!
(10) Come out, out, out, there is a weak leg here!
(11) Something puzzles[83] a boy: there is a weak leg here!
(12) Come out, out, out, there is a weak leg here!
(13) Come out, out, out, there is a weak leg here!

---

80) I. e. after a very short while.

81) *kum*, v. 'to cry, to weep, to mourn' (in the traditionally prescribed manner), cf. glossary.

82) *gbaaling*, adj. 'weak, sick, sickly, ailing, infirm (used for persons and animals)' (Kröger BED).

83) *kperi*, v. 'to be a problem, to be difficult or insoluble, to bring (s.b.) into difficulties, to frustrate (sb.), to perplex, to bewilder, to puzzle, to trouble [...]' (Kröger BED).

(14) *Wari a kperi biik ga ka nang gbaaling de!*
(15) *Ku nyini, nyini, nyini ka nang gbaaling de!*
(16) *Ku nyini, nyini, nyini ka nang gbaaling de!*
(17) *Wari a kperi biik ga ka nang gbaaling de!*
(18) *Ku nyini, nyini, nyini ka nang gbaaling de!*
(19) *Ku nyini, nyini, nyini ka nang gbaaling de!*
(20) *Wari a kperi biik ga ka nang gbaaling de!*

(21) Ate jaab a nyin wen a jam, a jam yin: (22) 'Ka boan wari, Asuom?' (23) Ain wa-kperikaliik ale kperi wa. (24) Wa cheng ka naa-yeri a ga faa wa nong. (25) Wa nganuwa be yin ka wa dan kpi, wa jam te ba maa gu wa. (26) Ba be yin wa kpi kama. (27) Wa ze wa ale wa nye diila.

(28) Ate jaamu ain waa: wa yiri a cheng wa dan ga paar-a, wa dan ga kum jo, wa nyini a zaan naawa tampoini zuk ain: (29) 'Awen-e, Awen-e! (30) Ta kui ale a kpa ja-buui, ale dung biik a jam ate n ta va nganuwa cheng a vuusi? (31) Ate bai ale nyiem a nye nna, abe ba ale ba a de jaabui la abe ba de ate ti nya.' (32) Asuom an zeri ya. (33) Wa yiri a cheng, wa moata, wa kum:

(14) Something puzzles a boy: there is a weak leg here!
(15) Come out, out, out, there is a weak leg here!
(16) Come out, out, out, there is a weak leg here!
(17) Something puzzles a boy: there is a weak leg here!
(18) Come out, out, out, there is a weak leg here!
(19) Come out, out, out, there is a weak leg here!
(20) Something puzzles a boy: there is a weak leg here!

(21) Then a [supernatural] being[84] came down from the sky[85], came and asked: (22) 'What is the matter, Hare?' (23) He said that something very serious was troubling him: (24) He had gone to the chief's house and married his girlfriend. (25) However, his mother-in-law had told him if she died, he should come so they would bury him as well. (26) And now it is said that she has in fact died. (27) He didn't know what to do.

(28) Then the [supernatural] being told him to get up and go to the chief's house and when he arrived [there], after he had cried and entered [the room where his mother-in-law's body lay], he should come out and stand on top of the chief's rubbish heap and shout: (29) 'Oh God, oh God! (30) Bring [me] a hoe and whatever a hoe produces[86] as well as an animal's young[87] so that I will take them and go with my mother-in-law and rest[88]. (31) And those who behave like this, [the people who are living,] let us see what they will eat!' (32) Hare did not object [to what the supernatural being suggested]. (33) He got up and set off and as he got nearer [to the chief's house], he cried[89]:

---

84) *jaab*, lit. a 'thing', 'something', cf. glossary.

85) *wen*, 'sky', 'heaven', 'Sky-God', cf. glossary.

86) I. e. farm products.

87) *dung*, n. [domestic] animal, used in Bulsa economy and in sacrifices, cf. glossary.

88) The teller probably refers here to the funeral custom of the Bulsa to kill one or more animals on the ash-heap before the compound. The animal(s) killed is (are) to accompany the dead on his or her journey into the realm of the dead where the ancestors live.

89) I.e. he sang his funeral dirge in the wailing manner which is customary with Bulsa funerals.

(34)	*Ku nyini, nyini, nyini ka nang gbaaling de!*
(35)	*Ku nyini, nyini, nyini ka nang gbaaling de!*
(36)	*Wari a kperi biik ga ka nang gbaaling de!*
(37)	*Ku nyini, nyini, nyini ka nang gbaaling de!*
(38)	*Ku nyini, nyini, nyini ka nang gbaaling de!*
(39)	*Wari a kperi biik ga ka nang gbaaling de!*
(40)	*Ku nyini, nyini, nyini ka nang gbaaling de!*
(41)	*Ku nyini, nyini, nyini ka nang gbaaling de!*
(42)	*Wari a kperi biik ga ka nang gbaaling de!*
(43)	*Ku nyini, nyini, nyini ka nang gbaaling de!*
(44)	*Ku nyini, nyini, nyini ka nang gbaaling de!*
(45)	*Wari a kperi biik ga ka nang gbaaling de!*

(46) Ate ba yig wa a ta cheng a ga jo. (47) Wa kum a ga nyin a jueli a zaan tampoini zuk: (48) 'Awen-e, Awen-e! (49) Ta kui ale a kpa ja-buui ale dung biik a jam ate n va nganuwa a cheng. (50) Abe ti yaa nya bai ale nyiem a nye nna, ba ale ba a de jaabui la, abe ti nya.' (51) Ate wa ta jam a te wa. (52) Ate wa nganuwa a yiri a zaan ain waa: wa kan ta ngantanga a cheng-i. (53) Ale wa daam a nye kama ain wa nya, ase wa ale sum a nye ku dila ya ase wa kan nye.

(34) Come out, out, out, there is a weak leg here!
(35) Come out, out, out, there is a weak leg here!
(36) Something puzzles a boy: there is a weak leg here!
(37) Come out, out, out, there is a weak leg here!
(38) Come out, out, out, there is a weak leg here!
(39) Something puzzles a boy: there is a weak leg here!
(40) Come out, out, out, there is a weak leg here!
(41) Come out, out, out, there is a weak leg here!
(42) Something puzzles a boy: there is a weak leg here!
(43) Come out, out, out, there is a weak leg here!
(44) Come out, out, out, there is a weak leg here!
(45) Something puzzles a boy: there is a weak leg here!

(46) They held him, took him and went and entered[90]. (47) He wailed and came out [of the house] and stood on top of the rubbish heap [crying]: (48) 'Oh God, oh God! (49) Bring me a hoe and the things a hoe produces (farm products) as well as an animal's young so that I will take [these things], follow my mother-in-law and go [away with them]. (50) Then we will see those who behave like this, [the people who are living,] what they will have left to eat; we shall see!' (51) And he [God] brought them [the things Hare asked for] and gave them to him. (52) Then his mother-in-law arose and stood and said that he shouldn't take the things with him and go [away]. (53) When she had acted [like this] the other day, [she had done it] to see whether he would really do it[91] or not.

---

[90] This refers to the funeral custom of the Bulsa to 'hold' (embrace) someone who comes wailing and weeping for the dead person, and to take the mourner into the compartment or room (*dok*) where the body of the dead person or some object symbolizing it, e.g. a rolled up straw mat, is exhibited. The mourning customs have to be observed in a particularly meticulous manner by the sons-in-law of the deceased. Insofar, the behaviour of Hare, as described in this story, corresponds well with the actual customs of the Bulsa.

[91] I.e. keep his promise.

(54) Dila ale soa ate ba yin waa, [...] (55) Dila nying ale soa ate ngandiinta boro. (56) Kan daa nganuwa nying-a, Asuom tue wogla, te yaa ti bo ka bolim po. (57) Wa te ta ba a taam.

(58) Mi sunsuelini miena la kpegtalegi.

(54) That is why it is said,...[92] (55) That is the reason why there is food. (56) Had it not been for the mother-in-law, Hare, the long-eared, would have put us into the fire. (57) He [Hare] would have taken them[93] along.

(58) This is the end of my story.

---

92) This sentence remained incomplete.

93) I.e. the agricultural implements and the domestic animals.

BULI TEXT (BUL-E0674)

(1) Jaabui ale soa ate kpiak a de ning a tom tuima miena la, jinla ti za ain ti wom.

(2) Naawen ale basi nurdoa ale nipok - daa nganta baye? - a pa kpiak, kpa-sari ale kpa-diak, a te nurwa ale wa powa. (3) Ba le ling cheng-a, Naawen alaa te ba ngandiinta, bala banaansi-oa. (4) Ate nurdoawa nyiem din sing vaari zaanga - nga soa nna -, a din ta sing daa te wa powa. (5) Wa din ta cheng tuika, wa ale kuri ale wa le poom kan kuri din soa se chaab la, wa gbi ya, kpiak de chag. (6) Ba miena ka bimbaansa le la te ba te ba - yo-o! - nwala biik, nipowa me nipok-liak, kpiaka me kpa-sari, kpa-diaka me kpa-da-palik.

01.06 Fowls and the Origin of Sacrifices

BUL-E0674 (ENGLISH TRANSLATION)

(1) The reason why a fowl is [the] first [sacrificial offering] used in performing all rituals[94] - this is what we are going to hear today.

(2) God created a man and a woman - are they not two beings?[95] - and [then] he took a fowl, a hen and a cock, and gave them to the man and his wife. (3) When they first went[96], God provided food for them, for those four. (4) And the man used to climb into [the grainstore] and collect the millet - there was as much as this![97] -, and then he would climb [again {continuous action} into the grainstore] and give it [the millet] to his wife. (5) She took it [the millet] to the mortar[98], and whether or not she pounded it properly, it was all the same[99] - when she had finished [and winnowed[100]] it, the fowl ate till it was satisfied. (6) They could all have had children - you

---

94) Lit.: '[...] a fowl is eaten first in doing all works'.

95) Lit.: 'isn't that two things?'.

96) I. e., when they first went down to the Earth.

97) This exclamation was probably followed by a gesture with the teller's hands or arms.

98) *tuik*, def. *tuika*, pl. *tuisa*, 'mortar'. 'Here it does not only refer to the mortar in which grain is pounded, but the word refers also to the spot or area, usually outside the compound, where the women go to pound their grain. Thus, one may hear for example: »'*Nipowa a cheng/taam ka tuik*', 'the woman has gone to the mortar'«, i.e. she has gone to the place where they pound grain.' (Pauline Akankyalabey).

99) I. e. even if she did her work slovenly, there was enough millet for all of them, the human couple and the chickens.

100) To expose (grain) to a current of air by tossing or fannying it so that the loose, dry outer part is blown away.

(7) Chi-pumin pe-pe-pe, kai alen ka saari siyewa la, ba kal ale kpiaka a jo nyo loebka jigi, age ba boro chim. (8) Ba a goa ale ka chaab, ba ze ba alaa nye ka dii la, alege kpa-diaka a jueli ka powa. (9) Kpa-sani ga loeb nue. (10a) Ba boro ... (10b) ... Ba a goa kama, ba kan gberi chaab-a? (11) Ba ze gberika! (12a) Ba ze ba ale ba nye ka dii la, ba nya ka nganta ale boro, wen me be ze dii te baa nye la, wa me nya kpiaka me, baa me alaa goa dila a nye dii la, ba be a goa ka chaab goota jig-a? (12b) Kpesa an poom a jueli daa kantueng-a? (13) Ta dila, ta dila ta-ta-ta, chiik jaa paara-a, wa kal ale kpiaka nyin ale chiisa; ka nyin ale chiisa. (14) Ba paai pi, va kpiaka ngaang, a de zaanga tuika po.

(15) Nipowa yaa kuri zaanga, yaa wieni ain waa: (16) 'Nya wa-kinkagle-e, Naawen ale basi te baye-baye! (17) Wa ling basi ka mi first, pa basi mi choro, a yin nurdoawala a nya mi. (18) Pai naa me niye-niye te ni a nya [chaab].' (19) Wa laa biisi dila la, ale

know! - the one [the man] being a young man, the woman also a young woman[101], the hen a young female[102] and a young cock too.

(7) Exactly one month passed; then when the second month came to an end, the fowl went into [the chicken coop] to put [eggs] into the place of the egg-laying hen, while they [the human beings] lived on quietly. (8) They [man and woman] went on sleeping together without knowing what they had to do, whereas the cock [continued to] copulate[103] with his wife. (9) The hen finished laying eggs. (10a) They [the human beings] lived on and on ... (10b [Question of the repeater:]) They slept and they did not know how to fuck one another? [Laughter among the audience] (11) They did not know fucking! (12a) They did not know how to go about it; they [only] saw 'things' [sexual organs] that were there; God himself even did not understand what they were doing; he [the man] even saw what the fowl did when they slept together - [but] did [the human couple and the fowls] sleep in the same sleeping place[104]? (12b) Do not chickens climb [=fuck] in the afternoon? (13) They lived on and on [like that] until another month had passed, and as she [the woman] was sitting there, the fowl came out with [its] chicks; she came out with chicks. (14) They [the chicks] numbered up to ten, and they were following the hen and eating the millet from the mortar.

(15) While the woman was pounding millet, she said: (16) 'Look, what a wonderful thing - God has created us in pairs! (17) First[105], he created me, then my husband, and then said that this man should take care of me. (18) He [God] created you [pl., the fowls] also as a pair, so that you could take care of each other.' (19) While she was saying this, the cock was absent - yes! -, and so she went on pounding her millet and

---

101) *nipok-liak*, 'girl, young woman who has not yet had children [...]' (Kröger BED).

102) *kpa-sari*, 'hen, female chicken' (Kröger BED), i.e. one that had not yet laid eggs.

103) *jueli*, 'to climb (up), to mount', here in the sense '(only said of animals) to copulate, to have sexual intercourse' (Kröger BED).

104) The teller means that they did not have the same sleeping place; therefore the human beings could not observe what the fowls were doing in the night. The repeater, however, argues in the next sentence that chickens do not copulate in the night, but in the afternoon.

105) The teller uses the Buli verb *ling*, 'to precede, to be first [...], to do first, [...] to come before' (Kröger BED), and also the English adverb 'first'.

kpa-diaka karo - yo-o!, waa kuri ka zaanga ale a biisi dila wa noai po. (20) Kpiaka a wom, kpa-sani ale ka bisanga a de zaanga ale a wom: (21) 'Kpiaka yaa nye se ta nurba soa nna alege wa ka nuro?' (22) Kpiaka yaa ain: (23) 'Ka dii!' (24) Yaa wom a yaa chigsi ka zuk, wan tulisi nipowa jigi - yo-o! - ale de zaanga ale cheng a jo. (25) A yaa jo wieni ka chorowa, kpa-diaka - yo-o! (26) Kpa-diaka a yin: (27) 'Di daa wari ya! (28) Fi dan kan biisi ale wa, mi dan nyini, n le biisi ale wa.' (29) Ba ale ngman jo la, ku an beni ya, chiisanga a pag.

(30) Nipowa ngman yin dila deg-dega. (31) Kpa-diaka yaa a yin waa: (32) 'Naa ze ba ale a nye dii la?' (33) Ain, wa be kuri zaanga a yali ate nga duag tengka a zuag, ate waa de zaanga chag, ate wa nye a sag ba. (34) Nipowa a siag, age nurdoa boro yiok.

(35a) Waa kuri, waa kuri, waa le yali ale wa le kan yali soa se chaab la, nyiem din gbeling chini a dueni teng, nga din nye: 'sara-ta-ta-ta!'. (35b) 'Aba-a!', (36a) kpa-diak da a ne, a ne, ne, ne ga chag - nya fook soa nna! - wa din yiri nag kinkanga 'pe-pe-pe!' ain: (37) 'Nurdoawade a kpa za la te-e-e-e... ummm!' (38) Fi wom kpadiak kumsanga? (39) Wa ale kum dila la, din dueni ka kingkangni teng din nye 'krrrr!'. (40) Kpa-nubini

saying this to herself[106]. (20) While they were eating the millet, the hen and her chicks heard her; they listened [to what the woman was saying]: (21) 'How did the fowl come by so many people[107] [chicks] while she [the woman] had none?' (22) Then the hen said: (23) 'Is that so?' (24) [She] listened and shook her head, [she] did not reply to the woman - okay! -, but [simply] ate the millet and went and entered [the house]. (25) [The hen] went in and told it to her husband, the cock - all right! (26) The cock said: (27) 'That is no problem! (28) If you didn't talk to her, I shall talk to her when I go out.' (29) They went in again and not long after that, the chickens matured.

(30) The woman said the same [words all over] again. (31) And the cock asked: (32) 'Don't you[108] know how this is done [to get children]?' (33) [He] said that she should pound the millet and winnow it so that a lot [of grains] fall to the ground, and when he [the cock] had eaten the millet and was satisfied, he would then do it and teach them [how to do it]. (34) The woman agreed, but the man lived on and was ignorant.

(35a) She pounded and pounded [her millet], and whether she winnowed it or not, it was all the same [to her]: she used to tilt the calabash towards the ground, then the millet scattered [on the ground] and it made a sound like: *'sara-ta-ta-ta!'*. (35b) *'Aba-a!'*[109], (36a) the cock quickly swallowed, swallowed, swallowed and swallowed till he was satisfied, - look, the [cock's] crop was as big as this[110]! - then he got up and flapped his wings: *'pe-pe-pe!'* and crowed: (37) 'This man should farm millet and give [it] to us *e-e-e...ummm!'* (38) Did you[111] hear the cock's crowing? (39) Having crowed in this way, he then placed his wing against the ground and made *'krrrr!'*[112].

---

106) Lit.: 'she was saying that in her mouth'.

107) *nurba*, pl. of *nur(u)*, lit. 'men', used here in the sense of 'relatives'.

108) *naa* < *ni a*, 'you', plural, i.e. you, the human beings.

109) Interjection by the repeater, Mr. Godfrey Achaw, meaning 'That will do! That's enough!' (cf. Kröger BED).

110) 'This is normally followed by a gesture on the part of the narrator.' (Pauline Akankyalabey).

111) The teller addressing the audience.

112) The swishing sound produced from the contact between the wing and the ground.

din ga duag din chub ka bitag-fiik nna, kpa-diaka din ga jue din nye tiig nipowa nimbie po.

(41) Wa din yig[113] *dok a jo. (42) Wa le din yig dok a jo la, din jo taam a yin wa duag la, nipok din ga pa nisa din yig nurdoa yoari ta gaa su wa badiaka po ale yin: (43) 'Bitag-fiik po la, badiak!' (44) Nurdoa din der-a gberi, nurdoa din der-a gberi, daa ngata puuk, daa ngata biik.*

(45) Wa le biag biika te biika ga a kal a kuug a cheng-a, nurdoawa yaa yiri, yaa a ka ain: (46) Wa le din yiri nya biikade nna, ka kpiak le soa ate wa nya biika. (47) Kpiak ale sag wa pok, te wa powa jo sag wa ate wa nya biika. (48) Wa ale biisi dila ... be biika seb kpiak!

(49) Wa ale gaa yin: 'Be biika seb kpiak!' la, ale Naawen jaa zi. (50) Ain wa-biok le la, te wa yaali ain wa nye. (51) Wa ale yin biika seb kpiak la, wa kan yin biika seb kpiak-a, biika somoa ale kpiak. (52) Nuru dan niag fu, te fu pai a tog a sag fi biik, faa

113) *yig = yiti.*

(40) Then the hen went and lay down and shook[114] her anus, the cock then went and climbed onto [the hen] and made [his semen] flow [into the hen's anus], right before the eyes of the woman.

(41) Then she got up, [went to her] room and entered it. (42) When she [the woman] had got up and gone into the room, she passed by [her husband] and as she was about to lay down, she took her hand and got hold of the man's penis, took it and put it into her vagina and said: (43) 'Into the anus or vagina [it's all the same]!'[115] (44) The man then started fucking and fucking, - after three days [there occurred] a pregnancy, after [another] three days [the woman bore] a child.

(45) When she had delivered the child and it began to sit and to crawl and to walk, the man got up and pronounced a curse saying: (46) When he had got up in order to obtain this child, it was a fowl who was responsible for his having got the child. (47) A fowl taught his wife, and his wife entered [the house] and taught it [sexual intercourse] to him, and he begot the child. (48) He said that ... the child should beware of[116] the fowl.

(49) As soon as he had said: 'The child should beware of the fowl!', God came down [from the sky]. (50) [God] told him that it was an evil thing[117] which he intended to do. (51) He [the man] had said that the child should beware of the fowl, [but] he should not have said that the child should beware of the fowl, [for] the fowl was the child's friend[118]. (52) If someone helps you and you want to inform your

---

114) *chubi*, v. 'to shake, to move [the anus or vulva] up and down, to make contractive movements [e.g. in sexual intercourse], to squeeze'.

115) I.e. she had observed that the cock copulated with the hen's anus, whereas she put the man's penis into her vagina.

116) *seb(i)*, v., lit. 'to know'; '*seba*! Be careful! Attention! *Ba seba*. They should be careful' (Kröger BED).

117) *wa-biok* < *wari*, word, thing, affair, *biok*, bad, wicked, wrong, evil, lit. 'bad deed or word', 'evil (physical and moral [...]), bad thing, bad affair, bad word, fault, (moral) mistake, sin (Christian sense)' (Kröger BED). In the present context, it may be translated: 'he was about, he was willing to commit a sin'.

118) *somoa*, def. *somo(a)wa*, pl. *soma*, '1. friend, neighbour, comrade (somebody 'who has done something important to help you and who you can always rely on') [...] 2. fellowship, comradeship, neighbourly kindness [...]' (Kröger BED).

yin ka: (53) Wa chum dan nya kpiak, wa niag. (54) Amaa kpiak ale nur-biik ale a wom chaab biik la ale soa, ate nuruwa poom boro a yin wa pai biemu a sag biika. (55) Nyin jinla cheng, ba kaa wom chaab biik ngman-a. (56) Gel-gel te kpiak kan ngmaa biisi ale nuro, te nuru me kan biisi ale kpiak-a. (57) Nurwa biika, te nurwa wien wa biika jigi la, biikala ale ngman biag biikai la, wa yaa wien ain: (58) Wa dan kpi, se ning nyono ka kpiak, te ba pa tom wa tuima te kpiak ga dula ga a sag.

(59) Ku kiri le la ate nuru dan kpi jinla, ban kan beg kpiak wari-a, ba kan beg naab war-a. (60) Ka kpiak ale sag te saaloa boro. (61) Ku kiri ale la ate kpiak a de ning.

child about it, you should rather say: (53) If he [the child] sees a fowl in future, he should help it [in return]. (54) It was because fowl and mankind understood each other[119)] that there was a child; but then the man was about to [tell his son] that he should commit an evil[120)] and teach [a curse on the fowl to] his son. (55) [God said:] From this day onwards, they will no longer understand each other's language. (56) Oh, well[121)], that was how it came about that fowl no longer talked to man and man no longer talked to fowl. (57) The man's child, the [child of the] one he [the father had already] spoken to[122)], the child that he [his son] begot [i.e. the man's grandson], then said: (58) When he [the grandchild] dies, the first thing[123)] should be a fowl; they should take [a fowl] to perform the sacrifice[124)], so that the fowl will go there [into the realm of the dead] and teach them[125)].

(59) That is the reason why when someone dies nowadays and they do not ask for a fowl [to be sacrificed][126)], then they will [also] not ask for a cow. (60) It was the fowl which taught mankind to live [to procreate]. (61) That is the reason why a fowl takes the first place[127)].

---

119) They understood each other's language, i.e. they were on good terms with one another (Pauline Akankyalabey).

120) Lit.: 'to take the evil', 'to commit the evil', i. e. to curse the fowl.

121) *gel-gel*, interjection, meaning lit. to suffer from carrying a heavy load, here: 'this is the problem'.

122) I. e. the son he had warned to beware of the fowl.

123) *ning nyono*, lit. 'owner of the first' or: 'the first owner, master, head, representative' or 'supreme leader, commander [...]' (Kröger BED), i.e. the thing or being preceding all others in rank and respect.

124) *Ba* [...] *tom wa tuima* [...], lit. 'They perform his work', i. e. they perform a sacrifice.

125) I. e. the fowl should teach the dead how to behave properly, even possibly meaning, how to have sexual intercourse; the dead (*kpilima*) are believed to live more or less like the living human beings.

126) I. e. if there is no sacrifice of an animal at all.

127) In all sacrificial rites when animals are being slaughtered.

02. GOD SAVES GIRLS FROM BEING SACRIFICED

02.01 BUL-E0008 Girl must not be killed (sacrificed) I

02.02 BUL-E0225 Girl must not be killed (sacrificed) II

02.03 BUL-E0259 Girl must not be killed (sacrificed) III

02.04 BUL-E0292 Girl must not be killed (sacrificed) IV

02.05 BUL-E0489 Girl must not be killed (sacrificed) V

02.06 BUL-E0572 Girl must not be killed (sacrificed) VI

02.07 BUL-E0761 Girl must not be killed (sacrificed) VII

02.08 BUL-E1267 Girl must not be killed (sacrificed) VIII

02.09 BUL-E1435 Girl must not be killed (sacrificed) IX

02.10 BUL-E0920 Girl must not be killed X

02. GOD SAVES GIRLS FROM BEING SACRIFICED

This chapter encompasses ten stories of the tale-type 'God Saves Girls from Being Sacrificed'. The variants of this tale-type may be classified into three sub-types: In sub-type 1 **all** girls must be killed (sacrificed), usually by the order of a chief; in sub-type 2, **one particular** girl must be killed, i.e. in most cases she must be slaughtered as a sacrifice to a *tanggbain*; in the aberrant sub-type 3, represented only by story BUL-E920, the girl intends to kill herself. In all types, the girl is finally saved by God, who sends an animal to be sacrificed in the girl's stead, or by some other supernatural being.

The motifs contained in these stories are listed in the ensuing tables. The first figure in these lists refers to the five episodes into which the story may be divided. The second figure designates the sub-type, with the figure 0 indicating motifs occurring in all or most sub-types. The third figure indicates the number of consecutive motifs in each episode.

A comparison of these lists shows that no less than 12 of the motifs occur in 50% and more of the stories analysed. These common motifs, printed in bold letters in the lists and compiled in the last list, may be called 'core motifs'. Thus, the tale type 'The Slaughtered Girl(s)' or 'The Girl(s) Saved by God (or another Supernatural Being) from Being Sacrificed' proves to be rather homogeneous in comparison with other Bulsa tale-types. Yet at the same time the Bulsa tellers show considerable variation in choosing different motifs when telling stories belonging to the same type and sub-type. The stories are presented here to exemplify the degree of variance found in Bulsa stories and how this variation is achieved.

EPISODES:

1. Initial situation
2. Dilemma
3. Further developments
4. Sacrifice/killing of girl
5. Intervention of God/Supernatural agent

SUB-TYPES:

0 00 All (most) sub-types
0 10 **All** girls must be killed
0 20 **One** particular girl must be killed
0 30 Girl kills herself

BUL-E	0008	0225	0259	0292	0489	0572	0761	0920	1267	1435	
1 01	**+a**	**+a**	**+p**	**+a**	**+p**	**+p**	**+p**	**+dl**	**+p**	**+d**	**Daughter(s)** (girl[s]) must be killed (a= all d.; d = dl. disliked by parents; p = d. promised to earth-shrine [*tanggbain*]).
1 12	+	+		+							**Kill, all** girls must be k.ed.
1 23			+		+	+	+		+	+	**Kill, one particular** girl must be k.ed
1 34								+			**Kill,** girl intends to k. (burn) herself.
2 01			+			+					**Husband** consults an earth-shrine (*tanggbain*) in order to make his barren wife fecund.
2 02		+	+		+	+	(+)		+		**Earth-shrine** (*tanggbain*), parents (promise to) sacrifice girl to an e. s. ([+] Earth)
2 03			**+f**		+	**+f**	**+f**		+		**Child(ren)** (f= first child) must be sacrificed to an earth-shrine (*tanggbain*).
2 04		+	+t			+t			+t		**Beget,** man b.s children, (t) after having consulted an earth-shrine (*tanggbain*)

BUL-E	0008	0225	0259	0292	0489	0572	0761	0920	1267	1435	
2 05	+	+	+t	+	+	+t	+t		+	+	**Birth,** (barren) wife gives b. to children, (t) after having promised a child to an earth-shrine (*tang-gbain*).
2 26					+w				+m		**Beautiful,** (w) woman gives birth/(m) man begets b. girl.
2 27					+l			+dl	+l		**Like/Dislike,** father (parents) like(s) (l)/ dislike(s) (dl) his (their) daughter.
2 28								+		+	**Father** wants to kill his daughter because he does not like her/ because he thinks that she is not of his family.
2 19	+	+		+m							**Hide,** parents (m = mother) h.(s) daughter, although all newborn girls must be killed.
3 01	+h	+h		+h	+b			+b	+b	+b	**Room,** girl is in a r. (house?): h = hidden by her parents; b = before she is taken out to be sacrificed.
3 02	+			+						+	**Cattle yard,** girl is taken into the c. y. before being killed.
3 03	+g	+b	+b	+Br	+Br	+m	+g	+Br	+g	+sBr	**Song** announcing girl's death sung by: b = bird; Br = brother; g = girl; m = mother.
3 04		+c	+e			+r	+r				**Ant** will destroy (c = cook: e = eat; r = remove) the intestines of the girl to be sacrificed [song].

BUL-E	0008	0225	0259	0292	0489	0572	0761	0920	1267	1435	
3 05	**+b**			**+Brs**	**+Brs**			**+Brs**		**+sBr**	**Brother** (Br) (sBr = senior brother; Brs = brothers; b = boy) has to bring girl out of house/room before she is killed.
3 06		**+**	**+**			**+**	**+**		**(+)**		**Millet beer,** girl ([+] people have) has to brew m. b. before she is sacrificed to an earth-shrine (*tanggbain*).
3 07			+			(+)	+				**Mother** orders her daughter to prepare millet beer before the girl is sacrificed / (+) Mother **and** daughter prepare millet beer together.
3 08		+	+				+				**Carry,** girl has to c. the millet beer she brewed to the earth-shrine (*tanggbain*) to which she will be sacrificed;
4 01			+			+	+		+		**Drink,** millet beer as sacrificial d. of an earth-shrine (*tanggbain*).
4 02		**+g**	**+f,g**		**+g**	**+f**	**+g**		**+g**	**+g**	**Sacrifice,** Earth-shrine (*tanggbain*) receives girl (g) / firstborn child (f) as a sacrifice.
4 03			**+**	**+**		**+**			**+**	**+**	**Knife,** girl to be killed (slaughtered) by cutting her throat with a k.
5 02	**+w**	**+G-r**	**+G-r**	**+r**	**+pa**	**+G-r**	**+G-a**	**+s**	**+w**	**+s**	**Death,** girl saved from d. by G = God (*Naawen*); a = animals sent by God; pa = paternal relative; r = ram; s = supernatural being; w = (old) woman;

BUL-E	0008	0225	0259	0292	0489	0572	0761	0920	1267	1435	
5 03		+r	+r	+r		+r	+				**God** sends animal (+) (r = ram) from the sky to be sacrificed to an earth-shrine (*tanggbain*) instead of a girl.

Motifs occurring in 50% and more of the analysed stories of the type 'GOD SAVES GIRL(S) FROM BEING SACRIFICED'

1 01 **Daughter(s)** (girl[s]) must be killed (a= all d.; d = dl. disliked by their parents; p = d. promised to Earth-shrine [*tanggbain*]).

2 02 **Earth-shrine** (*tanggbain*), parents (promise to) sacrifice girl to an e. s. ([+] Earth).

2 03 **Child(ren)** (f= first child) must be sacrificed to an earth-shrine (*tanggbain*).

2 05 **Birth,** (barren) wife gives b. to children, (t) after having promised a child to an earth-shrine (*tanggbain*).

3 01 **Room,** girl is in a r. (house?): h = hidden by her parents; b = before she is taken out to be sacrificed.

3 03 **Song** announcing girl's death sung by: b = bird; Br = brother; g = girl; m = mother.

3 05 **Brother** (Br) (sBr = senior brother; Brs = brothers; b = boy) has to bring girl out of house/room before she is killed.

3 06 **Millet beer,** girl ([+] people have) has to brew m. b. before she is sacrificed to an earth-shrine (*tanggbain*).

4 02 **Sacrifice,** earth-shrine receives girl (g) / firstborn child (f) as a sacrifice.

4 03 **Knife,** girl to be killed (slaughtered) by cutting her throat with a k.

5 02 **Death,** girl saved from d. by G = God (*Naawen*); a = animals sent by God; pa = paternal relative; r = ram; s = supernatural being; w = (old) woman;

5 03 **God** sends animal (+) (r = ram) from the sky to be sacrificed to an earth-shrine (*tanggbain*) instead of a girl.

BUL-E0008 (BULI TEXT)

(1) Ain naab le boro ain ba dan biag nipok-bili ba ko, ba dan biag nurdoa-bili ba tanla[128]*, a yaa boro, teee! - ate wa pok-bili jam biag nipok.*

(2) Ba yaa pa nipok-bini sug, a yaa din nyini yueni yeni dema ain wa powa biag kaasi kama. (3) Yeni nyama ain too[129] *di da wari ya, a biag kaasim dee*[130]*, ka wen le taa jam yoo.*

(4) A boro, boro, boro, biika pag ya, wan ngman bag-a a sugi. (5) Nurdoa-bili yaa jo ain wa moag bolim. (6) Wa yaa jo a paari le wa kala, wa yaa pilim nyin yueni yeni nyonowa ain waa: (7) 'Ase naawa velim kama ain ba dan biag nipok-bili ba ko la, naawa powa biag ka nipok-bili!' (8) Yeni nyonowa ain waa velim; [biika] ain ka wensie! (9) Yeni nyonowa yaa wu naawa ain: baa yaa ba meena kusung. (10) Ba yaa taam, ba yaa beg naawa ain biika le yuen waa: (11) 'Fi powa biag ka nipok-bili ate fi pa sug age paasi nurma ate baa ko ba liema?' (12) Ain waa: (13) 'Biika velim ya!' (14) Biika ain: (15) 'Wa boro, midek le nya wa!' (16) Ba yaa nye dila: yaa deri ga ta bai laa ko nurma

---

128) Colloquial form of *tara* or *ta la*, 'have', 'keep' [s.th.], imperative.

129) *too*, Hausa: 'yes, alright, well!'

130) *dee*, Hausa, 'concerning s.th.'

02.01 Girls must not be killed (sacrificed) I

BUL-E0008 (ENGLISH TRANSLATION)

(1) It is said that there was a chief who said that if a girl is born[131], they [his people] should kill [her], but if a boy is born, they should keep him [alive], and they went on and on to live[132]; well! - when [one day] his junior wife[133] happened to give birth to a girl.

(2) And they [the parents] took the girl and hid her, and they went out [of the room] and told the people in the house that his [the chief's] wife had born a child who had died. (3) The elders said, all right, that doesn't matter; as far as miscarriage is concerned, it is God's will[134]. [Laughter[135] among the audience].

(4) They went on and on and on to live, and the child grew up and she couldn't hide [herself] any longer. (5) A boy entered [the girl's room] in order to fetch fire. (6) He entered and met her sitting, and when he went out again, he told the house owner: (7) '[It is] as if the chief was telling lies when he said that when a girl is born, she should be killed, [but] the chief's wife has given birth to a girl!' (8) The house owner said that he [the boy] was telling a lie; [the boy] said that it was the truth! (9) The house owner then called the chief and said: they [the elders] wanted [to assemble] everybody in the *kusung*[136]. (10) They came along and asked the chief [whether it was true or not] what the boy had said: (11) 'Your wife had given birth to a girl, but you were hiding [her] while [you] deceived the [other] people into killing their [own] daughters?' (12) [The chief] answered: (13) 'The boy is telling lies!' (14) [But] the boy replied: (15) 'She [his daughter] was there, I myself have seen her!' (16) Thereupon

---

131) Lit.: '... if they give birth to a girl'.

132) I.e. nothing extraordinary happened.

133) She is usually the favourite wife.

134) Lit.: 'it is God who brings it indeed.'

135) The laughter refers to the Chief's skilful trickery in hiding his daughter.

136) A shelter or shade in front of the compound; see glossary.

la, a jam yoo! (17) A yaa za tamponi zuk ain: (18) Ba yaa be ta nipok-bini nyini ate ba ko.

(19) Ba yaa tom nurdoa-bini yuen waa, nurdoa-bili wai le bobri la, wa ga wi nipok-bini ain wa nyini ate ba ko wa. (20) Wa din ngman pilim chali a cheng yaa ga yueni waa ain: (21) 'Ba yuen fi nyini ate ba ko fi!' (22) Nipok-bini a yaa vaari yiti:

(23) Ain nyini ba ko-a, nyini ba ko-a, nyini ba ko-a, nyini ba ko-a!

(24) Ain wee: sug boro, sug boro!

(25) N tin sug boro, a gisi boa? Ni yin mi sug boro, n-yaa!

(26) N sug boro ka se-a? A sug boro, n-yaa!

(27) N sug boro, a gisi boa? Ni yuen mi sug boro n-yaa!

(28) Sug boro ka boa? A sug boro, n-yaa!

(29) N sug boro, a gisi boa? A sug boro, n-yaa!

(30) A sug boro ka se? A sug boro, n-yaa!

(31) A sug boro, a de ka boa dewa? A sug boro, n-yaa!

(32) Nangkpieng deng-teng, wei! (33) Wa nyini ya, kunkuteng zaa nangkpiengka po:

they did this: at once they went and brought those who had [already] killed people [their daughters], and they came, all right! (17) And [those who were to kill the girl] stood on the rubbish heap[137] saying: (18) They [the people in the chief's house] should bring the girl out so that they could kill [her].

(19) They sent the boy, saying that the boy who betrayed her should go and call her, telling her to come out so that they [could] kill her. (20) And he again ran, went and said [to the girl]: (21) 'They said that you should come out so that they may kill you.' (22) The girl got up quickly:

(23) [They] said: come out, they will kill [you], come out, they will kill [you], come out, they will kill [you], come out, they will kill [you]!

(24) [I] say: [I] hid and lived, hid and lived!

(25) If I hid myself and lived, what for? You [pl.] say I should hide and live, *n-yaa*[138]!

(26) How did I hide and live[139], how is it? [I] hid and lived, *n-yaa*!

(27) I hid myself and lived, for what? You [pl.] say I should hide and live, *n-yaa*!

(28) What did I hide and live for? [I] hid and lived, *n-yaa*!

(29) I hid myself and lived, for what? [I] hid and lived, *n-yaa*!

(30) How did I hide and live, how is it? [I] hid and lived, *n-yaa*!

(31) [I] hid and lived, what am I eating here? [I] hid and lived, *n-yaa*!

(32) [She came out of the courtyard] into the cattle-yard, upright, dear me! (33) She came out on elevated ground and stood in the cattle-yard:

---

137) The ash and rubbish heap (*tampoi*, def. *tamponi*) is in front of the Bulsa compounds, usually to the left of the entrance, behind the closed *kusung*.

138) *n-yaa!* are meaningless words sung as the wailing at the end of a mourning song (funeral dirge).

139) I.e. under what bad circumstances was I hiding myself? She would have loved to come out earlier. Now it was of no avail.

(34) *Ain nyini ba ko-a, nyini ba ko-a, nyini ba ko-a, nyini ba ko-a!*

(35) *A yuen wa bo dula, n poom seb le nye dii, chiak-gbiri ngmirisi, ka ngmirisika!*

(36) *Ain mi sug boro, sug boro!*

(37) *Ain mi sug boro-a, sug boro-a, n-yaa!*

(38) *N tin sug boro, a pa fi boa? Ni yuen mi sug boro, n-yaa!*

(39) *N sug boro-a, a de ni boa? A sug boro, n-yaa!*

(40) *N tin maa boro, a gisi boa? N tin maa boro-a, n-yaa!*

(41) *Sug boro a pa ni boa?*

(42) *A sug boro n-yaa!*

[Interference from the audience: the teller is asked by James Agalic and two women to continue the song, so she starts again:]

(43) *Ain mi sug boro, sug boro!*

(44) *Ain mi sug boro, sug boro!*

(45) *Ain nyini ba ko-a, nyini ba ko-a!*

(46) *Ain nyini ba ko-a, nyini ba ko-a!*

(34) [They] said: come out, they will kill [you], come out, they will kill [you], come out, they will kill [you], come out, they will kill [you]!

(35) [They] said: she is there, do I know what I have done? The [skin of my] waist is so much decorated[140] that there is no more room for decoration!

(36) [They] said I hid and lived, hid and lived!

(37) [They] said I hid and lived, hid and lived, *n-yaa*!

(38) When I hid and lived, what did I take [away from] you [sing.][141]? You [pl.] said that I hid and lived, *n-yaa*!

(39) I hid and lived, what did I eat of your [pl.] [foodstuff]? [I] hid and lived, *n-yaa*!

(40) When I also live, for what? I also live, *n-yaa*!

(41) Hide and live to take what?

(42) [I] hid and lived, *n-yaa*!

[Interference from the audience: the teller is asked by James Agalic and two women to continue the song, so she starts again:]

(43) [They] said, I hid and lived, hid and lived!

(44) [They] said, I hid and lived, hid and lived!

(45) [They] said: come out, they will kill [you], come out, they will kill [you]!

(46) [They] said: come out, they will kill [you], come out, they will kill [you]!

---

140) *ngmirisi*, v. 'to decorate (e.g. face with ornamental scars; walls or pots with incisions, decorative patterns etc.) ...' (Kröger BED). In the present context it means that the lower part of the girl's waist had been tatooed or ornamented with scarifications.

141) I.e. what harm did the girl cause while she was hiding?

(47) *A yuen wa bo dula, n poom seb le nye dii, chiak-gbiri ngmirisi, ka ngmirisika!*

(48) *Ain mi sug boro, mi tin sug boro, a pa fi boa?*

(49) *A sug boro, n-yaa!*

(50) *N tin maa boro, a de ni boa?*

(51) *A sug boro, n-yaa!*

(52) *N tin sug boro, a pa ni boa?*

(53) *A sug boro, n-yaa!*

(54) *N maa boro a de ni boa?*

(55) *A sug boro, n-yaa!*

(56) ... tamponi zuk deng-teng ale nipok din nyini wen din nye nna 'lak-lak-lak-lak' din jam zi ain waa gaari. (57) Ain ba kan nagi, ba zanla[142)] *ate wa yueni wari ate ba wom: (58) Ba dan biag ba miena, ba tanla, amaa*[143)] *ba laa nye nna, da-ngaye nurdoa*

---

142) Coloquial form of *zaani la* or *za la*, 'stand', 'wait', imperative.

143) *amaa*, Hausa: 'but, if, when'.

(47) [They] said: she is there, do I know what I have done? The [skin of my] waist is so much decorated that there is no more room for decoration!

(48) [They] said: I hid and lived, when I hid and lived, what did I take [away from] you [sing.]?

(49) [I] hid and lived, *n-yaa*!

(50) When I also live, what did I eat of your [pl.] [foodstuff]?

(51) [I] hid and lived, *n-yaa*!

(52) When I hid and lived, what of your [things] did I take?

(53) [I] hid and lived, *n-yaa*!

(54) I also live, what did I eat of your [foodstuff]?

(55) [I] hid and lived, *n-yaa*!

(56) ... [the girl] stood upright on the rubbish heap, when a woman came out of the sky and was making [the flying sound of] '*lak-lak-lak-lak*', then came and landed in order to separate[144] [them and to stop them from killing her]. (57) [She said] that they should not beat [and kill the girl], [but] that they should wait so that she would tell them something to which they should listen: (58) If they had born them all [both boys and girls], they should keep [them]; if, however, they continued to do it this way[145],

144) *gaari*, v. 'to separate, to isolate ... *gaari kpalingka*, to stop a fight (by separating the fighters) ...' (Kröger BED).

145) I.e. if they continued to kill newborn girls.

ngman ka buudi. (59) Hali[146] *badek le bo Naawen yeri la, baa dam ka chaab, donsi*[147] *ba nye wa gaafara*[148]*. (60) Ba deri pa nipok-bini basi.*

(61) Di nna kpegtalegi.

146) Hausa: 'even so, even that, the reason for s.th.'

147) Hausa: 'for that reason.'

148) Hausa: 'excuse!'

in two day's time[149] a man would no longer have a family[150]. (59) Even they themselves[151] who live in God's house, they are mixed [men and women], therefore they should exempt her [the girl, from being killed]. (60) They at once left the girl [in peace].

(61) That is the end [of the story].

---

149) I.e. in a very short time.

150) *buuri* or *buudi*, n., kind, genus, family, lineage, clan, posterity; cf. glossary.

151) The celestial woman and her consorts.

BUL-E0225 (BULI TEXT)

(1) Ain dilapowa, ba jam biag nipok-bilisanga a ko kama[152]*, alege a biag nidoa-bilisanga a tanla.*

(2) Naab a yaa biag wa lie a yaa basi wa doku po, a yaa pa sug. (3) Ate liewa yaa boro a yaa ga pag. (4) Yeni dema yaa chui nya wa ain liewa ale pag bo doku po la, [ain]: (5) 'Fi ale wieni ain: (6) 'Waa miena wuu a dan biag nipok-bili, ba yig ko', alege fi a yaa le biag nipok-bini la, a yaa pai sug la ate wa pag la,' yog-yogla ba yaa ba ko wa kama.

(7) Ba yaa ta naawa a nyin kusung a nyin yueni: (8) Naawa yaa yiti a yaa jo wieni wa powa ain yog-yoglude wa-dek le wieni ain ba biag nipok-bilisa a ko, abe ba biag nidoa-bilisa a tanla. (9) Yog-yogla nipowa a biag nipok-bili ate wa pag la, ate yeni dema yaa zer ain, se wa liewa me baa ko kama; ba kan basi wa.

(10) Ba yaa yiti pai kpaama te wa ain wa cheng ga ngari nyiam. (11) Nipoowa yaa ta kpaamanga a jo nanzuk. (12) Nuim, yoo! - bu yue le gbiin - a yaa jue a kal nanzuk mimpini zuk:

---

152) *ko kama* is pronounced [koɣma].

02.02 Girls must not be killed (sacrificed) II

BUL-E0225 (ENGLISH TRANSLATION)

(1) It is said that in former times, when people brought forth girls, they killed them, but when they brought forth boys they left them [alive].

(2) A chief then begot a daughter and left her in a room and hid her. (3) The daughter lived and grew up. (4) The people of the house peeped [into the room], saw that the [chief's] daughter had grown up in the room, [and said to the chief:] (5) 'It is you who said: (6) "If someone brings forth a girl, she should be taken and killed', but you [yourself] begot a girl, took her and hid her and she has grown up"; now they [the chief's people] wanted to kill her.

(7) They sent the chief outside [the house] to the *kusung*, and spoke to him: (8) The chief got up and entered [the house] telling his wife that from now on[153)] - he himself said[154)] that if they brought forth girls they should kill them, but if they brought forth boys they should let them live. (9) And now that his [own] wife has borne a girl and she has grown up, the people of the [chief's] house disagree [to make an exception with the chief's daughter] and say that his daughter should also be killed; they would not let her live.

(10) And so they got up, took some malt[155)], gave it to her and said that she should go and fetch water. (11) The woman [the girl] took the malt and went into the grinding room. (12) A bird, oho! -called *gbiin*[156)] - flew up and sat down on the grass roof[157)] of the grinding room:

---

153) This sentence, comprising reported speech twice, is somewhat distorted.

154) Translation of Miss Pauline Akankyalabey: '[...] it was he himself who had given the order [...]'.

155) *kpaama*, n. pl. 'malt, germinated millet or guinea corn grains (first stage of brewing pito)' (Kröger BED).

156) *gbiim* or *gbiin*, cf. glossary, *gbiin*.

157) *mipili* or *mimpili*, 'sloping roof, hut with a sloping (straw) roof' (Kröger BED); usually conical in form.

[Solo]

(13) *Adugpaalie, 'dugpalie,*

(14) *faa ngab fi kum kpaam-ee!*

[Refrain:]

[Solo]

(15) *Ate kingkering cha-moaning-a dig fi nyuet-ee!*

[Chorus]

(16) *'dugpaal-a!*

[Solo]

(17) *Ate kingkering cha-sobl-a dig fi nyuete-e!*

[Chorus]

(18) *'dugpaal-a!*

[Solo]

(19) *Ate kingkering cha-moaning-a dig fi nyueta-a!*

[Chorus]

(20) *'dugpaal-a!*

[Solo]

(21) *Ate kingkering cha-sobl-a dig fi nyueta-a!*

[Chorus]

(22) *'dugpaal-a!*

[Solo]

(13) Adugpalie[158], 'dugpalie,

(14) you are grinding the malt of your death!

[Refrain:]

[Solo]

(15) And an ant[159] with a red waist will cook your intestines!

[Chorus]

(16) 'dugpaal-a!

[Solo]

(17) And an ant with a black waist will cook your intestines!

[Chorus]

(18) 'dugpaal-a!

[Solo]

(19) And an ant with a red waist will cook your intestines!

[Chorus]

(20) 'dugpaal-a!

[Solo]

(21) And an ant with a black waist will cook your intestines!

[Chorus]

(22) 'dugpaal-a!

---

158) Proper name of the girl to be killed. The meaning of the name is not known.

159) *kingkering*, in this case, a very tiny ant in two varieties: with a red and dark 'waist', i.e. back part.

[Refrain (15-22) repeated 3 times]

(23) Wa ngab kpaamanga ga nue a nyin pa wa liik a cheng beli. (24) Gbiinka a ngmaa cheng a ga lig beni siuku ning:

[Solo]

(25) *Adugpaalie, 'dugpalie,*

(26) *nya faa ngar fi kum nyiam-oo!*

[Refrain:]

[Solo]

(27) *Ate kingkering cha-moaning-a dig fi nyuet-aa!*

[Chorus]

(28) *'dugpaal-a!*

[Solo]

(29) *Ate kingkering cha-sobl-a dig fi nyuete-e!*

[Chorus]

(30) *'dugpaalie-e!*

[Solo]

(31) *Ate kingkering cha-moaning-a dig fi nyueta-a!*

[Chorus]

(32) *'dugpaal-a!*

[Solo]

(33) *Ate kingkering cha-sobl-a dig fi nyueta-a!*

[Refrain (15-22) repeated 3 times]

(23) She finished grinding the malt, went out, took her earthenware vessel[160] and set out for a river. (24) The *gbiin* bird came again and blocked the way to the river:

[Solo]

(25) Adugpalie, 'dugpalie,

(26) look, you are fetching the water of your death!

[Refrain:]

[Solo]

(27) And an ant with a red waist will cook your intestines!

[Chorus]

(28) 'dugpaal-a!

[Solo]

(29) And an ant with a black waist will cook your intestines!

[Chorus]

(30) 'dugpaalie-e!

[Solo]

(31) And an ant with a red waist will cook your intestines!

[Chorus]

(32) 'dugpaal-a!

[Solo]

(33) And an ant with a black waist will cook your intestines!

160) *liik*, 'earthenware vessel with a narrow mouth (generally used for storing liquids)' (Kröger BED).

[Chorus]

(34) *'dugpaal-a!*

[Refrain (27-30) repeated 3 times, with slight variations of final vowels between *-e-e* and *-a-a*]

(35) Wa ngari nyiamu a yaa ta jam, a yaa jam borigi daamu, a yaa dam daamu; wa [bu] yaa ngman jam a kal jaamu zuk:

[Solo]

(36) *Adugpaalie, 'dugpalie,*

(37) *faa dam fi kum daam-oo!*

[Refrain:]

[Solo]

(38) *Ate kingkering cha-moaning-a dig fi nyuet-aa!*

[Chorus]

(39) *'dugpaal-a!*

[Solo]

(40) *Ate kingkering cha-sobl-a dig fi nyuete-e!*

[Chorus]

(41) *'dugpaalie-e!*

[Solo]

(42) *Ate kingkering cha-moaning-a dig fi nyueta-a!*

[Chorus]

(34) 'dugpaal-a!

[Refrain (27-30) repeated 3 times]

(35) She fetched the water and brought it [to the house] and then mixed the flour with the millet-beer, put it on the fire and [began] to stir[161] the millet-beer; it [the bird] came again and sat down on the thing [the straw roof]:

[Solo]

(36) Adugpalie, 'dugpalie,

(37) you are stirring the millet-beer of your death!

[Refrain:]

[Solo]

(38) And an ant with a red waist will cook your intestines!

[Chorus]

(39) 'dugpaal-a!

[Solo]

(40) And an ant with a black waist will cook your intestines!

[Chorus]

(41) 'dugpaal-a!

[Solo]

(42) And an ant with a red waist will cook your intestines!

---

161) The process called *borigi*, 'to stir millet-beer' includes: to mix the flour with the water in the pot, to put fire to it and then to stir it constantly.

[Chorus]

(43) *'dugpaal-a!*

[Solo]

(44) *Ate kingkering cha-sobl-a dig fi nyueta-a!*

[Chorus]

(45) *'dugpaal-a!*

[Refrain (38-41) repeated 6 times, with the said variations]

(46) Wa ngmaa zaa kuur daamu; wa [bu] ngman jam kal:

[Solo]

(47) *Adugpaalie, 'dugpalie,*

(48) *nya faa kuur fi kum daam-oo!*

[Refrain:]

[Solo]

(49) *Ate kingkering cha-moaning-a dig fi nyuet-aa!*

[Chorus]

(50) *'dugpaal-a!*

[Solo]

(51) *Ate kingkering cha-sobl-a dig fi nyuete-e!*

[Chorus]

(52) *'dugpaalie-e!*

[Chorus]

(43) 'dugpaal-a!

[Solo]

(44) And an ant with a black waist will cook your intestines!

[Chorus]

(45) 'dugpaal-a!

[Refrain (38-41) repeated 6 times]

(46) Then she stood and removed the millet-beer from the pot and put it into another vessel [in order to let it cool]; it [the bird] came again and sat down [on the roof]:

[Solo]

(47) Adugpalie, 'dugpalie,

(48) you are taking out the millet-beer of your death!

[Refrain:]

[Solo]

(49) And an ant with a red waist will cook your intestines!

[Chorus]

(50) 'dugpaal-a!

[Solo]

(51) And an ant with a black waist will cook your intestines!

[Chorus]

(52) 'dugpaal-a!

[Solo]

(53) *Ate kingkering cha-moaning-a dig fi nyueta-a!*

[Chorus]

(54) *'dugpaal-a!*

[Solo]

(55) *Ate kingkering cha-sobl-a dig fi nyueta-a!*

[Chorus]

(56) *'dugpaal-a!*

[Refrain (49-52) repeated 3 times, with said variations]

(57) Wa ngman zaa chagsi daamu; wa [bu] ngman zaa kal:

[Solo]

(58) *Adugpaalie, 'dugpalie,*

(59) *nya faa chagsi fi kum daam-oo!*

[Refrain:]

[Solo]

(60) *Ate kingkering cha-moaning-a dig fi nyuet-aa!*

[Chorus]

(61) *'dugpaal-a!*

[Solo]

(62) *Ate kingkering cha-sobl-a dig fi nyuete-e!*

[Chorus]

(63) *'dugpaalie-e!*

[Solo]

(53) And an ant with a red waist will cook your intestines!

[Chorus]

(54) 'dugpaal-a!

[Solo]

(55) And an ant with a black waist will cook your intestines!

[Chorus]

(56) 'dugpaal-a!

[Refrain (49-52) repeated 3 times]

(57) She began to filter the millet beer; it [the bird] again sat [on the roof]:

[Solo]

(58) Adugpalie, 'dugpalie,

(59) you are filtering the millet-beer of your death!

[Refrain:]

[Solo]

(60) And an ant with a red waist will cook your intestines!

[Chorus]

(61) 'dugpaal-a!

[Solo]

(62) And an ant with a black waist will cook your intestines!

[Chorus]

(63) 'dugpaal-a!

[Solo]

(64) *Ate kingkering cha-moaning-a dig fi nyueta-a!*

[Chorus]

(65) *'dugpaal-a!*

[Solo]

(66) *Ate kingkering cha-sobl-a dig fi nyueta-a!*

[Chorus]

(67) *'dugpaal-a!*

[Refrain (60-63) repeated 3 times, with said variations]

(68) Wa ngman zaa su daamu; wa [bu] ngman kal:

[Solo]

(69) *Adugpaalie, 'dugpalie,*

(70) *nya faa su fi kum daam-oo!*

[Refrain:]

[Solo]

(71) *Ate kingkering cha-moaning-a dig fi nyuet-aa!*

[Chorus]

(72) *'dugpaal-a!*

[Solo]

(64) And an ant with a red waist will cook your intestines!

[Chorus]

(65) 'dugpaal-a!

[Solo]

(66) And an ant with a black waist will cook your intestines!

[Chorus]

(67) 'dugpaal-a!

[Refrain (60-63) repeated 3 times]

(68) She again stood and put the millet-beer little by little with a calabash into another vessel[162] and added some yeast to it to ferment; it [the bird] sat again [on the straw roof]:

[Solo]

(69) Adugpalie, 'dugpalie,

(70) look, you are preparing to ferment the millet-beer of your death!

[Refrain:]

[Solo]

(71) And an ant with a red waist will cook your intestines!

[Chorus]

(72) 'dugpaal-a!

---

162) This vessel will be a pot in which the millet beer is to cool and in which will be sent to the market to be served out to customers.

[Solo]

(73) *Ate kingkering cha-sobl-a dig fi nyuete-e!*

[Chorus]

(74) *'dugpaalie-e!*

[Solo]

(75) *Ate kingkering cha-moaning-a dig fi nyueta-a!*

[Chorus]

(76) *'dugpaal-a!*

[Solo]

(77) *Ate kingkering cha-sobl-a dig fi nyueta-a!*

[Chorus]

(78) *'dugpaal-a!*

[Refrain (71-74) repeated 4 times, with said variations]

(79) Vani yaa vienti, ba yaa wu chaab nyini nansiungku noai a yaa jo koati daamu a ji Adugpaala-dek ain wa ji ate ba cheng tanggbani ate ba ga ko. (80) Ba yaa ji wa ta cheng tanggbani, a yaa ga gilim kala ain: (81) 'Daamwa naawa ale wieni ain ba biag nipok-bilisa a ko, abe ba biag nidoa-bilisa a tanla.' (82) Yog-yoglade ba ko ba nipok-bilisanga nue kama, alege naawa a pai wa liewa sug ate wa pag la, ba me yaa zeri ain se

[Solo]

(73) And an ant with a black waist will cook your intestines!

[Chorus]

(74) 'dugpaalie-e!

[Solo]

(75) And an ant with a red waist will cook your intestines!

[Chorus]

(76) 'dugpaal-a!

[Solo]

(77) And an ant with a black waist will cook your intestines!

[Chorus]

(78) 'dugpaal-a!

[Refrain (71-74) repeated 4 times]

(79) At daybreak, they [the people] called one another to come out [and assemble at] the entrance of the house; then they entered, lifted the millet-beer[163] and put it on Adugpaalie's head, saying that she [herself] should carry it, and that they will go to the *tanggbain*[164] to kill [the girl]. (80) They sent her to the *tanggbain*, then sat around it and said: (81) 'Formerly, the chief had said [ordered] that if someone brought forth a girl, she should be killed, whereas if someone brought forth a boy, he should be left [to live]. (82) Now they have killed all their girls, yet the chief took his daughter and hid her so that she grew up; [but] they disagreed [with him] and [insisted] that he should

---

163) Millet-beer is carried in big clay pots to the market or other places where it is being consumed.

164) An earth-shrine, or 'spirit of an earth-shrine [...]' (Kröger BED), cf. also glossary.

wa ko wa liewa. (83a) Jinla ba yaa ta jam kal ain ba te tanggbani. (83b) [...] ain tanggbani ngoa. (84) Gbiingka ngman jam jueli a kal tanggbani zuk:

[Solo]

(85) *Adugpaalie, 'dugpalie,*

(86) *faa kali fi kum kalike-e!*

[Refrain:]

[Solo]

(87) *Ate kingkering cha-moaning-a dig fi nyuet-aa!*

[Chorus]

(88) *'dugpaal-a!*

[Solo]

(89) *Ate kingkering cha-sobl-a dig fi nyuete-e!*

[Chorus]

(90) *'dugpaalie-e!*

[Solo]

(91) *Ate kingkering cha-moaning-a dig fi nyueta-a!*

[Chorus]

(92) *'dugpaal-a!*

[Solo]

(93) *Ate kingkering cha-sobl-a dig fi nyueta-a!*

[also] kill his daughter. (83a) Today they had brought [her] and they were sitting [round the *tanggbain*] so as to give her [as a sacrificial offering] to the *tanggbain*; (83b) the *tanggbain* should receive her. (84) The 'sitting thing'[165] then also sat down on top of the *tanggbain*:

[Solo]

(85) Adugpalie, 'dugpalie,

(86) you are sitting on the resting place of your death!

[Refrain:]

[Solo]

(87) And an ant with a red waist will cook your intestines!

[Chorus]

(88) 'dugpaal-a!

[Solo]

(89) And an ant with a black waist will cook your intestines!

[Chorus]

(90) 'dugpaal-a!

[Solo]

(91) And an ant with a red waist will cook your intestines!

[Chorus]

(92) 'dugpaal-a!

[Solo]

(93) And an ant with a black waist will cook your intestines!

---

165) The *gbiin* bird.

[Chorus]

(94) 'dugpaal-a!

[Refrain (85-88) repeated 4 times, with said variations]

(95) Ba yaa boo daamu a te tanggbani a yaa ga maa chaab yig nipowa ain ba duen. (96) Ate pa-diak a yaa nyin Naawen a yaa jam zi tanggbani teng ain ba kan ko nipok-bini, abe ba yig wa [ka] ko, abe ba basi nipok-bini.

(97) Dila ale soa ate yog-yoglade ate ba yaa biag nipok-bili a tanla, ale nipok-bili daam ka tanggbain ji-koorik, ba pa kama wala a kaab bogluk. (98) Daamwa alaa nye dii la ale la.

[Chorus]

(94) 'dugpaal-a!

[Refrain (87-90) repeated 4 times]

(95) Then they [the people] poured [some of the] millet-beer and gave it [sacrificed it] to the *tanggbain*[166] and then went together and seized the woman [the girl] in order to put her down [on the *tanggbain*]. (96) Then a ram came from God and landed beside the *tanggbain* saying that they should not kill the girl; they should rather seize it [the ram] and kill it and let the girl [live].

(97) This is the reason why nowadays, when they bring forth a girl, they let her [live]; in former times, a girl was something to be offered in sacrifice to a *tanggbain*; they took her to be offered as a sacrifice to a shrine (*bogluk*[167]). (98) This was what they did in former times.

---

166) They poured a libation for the *tanggbain*.

167) See glossary.

BUL-E0259 (BULI TEXT)

(1) Nipok le boro, wa ale wa choro-a; nipowa kan biagi, alege wa ta nipok me vi wa zuk. (2) Ba me a biag; wa be a yaali ka wai le kaa biag la, nipowa me a kum, ate wa ta wa jue tanggbain, ain wa nya wa yaa ka bisa. (3) Tanggbaini ain: 'Nguu!', wa le te wa bisa; wa le wa chorowa siag a kaab te wa.

(4) Ba kuli a ga paari, ga ain wa gberi la nipok-liak, pilim wa gberi la nurdoa - bisa bayuebi.

(5) Wa cheng ga wieni tanggbaini nyonowa ain wa nya jinla wa yaali ain wa jam kaabi wa bogluku. (6) Ba me siag, ba nya ku a kaab ka daam abe wa ta jam. (7) Ate wa

02.03 Girl must not be killed (sacrificed) III

BUL-E0259 (ENGLISH TRANSLATION)

(1) Once there lived a woman and her husband; the woman could not give birth, but he [the husband] had [taken] another wife in addition [to her]. (2) [Although] they [his wives[168)]] gave birth, he loved the one who did not give birth, and the [barren] woman wept and so he took her up to a *tanggbain*[169)]; he told it [the *tanggbain*][170)] that he wanted [to have] children [from his barren wife]. (3) The *tanggbain* said: 'Yes!', he[171)] [it] would give her children; she and her husband agreed and sacrificed [something] to him [it][172)].

(4) They went home and after having arrived there, he had sexual intercourse [with his wife] and begot[173)] a girl, and he again begot a man [boy] - [altogether] six children.

(5) He went and told the 'owner'[174)] of the *tanggbain* that today he wanted to come and to make a sacrifice to his shrine. (6) They [the 'owners' of the *tanggbain*]

---

168) The teller speaks of wives in the plural although he had previously mentioned only one wife besides the barren one.

169) An earth-shrine (cf. glossary), probably lying on a hill or on elevated ground.

170) I.e. he addressed his wishes to the *tanggbain*, promising it a sacrificial gift.

171) The teller uses the personal pronoun of the 1st class, reserved mostly for human beings.

172) Here the teller probably refers to some initial sacrifice to the *tanggbain*. The teller uses the personal pronoun of the 1st (*wa/ba*) class in referring to the *tanggbain*, thus declaring it to be a personalized being like a human being.

173) The teller uses the word *gberi*, 'to have sexual intercourse, to have sex, to fuck, to copulate' (Kröger BED). Apparently the verb *gberi* may be used in Buli in a transitive sense and its meaning includes the possible produce of sexual intercourse. The translator, Mr. Akamara, consequently rendered this passage: 'they went about to fuck a beautiful girl'.

174) I.e. the one responsible for the *tanggbain* and the observance of the proper procedure in prayers and sacrifices to the *tanggbain*.

jam wieni wa pooma ain wa le te kpaama ate ba ta jo nanzuk. (8) Ba siag ain nipok-bini dek le maa num. (9) Ba dan kpaamanga, ate nuim a jam a kali nawani zuk a kum; bu la kum la, bu a poli se ain wa le wa kum te wa la. (10) Wa la la bogluku be le la, ba yaa ba kaab te wa. (11) Nipok-bini yaa beg wa mawa ain: (12) 'N ma, a wom-u!' (13) Nipok-bini yaa kali tiesi wa poi po; nuimu yaa kum ain waa:

(14) *Waa Atubalie, 'tubalie,*
(15) *faa dani ka fi kum kpaama, 'tubalie-e!*
(16) *Atubalie, 'tubalie,*
(17) *faa dani ka fi kum kpaama, 'tubalie!*
(18) *Nan-gbang tapirig-a a dig wa nyueta, 'tubalie,*
(19) *a kinkering moaning a dig wa nyueta, 'tubalie!*

agreed, and they [made him] understand that its sacrificial drink is millet-beer, therefore he should bring it. (7) And he came [home] and told his wives that he would give them guinea corn malt, and they should take it and enter the grinding room[175]. (8) They agreed, saying that the girl herself should help them to grind [the malt]. (9) [As] they dried[176] the guinea corn malt, a bird came and sat on the edge of the wall [of the platform roof] and cried [sung][177]; as it was crying, it [the bird] thought that is was crying [mourning] for her [the girl]. (10) It was to her shrine[178] they wanted to make an offering. (11) The girl then asked her mother, saying: (12) 'My mother, listen!' (13) The girl sat down and meditated; the bird then cried, saying:

(14) Look, Atubalie, Atubalie,
(15) you are drying your death malt, Atubalie!
(16) Atubalie, Atubalie,
(17) you are drying your death malt, Atubalie!
(18) A dove[179] will cook her[180] intestines, Atubalie,
(19) a red ant will cook her intestines, Atubalie!

---

175) I.e. he told them that they should grind the malt.

176) The verb *dan(i)* means 'to spread (e.g. sheanuts, millet, groundnuts etc.) on a clean place (e.g. courtyard or flat roof) for drying, or: to dry (by spreading)' (Kröger BED).

177) The verb *kum(i)* means 'to mourn, to condole, to cry, to weep, to lament', but also 'to sing, twitter, chirp' of birds, cf. glossary. In the present context, the bird announces by its 'crying' (singing) the death of the girl.

178) *bogluk*, see glossary.

179) Probably *nan-gbang tapilierik*, 'red billed wood-dove (Turtur afer?)' (Kröger BED).

180) In the song, the teller changes between the personal address *'Waa Atubalie, 'tubalie!'* (Look, Atubalie, Atubalie!), using also the personal and possessive pronoun *fi*, 'you' (sing.) in the first four lines and, on the other hand, the pronoun *wa*, 'she' in the refrain of the last two lines of the verses. The first four lines change with the description of the different phases of millet beer brewing, whereas the last two lines remain constant throughout the repetition of the song. The threat expressed in the last two lines may be considered to be more 'objective' than the personal threats expressed in the first four lines.

(20) Nipowa [nipok-bini] ain: (21) 'Ama wom-u, nuimu a kum ka boa la?' (22) 'Faa lerigi kama, vaa kpaamanga ta sing!' (23) Wa vaa ta sing ta jo nanzuku. (24) Wa ga ain wa num:

(25) Atubalie, 'tubalie,
(26) faa num ka fi kum kpaama, 'tubalie-e!
(27) Waa Atubalie, 'tubalie,
(28) faa num ka fi kum kpaama, 'tubalie!
(29) Nan-gbang tapirigi a dig wa nyueta, 'tubalie,
(30) kingkering moaning a dig wa nyueta, 'tubalie!

(31) 'N ma, wom nuimu la kum la!' (32) 'Faa lerigi; num kpaamanga!' (33) Wa num vaari nyin. (34) 'Ni cheng beli!' (35) Nuimu ngman taam a zaani:

(36) Waa Atubalie, 'tubalie,
(37) faa ngari ka fi kum nyiamu-a, 'tubalie!
(38) Waa 'tubalie, 'tubalie,
(39) faa ngari ka fi kum nyiamu-a, 'tubalie!
(40) Nan-gbang tapirigi a dig wa nyueta, Atubalie,
(41) kingkering moaning dig wa nyueta, 'tubalie!

(42) 'Ama wom, nuimu la kum la!' (43) 'N kan yaa lerigika!' (44) Ba ngari jam, ain wa dam. (45) Wa gaa ain wa dam la, nuimu taam kala a daa kum:

(20) The woman [the girl] said: (21) 'Mother, listen, what is the bird crying?' (22) 'You talk too much, collect[181] the malt and take it down!' (23) She collected the malt, took it down [from the platform roof] and entered the grinding room. (24) She was about to grind [when the bird sang again]:

(25) Atubalie, Atubalie,
(26) you are drying your death malt, Atubalie!
(27) Atubalie, Atubalie,
(28) you are drying your death malt, Atubalie!
(29) A dove will cook her intestines, Atubalie,
(30) a red ant will cook her intestines, Atubalie!

(31) 'My mother, listen to what the bird cries!' (32) 'You talk too much; grind the malt!' (33) She [the girl] ground [the malt] and swept [the flour] together and came out. (34) [The mother ordered the girl:] 'Go [and fetch water] from the river!' (35) The bird passed by again and rested [singing]:

(36) Look, Atubalie, Atubalie,
(37) you are fetching your death water, Atubalie!
(38) Look, Atubalie, Atubalie,
(39) you are fetching your death water, Atubalie!
(40) A dove will cook her intestines, Atubalie,
(41) a red ant will cook her intestines, Atubalie!

(42) 'Mother, listen to what the bird cries!' (43) 'I don't want too much talking!' (44) They fetched [water] and came and told [the girl] that she should mix[182] [the millet flour with water]. (45) As she was going to stir [the millet beer], the bird passed by, sat down and cried:

---

181) *vari*, v. 'to collect (e.g. rubbish), to sweep' (Kröger BED). In the present context, the girl is asked by her mother to sweep together the malt which has dried on a platform roof.

182) *dam*, v. means in this context that the millet flour is mixed with water; later on it has to be stirred from time to time after having been put on the fire.

(46) *Waa Atubalie, 'tubalie,*
(47) *faa gaa dam-u ka fi kum daam-oa, 'tubalie!*
(48) *Nan-gbang tapirigi a dig wa nyueta, 'tubalie,*
(49) *kingkering moaning dig wa nyueta, Atubalie!*
(50) *Nan-gbang tapirigi a dig wa nyueta, 'tubalie,*
(51) *kingkering moaning dig wa nyueta, 'tubalie!*

(52) 'Ama, nuimu taa kum ain ka boa?' (53) 'N kan yaali lerigika; dam daamu!' (54) Wa dam nue. (55) 'Maa yaa fi chiem bolim!' (56) Wa chiem, dalisi dig du; nuimu ngman jam a kali:

(57) *Waa Atubalie, 'tubalie,*
(58) *faa dalisi ka fi kum daam-oa, 'tubalie!*
(59) *Waa Atubalie, 'tubalie,*
(60) *faa dalisi ka fi kum daam-oa, 'tubalie!*
(61) *Nan-gbang tapirigi a dig wa nyueta, 'tubalie,*
(62) *kingkering moaning dig wa nyueta, 'tubalie!*

(63) 'Ama wom-u!' (64) 'N kan yaa lerigika!' (65) Wa dalisi dig du. (66) 'Taam dam daamu!' (67) Ga wa dam la, nuimu jaa kali:

(68) *Waa Atubalie, 'tubalie,*
(69) *faa dam ka fi kum daam-oa, 'tubalie!*
(70) *Nan-gbang tapirigi a dig wa nyueta, 'tubalie,*
(71) *kingkering moaning dig wa nyueta, 'tubalie!*
(72) *Nan-gbang tapirigi a dig wa nyueta, 'tubalie,*
(73) *kingkering moaning dig wa nyueta, 'tubalie!*

(46) Look, Atubalie, Atubalie,
(47) you are stirring your death millet beer, Atubalie!
(48) A dove will cook her intestines, Atubalie,
(49) a red ant will cook her intestines, Atubalie!
(50) A dove will cook her intestines, Atubalie,
(51) a red ant will cook her intestines, Atubalie!

(52) 'Mother, what does the bird say when it cries?' (53) 'I don't want too much talk; stir the millet beer!' (54) She finished stirring [the millet beer]. (55) 'I want you to light a fire!' (56) She [the daughter] lit it, skimmed [the millet beer], and put it on [the fire]; the bird came again and sat down [singing]:

(57) Look, Atubalie, Atubalie,
(58) you are skimming your death millet beer, Atubalie!
(59) Look, Atubalie, Atubalie,
(60) you are skimming your death millet beer, Atubalie!
(61) A dove will cook her intestines, Atubalie,
(62) a red ant will cook her intestines, Atubalie!

(63) 'Mother, listen!' (64) 'I don't want too much talking!' (65) She skimmed [the millet beer] and put it on the fire. (66) [The mother ordered her:] 'Go and stir the beer!' (67) As she was about to stir, the bird came and sat down:

(68) Look, Atubalie, Atubalie,
(69) you are stirring your death millet beer, Atubalie!
(70) A dove will cook her intestines, Atubalie,
(71) a red ant will cook her intestines, Atubalie!
(72) A dove will cook her intestines, Atubalie,
(73) a red ant will cook her intestines, Atubalie!

(74) 'Ama, wom-u!' (75) 'N kan yaali lerigika! (76) Daamu be, kuuri!'

(77) Waa Atubalie, 'tubalie,
(78) faa kuui ka fi kum daam-oa, 'tubalie!
(79) Waa Atubalie, 'tubalie,
(80) faa kuui ka fi kum daam-oa, 'tubalie!
(81) Nan-gbang tapirigi a dig wa nyueta, 'tubalie,
(82) kingkering moaning dig wa nyueta, 'tubalie!

(83) 'Ama wom-u!' (84) 'N kan yaali lerigika!' (85) Wa kuui, vari vienti chagsi daamu.

(86) Waa Atubalie, 'tubalie,
(87) faa chagsi ka fi kum daam-oa, 'tubalie!
(88) Atubalie, 'tubalie,
(89) faa chagsi ka fi kum daam-oa, 'tubalie!
(90) Nan-gbang tapirigi a dig wa nyueta, 'tubalie,
(91) kingkering moaning dig wa nyueta, Atubalie!

(92) 'Ama, wom-u!' (93) 'N kan yaali lerigika! (94) Chagsi daamu!' (95) Wa chagsi nueri, daamu a vaasi, taam nya daamu.

(96) Waa Atubalie, 'tubalie,
(97) faa nya ka fi kum daam-oa, 'tubalie!
(98) Ti kingkering moaning dig wa nyueta, 'tubalie,

(74) 'Mother, listen!' (75) 'I don't want too much talking! (76) The millet beer is ready, take it out of[183] the pot!' [The bird sang again:]

(77) Look, Atubalie, Atubalie,
(78) you are collecting your death millet beer, Atubalie!
(79) Look, Atubalie, Atubalie,
(80) you are collecting your death millet beer, Atubalie!
(81) A dove will cook her intestines, Atubalie,
(82) a red ant will cook her intestines, Atubalie!

(83) 'Mother, listen!' (84) 'I don't want too much talking!' (85) She removed [the millet beer from the pot]; at daybreak, she [should] sift[184] the millet beer. [The bird started to sing again:]

(86) Look, Atubalie, Atubalie,
(87) you are sifting your death millet beer, Atubalie!
(88) Atubalie, Atubalie,
(89) you are sifting your death millet beer, Atubalie!
(90) A dove will cook her intestines, Atubalie,
(91) a red ant will cook her intestines, Atubalie!

(92) 'Mother, listen!' (93) 'I don't want too much talking! (94) Sift the millet beer!' (95) When she had finished sifting [it], and the millet beer was boiling, [her mother ordered her to] go and take a look at the millet beer.

(96) Look, Atubalie, Atubalie,
(97) you are looking at your death millet beer, Atubalie,
(98) And a red ant will cook her intestines, Atubalie!

---

183) The verb *kuuri* means: '1. to ladle, to scoop (with a spoon or a calabash; used for solid, viscous and liquid stuff, but not for water [...], to take sth. from a pot [...] with a calabash or spoon [...]' (Kröger BED).

184) *chagsi*, v. 'to sift, to (pass through a) sieve, to strain, ... to filter' (Kröger BED).

(99)	*Nan-gbang tapirigi a dig wa nyueta, 'tubalie!*
(100)	*Ti kingkering moaning dig wa nyueta, 'tubalie!*

(101) 'Ama, wom-u!' (102) 'N kan yaali lerigika!' (103) Ain: 'Taam su!' (104) Wa ga ain wa su; nuimu ngman jam a kali:

(105)	*Waa Atubalie, 'tubalie,*
(106)	*faa su ka fi kum daam-oa, 'tubalie!*
(107)	*Waa Atubalie, 'tubalie,*
(108)	*faa su ka fi kum daam-oa, 'tubalie!*
(109)	*Nan-gbang tapirigi a dig wa nyueta, 'tubalie,*
(110)	*kingkering moaning dig wa nyueta, 'tubalie!*

(111) Wa su ga nue. (112) Vari vienti, ain wa ji daamu. (113) Biika koati ji, ain ba cheng, biika koati ji, nuimu taam a kali:

(114)	*Waa Atubalie, 'tubalie,*
(115)	*faa ji ka fi kum daam-oa, 'tubalie!*
(116)	*Waa Atubalie, 'tubalie,*
(117)	*faa ji ka fi kum daam-oa, 'tubalie!*
(118)	*Nan-gbang tapirigi a dig wa nyueta, 'tubalie,*
(119)	*kingkering moaning dig wa nyueta, 'tubalie!*

(120) Wa ga paa tanggbaini jigini, tuili daamu zaani, nuimu taam a kali. (121) Nurba sueri: 'gila-gila'; wa tui zaani, nuimu kali me a ngman kum:

(99) A dove will cook her intestines, Atubalie!
(100) And a red ant will cook her intestines, Atubalie!

(101) 'Mother, listen!' (102) 'I don't want too much talking!' (103) [She] said: 'Go and add yeast[185] [to the millet beer]!' (104) She went and was about to put in the yeast, [when] the bird came again and sat [down]:

(105) Look, Atubalie, Atubalie,
(106) you are pouring your death millet beer, Atubalie!
(107) Look, Atubalie, Atubalie,
(108) you are pouring your death millet beer, Atubalie!
(109) A dove will cook her intestines, Atubalie,
(110) a red ant will cook her intestines, Atubalie!

(111) She finished putting the yeast [into the millet beer]. (112) At daybreak, she [the mother] told her to carry the millet beer. (113) The child lifted [the pot full of millet beer] and carried [it] and [the mother] said that they [the girl and the people in the compound] should go; [and when] the child lifted [the pot full of millet beer] and carried [it], the bird came and sat down [singing]:

(114) Look, Atubalie, Atubalie,
(115) you are carrying your death millet beer, Atubalie!
(116) Look, Atubalie, Atubalie,
(117) you are carrying your death millet beer, Atubalie!
(118) A dove will cook her intestines, Atubalie,
(119) a red ant will cook her intestines, Atubalie!

(120) She went and arrived at the place of the *tanggbain*, she put the [pot with the] millet beer down, and the bird came by and sat down. (121) People filled the place,

---

185) The verb *su* means '1. to put (into, in) ... 3. to decant, to pour into another vessel (usually from a large container into a smaller one, e.g. pito from a *chari* into a *gong*), to store, to fill up (from a big pot)' (Kröger BED). It also means to add the yeast (*da-puuk*) to the boiled beer after it has cooled down. Afterwards, the beer will start to ferment. This is the last stage of beer brewing.

(122)	*Waa Atubalie, 'tubalie,*
(123)	*faa tui ka fi kum daam-oa, 'tubalie!*
(124)	*Waa Atubalie, 'tubalie,*
(125)	*faa tui ka fi kum daam-oa, 'tubalie!*
(126)	*Nan-gbang tapirigi a dig wa nyueta, 'tubalie,*
(127)	*kingkering moaning dig wa nyueta, 'tubalie!*

(128) Wa tuili zaani. (129) Wa le ga zaani la, ba beg tanggbaini a beg wa nyonowa me, ba jam ya, nurdoawa pai chigsi wa.

(130) Wa daam kum ya ain wa yaali ka saaloa, a jam tanggbaini nyonowa jigi, a wieni wa, wa siag, wa le cheng la, wa nya bisa bayuebi. (131) Se, wa first lie ale nna, wa piilim biamu biik kpagni, wa yaa wa pa te tanggbani; ba nya ka wa lala le la! (132) Duerima tog yaali kama, ate wa zer ain waa: waa yaa wa pa te ka tanggbain abe tanggbaini ngoa. (133) Wa nya jinla wa ta jam kama, ba ngoa te wa, wa niag wa kama, ba nag ni-puuk ate wa.

(134) Ba me dek bomsi chaab a taam ga tu; ain wa le wa yig nipok-bini la, wa taam ga yig. (135) Nur taam ji nna wa, wanyi wa lig wa nina. (136) Ba ta gebika chien ain ba ko; ba le chien ba togri la, jaab zaani wen ain 'nnn' ain ba basi. (137) Wa ta ka wa biik a wa biisi te ba, before [(137b) abe] ba yaa ko. (138) Ku kum 'giri-giri-giri' a jam sing. (139) Ase ka pa-diak, nuru ngman kpabi wieni ain ba ko pa-diaka abe ba

surrounding it; [when] she had put down the [pot with the] millet beer, the bird also sat down and cried again:

(122) Look, Atubalie, Atubalie,
(123) you are putting down your death millet beer, Atubalie!
(124) Look, Atubalie, Atubalie,
(125) you are putting down your death millet beer, Atubalie!
(126) A dove will cook her intestines, Atubalie,
(127) a red ant will cook her intestines, Atubalie!

(128) She put down the [pot with the] millet beer. (129) After she had put it there, they asked the *tanggbain* and they also asked its owner, [saying that] they had come and the man [the girl's father] took [the offering] and placed it in front of [the *tanggbain*].

(130) [The girl's father said:] He [the *tanggbain*] had cried some time ago that he wanted a human being [as an offering] and after he [the girl's father] had come to the place of the *tanggbain* owner, telling him [what he wanted], he [the *tanggbain*] had agreed, and when he [the man] had gone [home], he had got six children. (131) So, the firstborn was a daughter; he had begun to bring forth [children beginning with this] eldest child, [this child] he wants to give to the *tanggbain*; so, there indeed she is! (132) Various suitors wooed her, [but] he had refused [to marry his daughter away], saying that he wanted to give her to the *tanggbain*, therefore the *tanggbain* should receive [her]. (133) Today he has brought [the girl], they should take her; he [the *tanggbain*] had blessed him [with children]; they [the crowd] applauded him by clapping their hands.

(134) They also deliberated among themselves, went and consulted one another; [they] said that whoever is going to hold down the girl, should come and hold her. (135) A man came and held her this way[186], another one closed her eyes. (136) They brought the knife to kill [the girl]; [but] when they were about to cut [the girl's] throat, something stood in the sky and said '*Nnn*![187]' - they should stop it. (137) It had something to tell them before they kill [the girl]. (138) It sounded like '*giri-giri-giri*' [the sound of thunder] and then it came down. (139) It was a ram, and a man hastened to

186) I.e. in the way an animal to be slaughtered is held down.

187) Meaning 'no!'.

ge nipok-bini. (140) Ba nag nipuuk te wa a togri pa-diaka ale ge nipok-bini. (141) Ate ba nag nisa ain baa te jiam, a te Naawen jiam, ain ba nya wen le saalim ain ba basi nipok-bini.

(142) Ale ba daam wieni ain ka fi dan biag fi piilim biam, fi pai te tanggbain. (143) Ka Naawen ale basi pa-diak ain ba kaab bogluku. (144) Di le soa ate baa kaab pa-diak bogluku la. (145) Kan daa di fi dan biag ning-biamu, fi paa a te ka tanggbain. (146) Naawen be le nya ale ku an nala ate wa yaa pa pa-diak a te, ate ba yaa a kaab bogluk.

(147) Ku noai le la.

say that they should kill the ram and leave the girl [alive]. (140) They applauded by clapping their hands for him and they cut the ram's throat and left the girl [alive]. (141) And they [applauded by] clapping their hands, saying that they should give thanks and that they should give thanks to God, and that they should realize that the sky (= God) asked [them] to leave the girl [alive].

(142) For in former times, it was said that if you beget your first child, you had to give it to a *tanggbain.* (143) It is God who sent a ram to use as sacrifice to a shrine. (144) That is why they offer a ram to the shrine. (145) Otherwise, if you had given birth to a first child, you would have to give it to a *tanggbain.* (146) God saw that this wasn't good and he gave a ram [to the people] in order that they should sacrifice [this] to the shrine.

(147) That is its [the story's] end.

BUL-E0292 (BULI TEXT)

(1) Nipok le boro, a yaa biag wa bisa; a yaa biag nur-doabilisa a yaa ga biag wa nipok-bili yeng.

(2) Ba wieni ain ba kaa biagi nipok-bilisa. (3) Wa yaa ta wa biika bo dok po a wuugi. (4) Biika yaa ga pag; ba yaa maasi nya biika. (5) Ba wieni ain nya wa ta ka nipok-bili, a ta bo doku po a wuugi. (6) Ba yaa wieni ain ba be yig ta nyini ate ba ko. (7) Ba yaa lagsi jam. (8) Nipok-bini yue ale Asugboro. (9) Wa toama yaa ba kum:

[Solo]

(10) *Wa Asugboro nyin te ba ko-a!*

[Chorus][188)]

(11) *Asugboro, n yaa!*
(12) *Fi sug bora-a nye ka boa-a?*
(13) *Asugboro, n yaa!*
(14) *Wa Asugboro nyin te ba ko-a!*
(15) *Asugboro, n yaa!*
(16) *Fi sug bora-a nye ka boa-a?*
(17) *Asugboro, n yaa!*
(18) *Asugboro nyin te ba ko-a!*
(19) *Asugboro, n yaa!*
(20) *Fi sug bora-a nye se?*

---

188) The solo voice, the teller, and the chorus, the audience, alternate throughout the song.

02.04 Girl must not be killed (sacrificed) IV

BUL-E0292 (ENGLISH TRANSLATION)

(1) Once there lived a woman who gave birth to her children; [she first] gave birth to boys and then gave birth to her only daughter.

(2) They [the people] had [however] said that one should not give birth to girls[189]. (3) So she [the woman] kept her child (daughter) in a room and nursed her. (4) The child grew up; then they [the people of the village] found out about the child. (5) They [the people] said that they had discovered that she had a girl whom she kept and nursed secretly in the room. (6) Then they said that they should seize her [the girl] and bring her outside in order to kill her. (7) They [the people] assembled. (8) The girl's name was Asugboro[190]. (9) Then her brothers began to cry[191]:

(10) Asugboro, come out so that they can kill you!
(11) Asugboro, *n-yaa*[192]!
(12) You hide and live - what are you doing?
(13) Asugboro, *n-yaa*!
(14) Asugboro, come out so that they can kill you!
(15) Asugboro, *n-yaa*!
(16) You hide and live - what are you doing?
(17) Asugboro, *n-yaa*!
(18) Asugboro, come out so that they can kill you!
(19) Asugboro, *n-yaa*!
(20) You hide and live - what are you doing?

---

189) Translation by Pauline Akankyalabey: 'They [the people] had, however, forbidden the delivery of girls.'

190) The name means 'hide and live', from the verbs *sugi* 'to hide' and *boro* 'to live'.

191) The verb *kum(u)* means '1. to mourn, to condole, to cry, to weep, to lament [...]' (Kröger BED), see also glossary.

192) The words *n-yaa!* are meaningless; they are sung in funeral dirges.

(21) *Asugboro, n-yaa!*
(22) *Asugboro nyin te ba ko!*
(23) *Asugboro, n-yaa!*
(24) *Fi sug boro a de ka boa?*
(25) *Asugboro, n-yaa!*

(26) Ba ta wa jam nyini nangkpiengka po, a ta wa a cheng kusungku. (27) Wa suoku ngmaa yiti:

[Song repeated]

(28) Ba yaa ta yiti a jue guuku zuk, a yaa jue lagsi kali. (29) Ba yaa gomsi magsi ba ko, nwala me ngmaa yiti:

[Song repeated]

(30) Ba yaa pai gebika, a yaa liti wa tutoku ain ba togri la, ale pa-diak nyin wen jam. (31) A jam sing ba ning ain ba ko wa abe ba basi nipowa.

(32) Dila te ba yaa ba ko piisanga. (33) Se daamwa, ba daam kan biag tama nipok-bilisa. [Great laughter among the audience] *(34) Ba daam dan biag tama nipok-bilisa, baa ko kama.* [Talking among the audience]

(35) Ku miena la.

(21) Asugboro, *n-yaa*!
(22) Asugboro come out so that they can kill you!
(23) Asugboro, *n-yaa*!
(24) You hide and live - what are you eating?
(25) Asugboro, *n-yaa*!

(26) They brought her out [from the room] into the cattle yard and took her into the *kusung*[193]. (27) Her brother again got up and [began to sing his song]:

[Song repeated]

(28) Then they took her and went up to the *guuk*[194] and there they gathered and sat down. (29) When they had got everything ready to kill [her], another [brother] also got up [and sang]:

[Song repeated]

(30) Then they took the knife, lifted her throat in order to slaughter[195] her, when a ram came down from the sky. (31) It landed in front of them and told them that they should kill it and that they should let the woman go.

(32) It is for this reason that thenceforth they have killed sheep. (33) In former times they never gave birth to us girls. [Great laughter among the audience] (34) Formerly, when they gave birth to us girls, they killed [us] indeed. [Talking among the audience]

(35) This is all [my story].

---

193) Shelter in front of the house, cf. glossary.

194) *guuk*, hillock where abandoned settlement formerly stood; see glossary.

195) *togri*, v. 'to cut the throat, to slaughter or kill an animal (only by cutting its throat)' (Kröger BED).

BUL-E0489 (BULI TEXT)

(1) Nuru le boro, a ta wa pooba. (2) A yaa ga puulim teng, ain wa powa dan biag, a piisi, wa te tengka nipok-liak.

(3) Nipowa din za-za-za nurdoa bulorta nyiini neuk, pai nipok, nipok-liak moaning gbang-gbang-gbang, a saari pi.

02.05 Girls must not be killed (sacrificed) V

BUL-E0489 (ENGLISH TRANSLATION)

(1) There lived a man who had many wives[196]. (2) He went and solemnly promised[197] the Earth[198] that if his wife[199] gave birth to many [children][200], he would give the Earth a young girl.

(3) The woman then [gave birth[201]] to nine ugly[202] men [boys] only, one after the other, [but] at last came a woman, a [beautiful] young girl with very, very fair skin[203], making ten [children] altogether.

---

196) [...] *a ta wa pooba*, lit. [...] [who] had his wives.

197) *puulim*, v. 'to promise, to make a vow' (Kröger BED).

198) *teng*, 'Earth (a god or a shrine [...])' (Kröger BED), see also glossary under *teng* and *tanggbain*.- In the present context, probably a *tanggbain*, 'earth-shrine' is meant. However, the teller uses the word *teng*, 'Earth', throughout this rather fragmentary story. - [...] *puulim teng* means 'to promise [something]' or 'to make a vow to the Earth'.

199) I.e. 'one of his wives' [?].

200) Lit.: 'if his wife gave birth and had many [children]', or: 'if [she] [...] multiplied'. The verb *piisi* means '1. to be numerous, to be many, to have many (much) [...] 2. to increase (in number), to multiply' (Kröger BED).

201) Lit.: 'nine ugly men came out' or '[...] came forth','[...] came into being'.

202) *buloruk*, pl. *buloruta* or *bulorta*, adj. 'ugly, nasty' (Kröger BED).

203) Lit.: with 'red skin' or 'light skin', 'fair complexion'. A (relatively) fair complexion corresponds to the ideal of beauty among the Bulsa.

(4) Nurdoawa me be kan ngmaa siag nipowa nying-a. (5) Tengka yaa jam ain wa tuni wa pamini.

(6) Wa yaa yiti nya wa ko-bisanga te ba jam, te wa toawa kpagni geng taam a zaani nansiungku noai. (7) Wa toawa yue le Asiateba.

(8) Asiateba, nyini, ba ko!
(9) Asiateba, nyini, ba ko!
(10) Nyini, ba ko!
(11) Nyini, nyini, ba ko!

(12) Asiateba, nyini, ba ko!
(13) Asiateba, nyini, ba ko!
(14) Nyini, ba ko!
(15) Nyini, nyini, ba ko!

(16) Te wai ale paai sang la, ngmaa taam:

(4) The man grew to like[204)] the woman [the girl, his daughter]. (5) Then the Earth[205)] came and asked the man to pay his debt[206)].

(6) So he got up and called together his paternal relatives[207)] and they came, and her [the girl's] senior brother passed by, stood at the entrance [and started singing]. (7) The name of his sister was Asiateba.

(8) Asiateba, come out, they [will] kill [you]!
(9) Asiateba, come out, they [will] kill [you]!
(10) Come out, they [will] kill [you]!
(11) Come out, come out, they [will] kill [you]!

(12) Asiateba, come out, they [will] kill [you]!
(13) Asiateba, come out, they [will] kill [you]!
(14) Come out, they [will] kill [you]!
(15) Come out, come out, they [will] kill [you]!

(16) And the next [eldest brother][208)] also passed by [and sang]:

---

204) The phrase, '*Nurdoawa me be kan ngmaa siag nipowa nying-a*' means literally the opposite: 'The man did **not** like his daughter.' In the present case, the negative *kan* expresses an intensification of the positive meaning.

205) Meaning probably the 'earth-shrine', *tanggbain*.

206) *tuni pami*, lit. 'to pay (*tuni*) one's debt (*pami*)'; this expression is used to refer to any act of reciprocity or *do ut des*. In a posisitve sense, it means that someone reciprocates a gift or some other good deed. But *tuni pami* means also 'to retaliate', 'to take revenge', 'to rival [someone]' etc. For a full discussion of this concept, central to Bulsa morals and ethics, cf. Schott 1980e, p. 182-184.

207) *ko-biik*, pl. *ko-bisa*, lit. 'father's child', paternal relative; see glossary.

208) Lit.: 'And the one who followed [the previously mentioned brother]'.

(17) *Naawen laa maari,*
(18) *ate wen laa maari,*
(19) *a maari sakpang maarika.*

(20) *Naawen laa maari,*
(21) *ate wen laa maari,*
(22) *a maari sakpang maarika.*

(23) Nwala ngman paai a sang:

[Song (8) - (15) repeated]

(24) Te nwala ngman paai a sang:

[Song (17) - (22) repeated]

[Song (8) - (15) repeated]

[Song (17) - (22) repeated]

(25) Te nwala ngman paai a sang:

[Song (8) - (15) repeated]

[Song (17) - (22) repeated]

(17) God will help,
(18) and God[209)] will help,
(19) he helps in a wonderful[210)] way.

(20) God will help,
(21) and God will help,
(22) he helps in a wonderful way.

(23) And the next [brother?] followed [and sang]:

[Song (8) - (15) repeated]

(24) And the next one followed [and began to sing]:

[Song (17) - (22) repeated]

[Song (8) - (15) repeated]

[Song (17) - (22) repeated]

(25) And the next one [brother?] also followed:

[Song (8) - (15) repeated]

[Song (17) - (22) repeated]

---

209) In the first line of the song, the teller uses the word *Naawen* for 'God' (lit. 'Chief of the Sky'), in the second line *wen*, lit. 'Sky', but meaning also 'God'. This shows that these two words can be used as synonyms; both refer to the concept of a sky-god. See also the glossary.

210) *sakpang* adj. wonderful, mysterious, supernatural. Cf. *sakpagni* n. 'witchcraft'; *sakpak*, n. 'witch, wizard, magician' (Kröger BED).

(26) Te nwala ngman a taam:

[Song (8) - (15) repeated]

[Song (17) - (22) repeated]

(27) Nipok-bini gaa zaani nansiungku noai; wa toa baangka taam a zaani:

[Song (8) - (15) repeated]

[Song (17) - (22) repeated]

(28) Wa ko-bisanga wanyi din ga vaa yiti, din zag kpalang yig toa baangka geng, buloruku, a fob lonsi. (29) Wa le sebi diila. (30) A zaani buntuem tengka ning, yaa le a basi liewa.

(31) Mi le nya dii la le la.

(26) And the next one [brother?] followed:

[Song (8) - (15) repeated]

[Song (17) - (22) repeated]

(27) The girl went and stood by the entrance, [when] her youngest brother passed by, [he] stood [and began to sing]:

[Song (8) - (15) repeated]

[Song (17) - (22) repeated]

(28) One of his paternal relatives got up, raised a club[211)], aimed at the youngest brother, the ugly one, and hit [knocked] him down [and killed him]. (29) That was what he knew[212)]. (30) Then he [the father's relative] placed ashes[213)] in front of the Earth [earth-shrine, *teng*] and the girl was left [alive].

(31) That is all that I have seen.

---

211) *kpalang*, n. 'throwing stick (not bent) used for hunting; stick shaped like a hockey bat, used for playing the local type of hockey [...]' (Kröger BED).

212) A euphemism for: 'he died'.

213) A symbolic gesture, denoting 'coolness' or 'peace'.

BUL-E0572 (BULI TEXT)

(1) Ka nurdoa le boro, a ta wa pok, ba kan biagi. (2) Te nurdoawa yaa yiti, a yaa ga jo tanggbain. (3) Wa le ka biag la, wa biag. (4) Tanggbani yaa yin di daa wari ya, wa le maa wa te wa biag.

(5) Wa yaa kul, wa dan kul a ga biag, wa la biag wai la, wa le soa. (6) Wa le piilim a biag wai la, wa ta jam te wa. (7) Wa yaa siag, a yaa kul la, a ga biag.

(8) Wa le piilim biag wai la nurdoa, a pilim a biag wai la nipok. (9) Ku le nye diila la: (10) Nipowa, wa yaa pag; wa ban baga a zeri tanggbani noani. (11) Wa yaa yiti a wien wa powa ain waa: (12) Wa num zom, ate ba yaa daam, ate ba ta biika, a ga te tanggbani. (13) Age fi dan nya nipokbini-a: 'Aiya!'. (14) Nipowa yaa siag. (15) Nurdoawa yaa gomsi ngantanga te nipowa. (16) Nipowa yaa yiti la... (17) Ba le din biag

02.06 Girls must not be killed (sacrificed) VI

BUL-E0572 (ENGLISH TRANSLATION)

(1) There lived a man who had a wife, but they didn't[214)] bring forth children. (2) So the man got up and went and consulted an earth-shrine (*tanggbain*)[215)]. (3) [He said to it:] He could not bring forth children, [but] he [would like] to bring forth [children]. (4) The earth-shrine said that this was no problem, he[216)] would help him to have children.

(5) And he [the man] went home, [but the *tanggbain* had told him that] if he went home and begot children, the one he begot [first], would be owned by him [the earth-shrine]. (6) Whoever he begot first, he should bring to him [the earth-shrine]. (7) He agreed and went home and begot children.

(8) His firstborn was a boy and the next child was a girl[217)]. (9) This is how it happened: (10) The girl matured and he could not go back on his promise to the earth-shrine. (11) So he [the man] got up and told his wife: (12) She [should] grind flour so that they will get [prepare] millet-beer, then they will take the child and go and give [her] to the earth-shrine. (13) Meanwhile, if you saw the girl, [you would exclaim:] 'No!'[218)] (14) The woman agreed [to what her husband proposed]. (15) The man prepared the things [to brew the millet-beer] and gave them to the woman. (16) The

---

214) Another translation: 'they couldn't have children'.

215) Lit.: 'he entered an earth-shrine'.

216) The *tanggbain* is referred to by the personal pronoun of the 1st (*wa/ba-*) class, thus speaking of it as if it were a human being.

217) Consequently, the boy should have been the one to be sacrificed to the *tanggbain*, but not the second born daughter. The teller seems to be confused: he probably mixes up two different motifs, the sacrifice of the first-born child (usually a son) and the sacrifice of (all) girl(s) to an earth-shrine.

218) I.e. 'What a pity to kill such a nice girl!'

nipok-bini din ga te yin nipok-bini yue le Asugboro. (18) Nipowa yaa ta zaanga jo wa num la, wa liewa yaa jo wa maa num. (19) Nipowa jiirim yaa a dari, wa yaa a piilim wa yiili, poom ka kumsa:

(20) Asugboro-a num ka wa kum zom-oa![219]
(21) Asugboro, n-yaa!
(22) Asugboro-a num ka wa kum zom-oa!
(23) Asugboro, n-yaa!
(24) Fi tin sug boro a nye ka se?
(25) Asugboro, n-yaa!
(26) Fi tin sug boro a nye ka se?
(27) Asugboro, n-yaa!
(28) Asugboro-a num ka wa kum zom-oa!
(29) Asugboro, n-yaa!
(30) Asugboro-a num ka wa kum zom-oa!
(31) Asugboro, n-yaa!
(32) Fi tin sug boro a nye ka se?
(33) Asugboro, n-yaa!
(34) Fi tin sug boro a nye ka se?
(35) Asugboro, n-yaa!

(36) Ba num zomu nueri. (37) Wa magsi kpaamanga ta jo-a, a jo ba ngab, a ngman piilim:

219) This line is sung by the teller, the next line by the chorus. The singing was very weak.

woman got up...[220)] (17) When they [had] brought forth the girl, they had given her the name Asugboro[221)]. (18) The woman then took the millet and entered [into her grinding room] to grind, and her daughter [also] entered [the grinding room] to help her grind [the millet]. (19) But the woman felt pity for her[222)] and she began her song, almost crying[223)]:

(20) Asugboro is grinding her death flour!
(21) Asugboro, *n-yaa*!
(22) Asugboro is grinding her death flour!
(23) Asugboro, *n-yaa*!
(24) While you are hiding, what are you doing?
(25) Asugboro, *n-yaa*!
(26) While you are hiding, what are you doing?
(27) Asugboro, *n-yaa*!
(28) Asugboro is grinding her death flour!
(29) Asugboro, *n-yaa*!
(30) Asugboro is grinding her death flour!
(31) Asugboro, *n-yaa*!
(32) While you are hiding, what are you doing?
(33) Asugboro, *n-yaa*!
(34) While you are hiding, what are you doing?
(35) Asugboro, *n-yaa*!

(36) They finished grinding the flour. (37) She [the girl's mother] measured the malt and took it inside [the grinding room] for grinding and began [to sing] again:

---

220) This sentence is anacoluthic.

221) Lit.: 'to hide and live'. The sense of this name does not become clear from the present version, but e.g. in version BUL-E0225 the father's girl, a chief, hides his daughter in his room where she grows up even though he has given the order to kill all girls after their birth.

222) Lit.: 'Compassion then moved her.'

223) *kumsa*, n.pl. 'mourning, weeping, crying' (Kröger BED), see also glossary: *kum*, v.

(38) *Asugboro-a num ka wa kum kpaama!*
(39) *Asugboro, n-yaa!*
(40) *Fi tin sug boro a nye ka se?*
(41) *Asugboro, n-yaa!*
(42) *Asugboro-a num ka wa kum kpaama!*
(43) *Asugboro, n-yaa!*
(44) *Fi tin sug boro a nye ka se?*
(45) *Asugboro, n-yaa!*

(46) Wa nye dila, ain ba kuri ka kpaam me. (47) A pai jigsanga ta nyin boro a bugsi-a, nipok-bini jam maa boro a bugsi, wa piilim:

(48) *Asugboro-a a kuri ka wa kum kpaam-oa!*
(49) *Asugboro, n-yaa!*
(50) *Fi tin sug boro a nye ka se?*
(51) *Asugboro, n-yaa!*
(52) *Asugboro-a a kuri ka wa kum kpaam-oa!*
(53) *Asugboro, n-yaa!*
(54) *Fi tin sug boro a nye ka se?*
(55) *Asugboro, n-yaa!*

(56) Ba nye kpaamu me nueri. (57) Ba chelimu dani-a, baa gomsi ba ngantanga miena; wa kowa yaa kali kusung:

(58) *Asugboro nyin te ti cheng-a!*
(59) *Asugboro, n-yaa!*

(38) Asugboro is grinding her death malt!
(39) Asugboro, *n-yaa*!
(40) While you are hiding, what are you doing?
(41) Asugboro, *n-yaa*!
(42) Asugboro is grinding her death malt
(43) Asugboro, *n-yaa*!
(44) While you are hiding, what are you doing?
(45) Asugboro, *n-yaa*!

(46) She [the mother] did that and said that they had to pound [shea-nuts and prepare] shea-nut oil as well. (47) She took out the shea-nuts[224] and [when she started] crushing them, the girl came to help her crush [the shea nuts], [and] she [the mother] again started:

(48) Asugboro is pounding her death oil
(49) Asugboro, *n-yaa*!
(50) While you are hiding, what are you doing?
(51) Asugboro, *n-yaa*!
(52) Asugboro is pounding her death oil
(53) Asugboro, *n-yaa*!
(54) While you are hiding, what are you doing?
(55) Asugboro, *n-yaa*!

(56) They also finished preparing the oil. (57) On the appointed day[225], they got all their things ready; her father then sat in the *kusung*[226] [and started singing]:

(58) Asugboro come out and let us go!
(59) Asugboro, *n-yaa*!

---

224) *jigsanga* or *jisinga*, sing. *jigsidi*, n. 'shea nut (pulp removed)' (Kröger BED).

225) Lit.: 'on the day of their travelling' or 'on the day of their journey'; *chelim*, def. *chelimu*, n. journey, walk, travel, expedition, tour, trip, excursion' (Kröger BED).

226) Shelter; see glossary.

(60)	*Fi tin sug boro a nye ka se?*
(61)	*Asugboro, n-yaa!*
(62)	*Asugboro nyin te ti cheng-a!*
(63)	*Asugboro, n-yaa!*
(64)	*Fi tin sug boro a nye ka se?*
(65)	*Asugboro, n-yaa!*
(66)	*Asugboro nyin te ti cheng-a!*
(67)	*Asugboro, n-yaa!*
(68)	*Fi tin sug boro a nye ka se?*
(69)	*Asugboro, n-yaa!*

(70) Nipok-bini nyin; ba cheng, ba ga paa tanggbani jigni. (71) Wa kowa a yieri gebika, a yaa wien nipok-bini ain wa taam koori.

(72)	*Asugboro koori te mi ko-a!*
(73)	*Asugboro, n-yaa!*
(74)	*Fi tin sug boro a nye ka se?*
(75)	*Asugboro, n-yaa!*
(76)	*Asugboro koori te mi ko-a!*
(77)	*Asugboro, n-yaa!*
(78)	*Fi tin sug boro a nye ka se?*
(79)	*Asugboro, n-yaa!*
(80)	*Asugboro koori te mi ko-a!*
(81)	*Asugboro, n-yaa!*
(82)	*Fi tin sug boro a nye ka se?*
(83)	*Asugboro, n-yaa!*
(84)	*Asugboro koori te mi ko-a!*
(85)	*Asugboro, n-yaa!*
(86)	*Fi tin sug boro a nye ka se?*
(87)	*Asugboro, n-yaa!*

(60) While you are hiding, what are you doing?
(61) Asugboro, *n-yaa*!
(62) Asugboro come out and let us go!
(63) Asugboro, *n-yaa*!
(64) While you are hiding, what are you doing?
(65) Asugboro, *n-yaa*!
(66) Asugboro come out and let us go!
(67) Asugboro, *n-yaa*!
(68) While you are hiding, what are you doing?
(69) Asugboro, *n-yaa*!

(70) The girl came out; they went and went and arrived at the place of the earth-shrine. (71) Her father took out the knife and told the girl that she should come along and bend over.

(72) Asugboro bend down so that I may kill [you]!
(73) Asugboro, *n-yaa*!
(74) While you are hiding, what are you doing?
(75) Asugboro, *n-yaa*!
(76) Asugboro bend down so that I may kill [you]!
(77) Asugboro, *n-yaa*!
(78) While you are hiding, what are you doing?
(79) Asugboro, *n-yaa*!
(80) Asugboro bend down so that I may kill [you]!
(81) Asugboro, *n-yaa*!
(82) While you are hiding, what are you doing?
(83) Asugboro, *n-yaa*!
(84) Asugboro bend down so that I may kill [you]!
(85) Asugboro, *n-yaa*!
(86) While you are hiding, what are you doing?
(87) Asugboro, *n-yaa*!

(88) Nipok-bini gaa koori, wa yin wa ko la, ba ngman gilim, wa nimbie, a koori ngman pilim yiti za:

(89)	*Asugboro duag te mi ko-a*
(90)	*Asugboro, n-yaa!*
(91)	*Fi tin sug boro a nye ka se?*
(92)	*Asugboro, n-yaa!*
(93)	*Asugboro duag te mi ko-a!*
(94)	*Asugboro, n-yaa!*
(95)	*Fi tin sug boro a nye ka se?*
(96)	*Asugboro, n-yaa!*

(97) Wa yaa nye dila ta geku[227] *tuag wa togri nipok-bini tutoku la, ale Naawen din ta pa-diak, din jam chigsi. (98) Ain tintuem le nna, te wa zaan wa ning. (99) Wa saalim kama, wa kan ko nipok-bini, be wa pai posuku, a ko te tanggbani.*

(100a) Ka ku ale nye dii, te ti pa dung-a a kaab bogluk la le la. (100b) Ka ku ale nye dii, te ti pa dung-a a kaab tanggbana la. (101) Saaloa-biik me te ba yin nya wa jo ka tanggbain a ta wa nganta, a ta wa nying-yogsa, ta wa nurba la, ba kan kisi jaabui yue puulim wuka. (102) Age Naawen-yaa le wieni ain fi daa puulim tanggbain fi puulim le

---

[227] Variant of the word *gebik*, def. *gebika* or *geku*.

(88) The girl bent over, [but when] he was about[228] to kill her, his eyes began to turn[229], so he bent down and [then] stood up again [and started his singing]:

(89) Asugboro lie down so that I may kill [you]!
(90) Asugboro, *n-yaa*!
(91) While you are hiding, what are you doing?
(92) Asugboro, *n-yaa*!
(93) Asugboro lie down so that I may kill [you]!
(94) Asugboro, *n-yaa*!
(95) While you are hiding, what are you doing?
(96) Asugboro, *n-yaa*!

(97) He did that and took the knife, but when he was about to cut the girl's throat, God took a ram and let it drop down [from the sky]. (98) [He, God] said that this [the ram] represents the ashes[230] which he has placed in front of him. (99) He [God] was begging him [the father] that he should not kill the girl, but that he should take the sheep [instead], kill it and give it to the earth-shrine (*tanggbain*).

(100a) That is how it happened that we take an animal and sacrifice it to a shrine. (100b) That is how it happened that we take an animal and sacrifice it to an earth-shrine[231]. (101) Concerning a human being, when they say: 'Look, he has consulted an earth-shrine[232] and has [received] riches, is healthy and has a lot of people [relatives]', it is not forbidden[233] that he should name anything and vow it [to the earth-shrine] by mentioning [it]. (102) However, God said that if you make a vow to an

228) Lit.: 'when he said that he would kill her [...]'.

229) I.e. he felt dizzy.

230) Ashes, i.e. something burnt out, are the symbol of coolness and peace according to the concepts of the Bulsa.

231) The teller uses the word *bogluk*, 'shrine', the repeater the word *tanggbain*, 'earth-shrine'. For both terms, see the glossary.

232) Lit.: 'entered an earth-shrine'.

233) *kisi*, 'to be tabooed', see glossary.

dung, kan pa nuru puulimu. (103) Ku kiri soa dii la le la. (104) Mi wani miena, miena le la.

earth-shrine, do promise [it] an animal, but do not take a human being as something promised with a vow. (103) This is the reason for it[234]. (104) This is all of my story.

234) I.e. why human beings are no longer promised to shrines and used in sacrifices, but four-legged domestic animals (and fowls) instead.

BUL-E0761 (BULI TEXT)

(1) Nipok ale boro, wa kan biagi. (2) Wa yaa cheng tengka a ga puulum ain waa: (3) Wa dan biag, wa laa biag biikai la, biikala wa ta chien ain wa te wa.

(4) Wa cheng kun paar da ngata, wa deri zaa biag. (5) Biika a deri pag; wa yue be le Atuubaanlie. (6) Wa mawa yaa pa za a te wa ain wa lusi. (7) Wa lusi kpaamanga. (8) Biika yaa cheng beni jam. (9) Kpaamanga a ko. (10) Ain wa ta jo ngab. (11) Biika jo a zaan nanzuku po-a:

(12)	*N ngab ka n kum kpaama-e!*
(13)	*N ngab ka n kum kpaama-e!*
(14)	*'te ba ta mi jue-e ba tengka-e!*

02.07 Girls must not be killed (sacrificed) VII

BUL-E0761 (ENGLISH TRANSLATION)

(1) There was a woman who could not give birth [to children]. (2) Then she went to the Earth [an earth-shrine, *teng*][235)] and made a vow saying: (3) If she gave birth [to a child], she would give that child away and offer it to him [the earth-shrine].

(4) She went [home] and in less than three days she gave birth [to a child]. (5) The child grew up quickly; she was named Atuubaanlie. (6) [One day] her mother took some guinea-corn[236)] and gave it to her so that she [might] soak [it][237)]. (7) She soaked the malt[238)]. (8) The child went to the river, [fetched water] and came [back]. (9) The malt dried. (10) [The mother] asked her to take it inside [the grinding room] and grind it. (11) The child [the girl] entered the grinding room [and began to sing]:

(12) I am grinding the malt of my death!
(13) I am grinding the malt of my death!
(14) Then they will take me up to their earth-shrine (*teng*)!

---

235) *teng*, def. *tengka*, here: 'Earth (a god or shrine [...])' (Kröger BED), i.e. the Earth as a religious power; see glossary. The Earth is venerated at certain spots, so-called 'earth-shrines' which may be representations of the Earth itself or of particular localized chthonic beings (*tanggbana*, sing. *tanggbain*).

236) Guinea-corn is called *za-moaning*, lit. 'red millet', from *zari*, def. *zani*, pl. *zaa*. The teller pronounces the word *za* with a short vowel; he probably uses the word as an abbreviation of *za-moaning*. Millet beer (pito) is, in fact, brewed from red millet (Sorghum sp.).

237) Guinea corn is soaked in water in order to prepare malt called *kpaama*, n.pl.: 'malt, germinated guinea-corn grains (first stage of brewing pito [millet beer])' (Kröger BED).

238) A short way of saying that the girl soaked the guinea-corn, which then germinated and thus turned into malt.

[Refrain]

(15) *'te kinkering di-gonanga yie mi nyueta!*
(16) *A yie mi nyueta, 'Tuubaanlie!*
(17) *'te kinkering nyue-geminga yie mi yuet-ee!*
(18) *A yie mi nyueta, 'Tuubaanlie!*
(19) *'te kinkering di-gonanga yie mi nyueta!*
(20) *A yie mi nyueta 'Tuubaanlie!*
(21) *'te kinkering nyue-geminga yie mi nyueta!*
(22) *A yie mi nyueta 'Tuubaanlie!*
(23) *'te kinkering di-gonanga yie mi nyueta!*
(24) *A yie mi nyueta 'Tuubaanlie!*
(25) *'te kinkering di-gonanga yie mi nyueta!*
(26) *A yie mi nyueta 'Tuubaanlie!*

(27) Wa ngab kpaamanga a nue, ain wa cheng beli. (28) Wa cheng beni-a:

(29) *N ngari ka n kum nyiam-oo!*
(30) *N ngari ka n kum nyiam-oo!*
(31) *'te ba ta mi jue-e ba tengka-e!*

[Refrain as above, sentence (15) foll.]

(32) *Wa yaa ga ngari jam, ain wa be moag bolim a chiem:*

(33) *N chiem ka n kum bolim-oo!*
(34) *N chiem ka n kum bolim-oo!*
(35) *'te ba ta mi jue-e ba tengka-e!*

[Refrain as above, sentence (15) foll.]

[Refrain]

(15) And the ant with the gourd-like forehead will remove my intestines!
(16) Will remove my intestines, 'Tuubaanlie!
(17) And the short-nosed ant will remove my intestines!
(18) Will remove my intestines, 'Tuubaanlie!
(19) And the ant with the gourd-like forehead will remove my intestines!
(20) Will remove my intestines, 'Tuubaanlie!
(21) And the short-nosed ant will remove my intestines!
(22) Will remove my intestines, 'Tuubaanlie!
(23) And the ant with the gourd-like forehead will remove my intestines!
(24) Will remove my intestines, 'Tuubaanlie!
(25) And the ant with the gourd-like forehead will remove my intestines!
(26) Will remove my intestines, 'Tuubaanlie!

(27) When she had finished grinding the malt, [her mother] asked her to go to the river [and fetch water]. (28) She went to the river [and began to sing]:

(29) I am fetching the water of my death!
(30) I am fetching the water of my death!
(31) Then they will take me up to their earth-shrine (*teng*)!

[Refrain as above, sentence (15) foll.]

(32) She went and fetched [water] and [when she] returned, [her mother] told her to fetch fire and to kindle [it under the pot]:

(33) I am kindling the fire of my death!
(34) I am kindling the fire of my death!
(35) Then they will take me up to their earth-shrine (*teng*)!

[Refrain as above, sentence (15) foll.]

(36) Wa chiem bolimu. (37) Ain wa yuiiri daamu a dig du:

(38) *N yuiiri n kum daam-oo!*
(39) *N yuiiri n kum daam-oo!*
(40) *'te ba ta mi jue-e ba tengka-e!*

[Refrain as above, sentence (15) foll.]

(41) Daamu nye [be], ain wa kati ate wa kati daamu. (42) Vani vienti ate bu miig, ain wa chagsi:

(43) *N chagsi n kum daam-oo!*
(44) *N chagsi n kum daam-oo!*
(45) *'te ba ta mi jue-e ba tengka-e!*

[Refrain as above, sentence (15) foll.]

(36) She lit the fire. (37) [Her mother] told her to mix the millet beer and put it to boil[239]:

(38) I am mixing the millet beer of my death!
(39) I am mixing the millet beer of my death!
(40) Then they will take me up to their earth-shrine (*teng*)!

[Refrain as above, sentence (15) foll.]

(41) The millet beer was cooked; [her mother] told her to scoop it out and transfer it to another vessel[240]; she [the girl] did this. (42) [When] day broke the millet beer was sour[241]; [her mother] told her to sieve[242] it:

(43) I am sieving the millet beer of my death!
(44) I am sieving the millet beer of my death!
(45) Then they will take me up to their earth-shrine (*teng*)!

[Refrain as above, sentence (15) foll.]

239) Pauline Akankyalabey: '*yuiiri*, v.: The first phase in the process of preparing millet beer. This involves mixing the malt flour with water and leaving it to settle for a few minutes. Some of the uppermost liquid is then removed and put aside whereas the thick mixture is put to boil and constantly stirred.'

240) Pauline Akankyalabey: *kati daamu*: 'This involves taking the thick porridge-like mixture calabash by calabash, one after the other and putting it into another pot. When it has cooled enough the uncooked liquid is then added and it is left till the next day'.

241) *miig*, v. 'to be or turn sour (e.g. cooked rice, flour-water, milk, pito etc.), to curdle (milk)' (Kröger BED).

242) *chagsi*, v. 'to sift, to (pass through a) sieve, to strain, [...] to filter' (Kröger BED). For filtering the beer, the Bulsa use woven basket-like sieves, called *chagsik*, pl. *chagsika*.

(46) Wa chagsi daamu a dig du. (47) Ain wa dobri daamu:

(48) N dobri n kum daam-oo!
(49) N dobri n kum daam-oo!
(50) 'te ba ta mi jue-e ba tengka-e!

[Refrain as above, sentence (15) foll.]

(51) A daamu nye [be], ain wa kati. (52) Wa kati daamu. (53) Bu yog, ain wa su:

(54) N su ka n kum daam-oo!
(55) N su ka n kum daam-oo!
(56) 'te ba ta mi jue-e ba tengka-e!

[Refrain as above, sentence (15) foll.]

(57) Wa nue, ate wa wieni ain wa be duag a goa ate vani vienti:

(58) N goa ka n kum goom-oo!
(59) N goa ka n kum goom-oo!
(60) 'te ba ta mi jue-e ba tengka-e!

(46) She sieved the millet beer and put it to boil. (47) [Her mother] told her to skim[243] the millet beer:

(48) I am skimming the millet beer of my death!
(49) I am skimming the millet beer of my death!
(50) Then they will take me up to their earth-shrine (*teng*)!

[Refrain as above, sentence (15) foll.]

(51) When the beer was cooked, [her mother] asked her to scoop it out and transfer it into another vessel. (52) She [the girl] scooped it out and transferred it into another vessel. (53) It cooled; [her mother] asked her to decant it [and prepare it for fermentation by adding yeast to it][244]:

(54) I am decanting the millet beer of my death!
(55) I am decanting the millet beer of my death!
(56) Then they will take me up to their earth-shrine (*teng*)!

[Refrain as above, sentence (15) foll.]

(57) She finished [brewing the millet beer] and she [her mother] told her to lie down and sleep until the next day:

(58) I am sleeping the sleep of my death!
(59) I am sleeping the sleep of my death!
(60) Then they will take me up to their earth-shrine (*teng*)!

---

243) *dobri*, v. '1. to take one thing from the other [...] 2. to skim (e.g. foam from pito), to take off [...]' (Kröger BED).

244) *su*, v.: '1. to put (into, in through) [...] 3. to decant, to pour into another vessel (usually from a large container into a smaller one, e.g. pito [millet beer] from a *chari* into a *gong*) [...]' (Kröger BED). - Pauline Akankyalabey: 'This is the last phase in the preparation of millet beer. It involves putting the millet beer into pots, then adding some yeast to it to make it ferment.'

[Refrain as above, sentence (15) foll.]

(61a) Vari vienti, ain wa ji daamu ate ba cheng: (61b) [...] ate ba cheng tengka:

(62) N vili ka n kum tulik-ee!
(63) N vili ka n kum tulik-ee!
(64) 'te ba ta mi jue-e ba tengka-e!

[Refrain as above, sentence (15) foll.]

(65) Wa ji:

(66) N be cheng ka n kum chelim-oo!
(67) N be cheng ka n kum chelim-oo!
(68) 'te ba ta mi jue-e ba tengka-e!

[Refrain as above, sentence (15) foll.]

(69) Wa nue. (70) Ba ga paai du, ain wa tui:

[Refrain as above, sentence (15) foll.]

(61a) The next day she [the mother] told her to carry[245] the millet beer so that they [could] go: (61b) [...] that they [could] go to the Earth [-shrine]:

(62) I am winding the carrying pad[246] of my death!
(63) I am winding the carrying pad of my death!
(64) Then they will take me up to their earth-shrine (*teng*)!

[Refrain as above, sentence (15) foll.]

(65) She carried [the millet beer]:

(66) I am indeed going on the journey of my death!
(67) I am indeed going on the journey of my death!
(68) Then they will take me up to their earth-shrine (*teng*)!

[Refrain as above, sentence (15) foll.]

(69) She came to an end[247]. (70) They got there; [her mother] told her to put [the millet beer] down[248]:

---

245) *ji*, v. 'to carry (usually on head), to charge, to put on head' (Kröger BED).

246) *tulik*, n. 'carrying pad' (Kröger BED). - Pauline Akankyalabey: 'A pad made of rags or woven with other material that is put on the head before any heavy load is carried.'

247) *nue(ri)*, v. 'to finish, to end, to conclude, to terminate [...]' (Kröger BED). The teller does not say what the girl finishes; I suppose that the verb is here used in an intransitive sense. - Throughout the story, the teller prefers very concise, sometimes even cryptic formulations.

248) *tuili* or (rarer) *tuiri*, v. 'to put down (e.g. a load from one's head), to unload, to deposit a charge' (Kröger BED).

(71) *N tui ka n kum daam-oo!*
(72) *N tui ka n kum daam-oo!*
(73) *'te ba ta mi jue-e ba tengka-e!*

[Refrain as above, sentence (15) foll.]

(74) A nue. (75) Ain: (76) 'Kala a vuusi ate ba ko fi!'

(77) *N kali ka n kum kalik-ee!*
(78) *N kali ka n kum kalik-ee!*
(79) *'te ba ta mi jue-e ba tengka-e!*

[Refrain as above, sentence (15) foll.]

(80) Ba din pa ta jue a ga ale ba togri la, Naawen a din pa kpesa-ee, piisa, kpiina, niiga, bala ale bala te ba jam sing. (81) A yaa wieni ain waa, waa saalim ba ngoa ngantanga a ko alege ba basi biika ale saaloa koka an nala.

(82) Ba yaa ko ngantanga alege bisanga ate bisanga yaa boro.

(83) Dii le soa ate nur bo tengka po la le la. (84) Nnapode ba te yig saaloaba a ko kama.

(85) Sunsuelini miena ale la.

(71) I am putting down the millet beer of my death!
(72) I am putting down the millet beer of my death!
(73) Then they will take me up to their earth-shrine (*teng*)!

[Refrain as above, sentence (15) foll.]

(74) [She] came to an end. (75) [Her mother] told her: (76) 'Sit down and take a rest before they kill you!'

(77) I am sitting on the place of my death!
(78) I am sitting on the place of my death!
(79) Then they will take me up to their earth-shrine (*teng*)!

[Refrain as above, sentence (15) foll.]

(80) When they took her up [to the earth-shrine] and were about to slaughter[249)] her, God[250)] took [lots of] fowls, sheep, guinea-fowls, cows and many other animals and birds and sent them down [to earth]. (81) And [God] then begged them to accept these 'things'[251)] [birds and animals] and to kill those, and they should leave the child, for the killing of a human being was not good.

(82) Since then they have killed the 'things' [animals and birds] and left the children and the children [continued] to live.

(83) This is the reason why man lives and exists on earth. (84) [Otherwise] they would still get hold of human beings and kill them indeed.

(85) This is the whole of my story. (Or: This completes my story.)

---

249) *togri*, v. 'to cut the throat, to slaughter or kill an animal (only by cutting its throat)' (Kröger BED).

250) *Naawen*, see glossary.

251) See glossary under the entry *jaab*, pl. *nganta*.

BUL-E1267 (BULI TEXT)

(1) Ka dilapo, dilapo ate nur jam boro, a ta nipok alege ba kan biag biik-a.

(2) Nurwa yaa ga dueni noai ale tanggbain a yuen: (3) Wa dan biag bisa, a maa biag nipok-bili moaning, wa ale te tanggbani biika wanyi.

(4) Wa le dueni noaini ale kuli la, kun beni ya, ba biag bisa piisi, a yaa maa biag lie moaning. (5) Nipok-bini a moaning nna yeg-yega, ate nurwa dek maring wa.

(6) Ku gaa paai ning, tanggbani yaa wien nurwa ain wa yig nipok-bini a kaab di. (7) Ba be le kaa de tanggbain pamini la, nur siag ain wa le kaab di ale wa liewa. (8) Ba yaa te nipok-bini yue ain Atogtibanyin. (9) Kun beni ya nipok-bini chim zuag, a yaa ngmansi nala nna yeg-yega.

(10) Nurwa yaa yuen sag nipok-bini wa le yin wa pai wa kaab tanggbani la. (11) A yaa yiri ate ba dig daam ain ba ta ga ling te daamu a te tanggbani. (12) Ngaam a sag ain ba sue a pienti ale di, abe wa ge a yaa te di di nurwa.

02.08 Girls must not be killed (sacrificed) VIII

BUL-E1267 (ENGLISH TRANSLATION)

(1) Once upon a time, there was a man who had a wife, but they did not bring forth children.

(2) The man then went and made a solemn promise[252) to a *tanggbain*[253) by saying: (3) If he begot children, and among them there was a fair-skinned[254) girl, he would give one of the children to the *tanggbain.*

(4) Not long after he had made this promise and returned home, they [the man and his wife] brought forth many children and they also brought forth a fair-skinned daughter. (5) The girl was so very fair that the man [her father] himself admired[255) her.

(6) After some time had passed, the *tanggbain* told the man that he should seize the girl and sacrifice her to it. (7) Since one cannot escape paying a debt to a *tanggbain,* the man agreed that he would sacrifice his daughter to it. (8) They named the girl Atogtibanyin[256). (9) In a very short time, the girl grew up and became even more beautiful.

(10) The man informed the girl about his intention to sacrifice her to the *tanggbain.* (11) He got up and made them[257) brew millet beer so that they could firstly

252) *dueni noai,* '(lit. to put down mouth) to swear, to take an oath, to promise, to conclude an agreement, to make a treaty [...]' (Kröger BED).

253) Earth-shrine, see glossary.

254) A (relatively) fair skin corresponds to the ideal of beauty among the Bulsa.

255) *maring,* v. 'to like, to love, to be fond of, to admire, to be interested in, to be pleased with, to enjoy, to be glad [...]' (Kröger BED).

256) The name supposedly means: 'Talk and they will go out.'

257) The people in his house.

(13) Dadidai ate ba ain ba be cheng la, nipok-bini yaa jo kal dok po a piilim wa yiili:

(14) *Ba waa Atog-tibanyinaa tibanyinaa tinyinbaani nya,*
(15) *Se wa mawa se wu bani-nyin, se wu chakuri-wu daari.*

(16) Ba nyin ya, baa cheng, baa cheng, a ga paai tanggbani. (17) Ba te daamu. (18) (Ba pa daamu kaab tanggbani bogluku)[258]*. (19) Ba ale nyu daamu nue la, nurwa din gaa pa wa gebik a saasi. (20) Wa yuen ain nipok-bini duag. (21) Nipok-bini duag. (22) Wa ale din ga ain wa togri la, ba nya ka nipok nisom kpak moaning ale din nyin wen a sing 'chaan-a!', ale daa nag wuliing ain: 'Wa yie-e-e-ei-ie!'. (23) A jam zi a yuen ain ba kan ko nipok-bini ale ka wadek ale la, abe ba basi wa. (24) Wa le yuen nue la,*

---

[258] Added in brackets by the writer.

go and give the millet beer to the *tanggbain*. (12) He did this as a preliminary act[259] to show that they [the parents of the girl] were happy with it [the *tanggbain*], before he [the father] could then give it its human being [the girl].

(13) On the day they were to go [to the *tanggbain*] the girl entered a room, sat down and began to sing[260]:

[(14-15) Song[261]]

(16) They came out and went on and on till they arrived at the *tanggbain*. (17) They gave out the millet beer. (18) (They offered the millet beer to the shrine[262] of the *tanggbain*). (19) When they had finished drinking the millet beer, the man went and took his knife and sharpened it. (20) [Then] he told the girl to lie down. (21) The girl lay down. (22) As he was about to slaughter[263] [her], they saw a very old, fair-skinned woman descending 'swish!'[264] from the sky; she was wailing[265]: *'Wa ye-eee-ei-eie!'* (23) She descended and told them not to kill the girl, for she [the old woman] was [the girl] herself[266], so they should let her go. (24) When she had said that, they heard her

---

259) I.e. he poured the libation of millet beer before he sacrificed the girl.

260) The writer translated: 'the girl[...] started her song', and he added in brackets: '(which carried the message about the sacrifice; it was a sorrowful song)'. The writer did not give a translation of the song.

261) The song is in a language other than Buli; it cannot be translated.

262) *bogluk*, 'shrine or sacred object that receives sacrifices, altar' (Kröger BED). In the present case, the word *bogluk* probably refers to the most sacred spot of the *tanggbain* where sacrificial offerings are placed.

263) *togri*, v. 'to cut the throat, to slaughter or kill an animal (only by cutting its throat)' (Kröger BED).

264) '*chaan-a!*', exclamation, imitating the sound of a bird coming down and landing with its wings outstretched.

265) *weliing* or *wuliing*, n. 'ululation, high pitched cry (e.g.) in praise of a dance or a speech (esp. uttered by women)' (Kröger BED).

266) I.e. she was identical with the girl.

ba ngman gaa nya ku ale kumu ain: 'Wa yie-e-e-ei-ie!'. (25) Nipowa ngman yiri jue wen alege ate ba yiri waang.

(26) Di ale soa ate ba yuen ain ba kan pai nuroa a kaab bogluk la.

wailing again[267]: '*Wa yie-e-e-e-ei-ie!*' (25) The woman rose up into the sky again and they [the people] got up and dispersed.

(26) That is why it is said that one does not take human beings and sacrifice them to a shrine.

267) [...] *ba ngman gaa nya ku ale kumu ain*: lit. 'they again went to see [=hear] it cry:', or 'how it sounded'. The verb *kum(u)* means '1. to mourn, to condole, to cry, to weep, to lament [...] 2. [...] to sound, to make a noise [...]' (Kröger BED).

BUL-E1435 (BULI TEXT)

(1) Ka nuro ale wa pok ale boro, a yaa biag ba biik. (2) Ba ale ling a biag wai la, nidoa-bili. (3) A kali vuusi, a ngman jaa yig logi a paa biag nipok-bili. (4) Ba le paa biak nipok-bini la, nipowa ale wa chorowa a yaa nya chaab-a, ain waa: (5) Nipok-bin-a, daa ba buuri po. (6) Ba yig wala a ko ale wa kan niesi ba buuri. (7) Ba yaa te dai ain ba le yig nipok-bini a ko. (8) Da neuk dani a dan paari, ba yig nipok-bini ko. (9) A saasi gebsa neuk, a limsi a yin da neuku a dan paari abe ba ko nipok-bini.

(10) Ba boro, ba boro, da neuku a yaa par-a, ate ba yaa yin ba jo a yig biika a ta nyini a ko-a. (11) Nipok-bini yue be le Afaati. (12) Ba yaa tom wa moa kpagni ain wa jo a ta wa suoku a nyin ate ba ko, ale daa ba buuri po.

02.09 Girls must not be killed (sacrificed) IX

BUL-E1435 (ENGLISH TRANSLATION)

(1) There was a man and his wife and they brought forth a child. (2) The first [child] they brought forth was a boy. (3) Then they sat down and rested, and [after some time the woman] became pregnant[268] again and gave birth to a girl. (4) After they had brought forth the girl, the woman and her husband looked at each other and they said (5) the girl was not of their clan[269]. (6) [They decided that] they should take her and kill her because she did not resemble[270] their kind. (7) So they fixed a day when they would take the girl and kill her. (8) They decided to take the girl and kill her on the ninth day. (9) And they sharpened nine knives and waited for the ninth day to come when they would kill the girl.

(10) They lived on[271] and [when] the ninth day arrived, they said [it was now time to] enter [the house or the room] and take the child out and kill her. (11) The girl's

---

268) *yig logi*, lit. 'to catch a belly'; *logi*, def. *logni*, pl. *loga* 'stomach, esp. if protruding), belly (visible shape, big belly as in pregnancy [...]), abdomen' (Kröger BED).

269) *buuri*, def. *buuni*, pl. *buura*, n. '1. kind, race, species, genus, type, sort [...]; 2. lineage of varying span [...]' (Kröger BED; see also glossary). - The present sentence may also be translated: 'The girl was not of their kind'. This may imply that the girl was considered to be a *kikiruk* (pl. *kikita*, see glossary), an ogre with superhuman faculties. Children suspected of being *kikita* were formerly killed by specialists among the Bulsa.

270) *niesi*, v. 'to resemble, be similar (only in appearance, not in action, cf. *nyesi* to resemble in action), to look like, to look alike [...]' (Kröger BED). - The sentence may also be translated: '[...] she did not resemble their clan, family' etc. See the preceding footnote and the glossary under the entry *buuri*.

271) *ba boro, ba boro,* lit. 'they were there' or 'they lived', 'they existed'. This is the stereotype formula used to describe a lapse of time in which nothing extraordinary happened; it may also be translated as 'days passed by'. In Bulsa tales, the formula *ba boro, ba boro* frequently marks the transition from one episode to another one or the gap between two episodes.

(13) Nidoa-bini a yaa yiri a jo. (14) Ale wa mawa biag Afaatiwa a ta bo dayiik po, wan diem a ta wa a nyini pielim-oa. (15) Wa moawa a yaa chali a jo dalongku po-a, a jo kali dula a piilim wa yiila:

[Song in Kasem]

(16) Afaati ya nung ba gua,
(17) Afaati ya nung ba gua,
(18) nung ba gua, sera nung ba gua.
(19) Afaati ya nung ba gua,
(20) Afaati ya nung ba gua,
(21) nung ba gua, sera nung ba gua.
(22) Di ba nu lag baara yeramu se wa ba kana lagi na
(23) Di ban ko lagi baara yeramu se wa ba kana lagi na
(24) Afaati ya nung ba gua,
(25) Afaati ya nung ba gua,
(26) nung ba gua, sera nung ba gua.

(27) Ba ta wa a nyini dalong-oa, biika ngman chali a nyin dabiak po. (28) A ngman nyini a zaan dabiaka po:

[Song in Kasem repeated]

name was Afaati. (12) They sent her senior brother to enter [the house or the room] and bring his sister out, so they could kill her, for [she was] not part of their family[272].

(13) The boy got up and went into [the house or the room]. (14) [Yet] after his mother had given birth to Afaati, she remained [with her] in the *dayiik*[273]; she had not yet taken her outside[274]. (15) Her senior brother then ran and entered the *dalong*[275] and sat there and started singing his song:

[Song in Kasem[276]]

(27) They brought her [the girl] out [of the *dayiik*] to the *dalong* and the child [her senior brother] ran out into the *dabiak*[277]. (28) He went out again and stood in the *dabiak* [singing]:

[Song in Kasem repeated]

---

272) Lit.: She was 'not in her family' (*buuri*, see glossary).

273) *dayiik*, 'inner room', sleeping room, can only be entered through the *dalong*, 'outer room'; see glossary for both terms.

274) Among the Bulsa, it is a custom to keep newborn babies inside the room where they have been born. Boys are kept inside for three days, girls for four days. After that they are ceremonially brought outside to be introduced to the family. For details of this *rite de passage* (rite of transition) cf. Kröger 1978: 54-55.

275) 'Outer room', cf. footnote no. 273.

276) This song was transcribed by Ms. Pauline Akankyalabey. She could, however, not translate it. Kasem is the language of the Kasena, a people living next to the Bulsa to the north of their territory.

277) 'Inner compound yard', see glossary.

(29) Ba ta wa nyin dabiak po, biika ngman yog zi nangkpieng po:

[Song in Kasem repeated]

(30) Ba ta wa nyin nangkpieng po; biika a chali a nyin kusung wa kowa jigi ale wa chani:

[Song in Kasem repeated]

(31) Ba ta biika nyin ate ba yig dueni a magsi togrika, a yaa ba piilim ba yiini. (32) A yaa ba pa gebika a su biika tutoku po:

[Song in Kasem repeated]

(33) Jaab a din nyin wen-a, a jam zi. (34) Ain waa: (35) Ba ale a yaali ain ba ko biika la, ka boan nying ate ba a yaali ain ba ko biika? (36) Jaamu ale jam a zi la-a, a zaan wa zuku-a, a ta va kuusin-a, a jam nyini wa siuku-a, a basi wa bitagi-fiik po-a, wa

(29) [Then] they brought her out into the *dabiak* and the child [her brother] jumped [over the wall[278)]] into the cattle-yard [and began to sing again]:

[Song in Kasem repeated]

(30) They brought her out to the cattle-yard; the child [her brother] ran outside with his pot[279)] to the *kusung* where his father was:

[Song in Kasem repeated]

(31) They took the child [the girl] out and laid her down, ready to be slaughtered[280)] and they started their song. (32) Then they took the knife and put it against the child's throat:

[Song in Kasem repeated]

(33) A being[281)] came down from the sky and landed. (34) It said [asked]: (35) For what reason did they want to kill the child?[282)] (36) The being which came [down from the sky] and landed, [looked like this:] From its head to its chest, down to its navel

---

278) The *dabiak* is separated from the cattle yard (*nangkpieng*) by a wall which, in Bulsa compounds, is usually so high that it can only be climbed over with ladders or steps (*tiila*) on both sides of the wall.

279) *chari*, def. *chani*, pl. *chaa*, 'unrestricted open clay vessel ([...] used, for example, for making shea-butter or as a grave-lid [...])' (Kröger BED).

280) *togri*, v. 'to cut the throat, to slaughter or kill an animal ([...] by cutting its throat)' (Kröger BED). The present form *togrika* is the verbal noun (*nomen actionis*), meaning '[the] slaughtering'.

281) *jaab*, lit. 'a thing', 'something', also 'animal [...], beast, creature [...]' (Kröger BED) etc., see glossary. In the present context, a supernatural being, half-human, half-animal, is concerned.

282) Lit.: 'As they wanted to kill the child, for what reason did they want to kill the child?'.

kauku-a, a chim nuro-a, kauku-a, a chim dung; fi ze ka aleka dungkai nyin kobta la. (37) A yug tintuem, ale yin biik kan ngari tintuemu, abe ba kan pa gebika a su biika tutowa. (38) Ale ba dan ko dila, ba buuri a kpegli kama. (39) Ba yaa pai biika a basi.

(40) Dila ale soa ate nipok a bo teng zuk, ale ba daam a yaali ain ba yig nipoma a ko kama. (41) Naawen abe le basi ate sabiila a jam yug tintuem a vari nipok basi ate wa maa bo teng zuk.

(42) Sunsuelini miena kpegtalegi.

and then to its anus - all that half was human, the [other] half was an animal; you wouldn't know what kind of animal it was that had [such] hair. (37) It threw ashes[283] and said that a child doesn't fetch ashes[284] and so they should not take the knife and put it against the child's throat. (38) For if they kill it, their clan will come to an end[285]. (39) Thereupon, they let go of the child.

(40) This is why women live[286] on earth; formerly they wanted to catch [all] the women and kill them. (41) It was God who sent down a servant[287] to come and throw ashes in order to save the woman, so that she can also live on earth.

(42) That is the end of the whole story.

---

283) This is a symbolic act which is meant to restore peace between fighting parties. Ashes, according to Bulsa creeds, are a symbol of 'coolness'.

284) The meaning of this proverbial saying is not clear.

285) I.e. their *buuri* (cf. glossary) will die out, become extinct.

286) Lit.: '[...] why women live on earth;'.

287) *sabilo*, def. *sabilowa*, pl. *sabiloba* (loanword Hausa?), n. 'servant'. '*Naawen sabilo*' in the language of Christian missionaries: 'angel' (Kröger BED).

BUL-E0920 (BULI TEXT)

(1) Ka nuru ne boro, a faa wa pok a biag wa bisa - bata, liewa wanyi.

(2a) Nurdoawa yaa ain wa kan yaa nipowa. (2b) [...] nipok-bini. (3) Wa mawa ain wa kan yaa nipowa. (4) Wa toawa wanyi yaa kan siagi ain: (5) 'Fi nin ta toa ne fi chim nuru, fi dan kan ta toa fi yaa nye se chim nuru?' (6) Ain ba kan yaa wa.

(7) Ba kowa yaa ain ba cheng goai ga yaa daata ta jam te wa. (8) Ba yaa ga yaa daatanga, a yaa fag, a yaa moag bolim ju. (9) A moag bolimu ju-a, ain nipowa nyini, wa toa kpagni za piilim wa yiili, a jue kingkangni teng:

[Song in Kasem[288)]]

(10)	*Atira tira nong ba gua nong ba gua anina lagra!*
(11)	*Atira tira nong ba gua nong ba gua anina lagra!*
(12)	*Ako wu lag bagra yeri mu sum bakana lag 'yoo'!*
(13)	*Ako wu lag bagra yeri mu sum bakana lag 'yoo'!*
(14)	*Atira tira nong ba gua nong ba gua anina lagra!*
(15)	*Atira tira nong ba gua nong ba gua anina lagra!*
(16)	*Ako wu lag bagra yeri mu sum bakana lag 'yoo'!*
(17)	*Ako wu lag bagra yeri mu sum bakana lag 'yoo'!*
(18)	*Atira tira nong ba gua nong ba gua anina lagra!*
(19)	*Atira tira nong ba gua nong ba gua anina lagra!*
(20)	*Ako wu lag bagra yeri mu sum bakana lag 'yoo'!*
(21)	*Ako wu lag bagra yeri mu sum bakana lag 'yoo'!*

288) Mr. Akamara Atogtemi tried to transcribe this song as rendered above. As Mr. Akamara did not know Kasem, he did not furnish a translation.

02.10 Girls must not be killed (sacrificed) X

BUL-E0920 (ENGLISH TRANSLATION)

(1) There once lived a man who married[289] and begot children - three of them; one of them [was] a daughter.

(2a) The man then said that he did not like the woman. (2b) [...] the girl. (3) Her mother [also] said that she did not like the woman [the girl]. (4) [But] one of her brothers did not agree [with his parents' opinion] and said: (5) '[Only] if you have a sister, are[290] you a man, [but] if you don't have a sister, how could you be a man?' (6) [But] they [the parents] said that they didn't like her.

(7) Their father told them[291] to go to the bush and fetch firewood and bring it to him. (8) And they went and fetched the firewood, piled it up [and then] set [it] on fire. (9) When they had set [it] on fire, [they] said that the woman [the girl] should come out [of the room or the house] and her senior brother started his song and climbed over the courtyard wall [and stood] beside it:

[(10) - (21) Song in Kasem (see footnote no. 276)]

---

289) Lit.: '[...] who married his wife'.

290) Lit.: 'you become (*chim*) a man'. The verb *chim* means: '1. to become, to grow, to change into [...] 2. to develop, to mature, to become an adult [...] 3. to be [...]' (Kröger BED).

291) It is not clear whether the tellers means by 'them' any people of his compound or the girl's brothers who call her to come out of the house later on.

(22) Wa nye dila, nipok-bini an nyin ya, nwala ngman pilim a jo:

[Song repeated]

(23) Wan yiri ya; nwala ngmaa jo, wai ne kaa siag wa nying la ne la, a za nansiungku noai, a kan siag wa jo. (24) Ane za dula jigni:

[Song repeated]

(25) Ngman pilim cheng a jo nangkpiengka dek po:

[Song repeated]

(26) Ngman paa kingkangni teng, nipok-bini yiri jengsi, ain wa wom se ka wai ne ka siag wa nying la ya? (27) Wa yiri kala; biika ngmaa jo, a ga paa kingkangni teng. (28) Wa be kan siag wa yueni, ku be a fe te wa yueni:

[Song repeated]

(22) He [the brother] did this, [but] the girl did not come out; another one [of her brothers] also entered [the house and started singing]:

[Song in Kasem repeated]

(23) She did not get up; [then] another one [of her brothers] also entered, [and also] the one who liked her was there and stood by the entrance, [but] he did not want to enter. (24) And he stood there [and began to sing]:

[Song repeated]

(25) [And he, the favourite brother] turned back into the cattle yard [singing]:

[Song repeated]

(26) [When he] approached the courtyard wall[292] again, the girl got up and peeped[293] to see whether it was the one who liked her. (27) She got up and sat [in her *dok*[294]]; the boy [her brother] also entered and reached the courtyard wall. (28) [Although] he did not want to tell her[295], he was compelled to say it:

[Song repeated]

---

292) *kingkangi*, n. 'inner wall of a compound' (Kröger BED), see glossary.

293) *jengsi*, v. 'to peep in the sense of to stand on tiptoe, trying to have a quick look'.

294) *dok*, pl. *diina* '1. room [...], 2. set of rooms around an inner courtyard (*dabiak*)' (Kröger BED), see glossary.

295) I.e. that she was going to be burnt.

(29) Wa din vaari yiri, vaari yiri, daa chal, daa chal, a din nyin tuag wa lo bolimu po, jaab din nyin wen, a jam chiag wa nna: 'kpiap!', a ta ga chigsi nakpiak. (30) Alege te nyiam deri a sing nna 'chubububu!', a jam kpimsi bolimu, alege te nipok-bini za. (31) Nipok-bini yaa le za la, wai le wi te wa nyin la, biikala a pa ka wa lala, a faa nipooba a sue yeri.

(32) Dila ne soa, ate fi dan nyin nurdoaba nyiini, alege n maa biag nipowa, nipowa sui a puuri, nurdoa-bilisanga [(32b) me] sui a puuri, ba le kan ta toa la nying. (33) Ba toawa ale vari ba basi nyin kini po. (34) Nipok-bini ale dueni wa mawa buuri nyini kini po.

(35) Mi sunsuelini miena kpegitalegi.

(29) She jumped up, jumped up and ran, ran and went out near [to the fire] and when she was [just about] to fall into the fire, a being[296] came down from the sky (God)[297], came and grabbed[298] her: *'kpiap!'*, and placed her aside[299]. (30) Suddenly water poured down *'chubububu!'* and quenched the fire while the girl stood by. (31) While the girl stood there, the one who called her outside, took her and married women and 'filled a house'[300].

(32) That is why, when you bring forth men only and do not also bring forth a woman, the woman [the girl] is always unhappy[301], and the boys are [(32b) also] unhappy because they do not have a sister. (33) For it was their sister who saved them[302] from the beginning. (34) The girl perpetuated her mother's clan from its beginnings.

(35) That is the end of my story.

---

296) *jaab*, lit. 'thing', 'something', here: a 'being', see glossary.

297) [...] *jaab din nyin wen*, lit. 'a thing then came down from the sky' or 'from God'. The word *wen* means both the 'sky' and the Sky-God; see glossary.

298) *chiagi*, v. 'to snatch, to seize, to grab, to take (away) suddenly, to carry away (e.g. as a hawk does a chicken)' (Kröger BED).

299) *chigsi nakpiak*, lit. 'dropped [her] outside'; *chigsi*, v. '1. to put into an upright position [...] 2. to drop, to put down (e.g. a child or a bundle of firewood from the flat roof to the floor of the courtyard, but only used if the object stands upright after dropping [...]'; *nakpiak*, n. 'exterior, external parts or side (e.g. of a building or a town), surrounding area, outskirts [...] (transl.:) apart (from), aside, beside, outside, near [...]' (Kröger BED).

300) Idiomatic phrase, meaning to 'fill a house' with women, children and riches of all kinds.

301) This phrase is obviously illogical.

302) *vari basi*, 'to save, to set free, to deliver, to rescue, to escape [...]' (Kröger BED). Here the phrase means probably : the sister 'ensured their existence'.

03. GOD MAKES MEN AND WOMEN MARRY

03.01 BUL-E1445 Women from the Sky Marry Hunter

03.02 BUL-E0426 Women from the Sky Marry Three Bachelors

03.03 BUL-E0182 Women from the Sky Marry Three Brothers

03.04 BUL-E0503 Half-Woman (God's Daughter) Marries Bachelor

03.05 BUL-E0514 Leper (God) Marries Chief's Daughter

03. GOD MAKES MEN AND WOMEN MARRY

The five stories of this chapter have one theme in common: God forces unmarried men and women to marry, i.e. to accept their social statuses as adult men and women. In the first three stories, bachelors are visited by women from the sky, i.e. from God. They secretly do the most important work a woman has to do: they prepare food for the men while they are in the bush hunting or farming. With the help of magic ashes, the men succeed in keeping the celestial women from returning to the sky. The men then marry the women. In two stories (BUL-E0426, BUL-E0182) the women want to see their parents in the sky. This corresponds to Bulsa custom: a daughter married elsewhere has to visit her parents from time to time. In the sky, the elder brothers are frightened by ferocious animals; they return to Earth. Only the youngest brother succeeds in overcoming all obstacles and ruses by means of which the people in the sky want to prevent him from taking their 'daughter' back to Earth. With the help of a grateful cat - a motif which occurs also in other Bulsa tales - he recognizes his wife amidst many other identical women. In both tales, the cannibalistic habits of witches are alluded to; one story (BUL-E0426) even ends with the etiological motif explaining how witches came to exist on earth.

In story BUL-E0503 a man refuses to marry any girl. He goes to collect firewood for his mother - a very unusual thing for a man to do. In the bush he meets a half-woman who later proves to be God's daughter. The man returns from the underground realm of God with many riches, accompanied by his most beautiful wife. The young man is made chief; the deposed chief, being jealous, entices the other men in his village to sleep with the young man's wife. The old chief has him publicly burnt. The young man's wife, God's daughter, resuscitates him from the ashes while his parents shrink back from saving their son out of the flames.

In story BUL-E0514, on the other hand, a girl, a chief's daughter, rejects all her suitors. Her father tells her that he will not force her to marry, but he ordains that his daughter is no longer to speak to any man. If she breaks this taboo, she must marry the one she has spoken to. God transforms himself into a leper and by a trick he makes the chief's daughter speak. Although she does not want to marry the leper, her father forces her to follow him as his wife. She maltreats him by spoiling his food and by smearing a slippery sauce on the ladder used in climbing over the compound wall. In spite of this obstruction, the leper succeeds in arriving at the woman's father's funeral. He touches the corpse of the chief, his father-in-law, with his magic tail and revives him. Then the 'leper' reveals himself as God. He hands his life-giving tail to the recuscitated chief so that he may revive dead people. God says that the tail must not be taken into a room. A wife of the chief pilfers the tail in order to revive her father. Being ignorant of God's order, he puts the tail into the rafters of a house where the tail's 'medicine' is spoilt at once. Ever since then, it has not been possible to revive dead people.

All five stories proclaim the 'message' that God is averse to men or women staying single and that God is Lord over life and death. In most of the stories in this chapter, God remains in the background. Except in the last story, God's daughters are active in his stead in making men take the yoke of married life.

BUL-E1445 (BULI TEXT)

(1) Kaa nidoa ale boro, bo wa yeri po, chim yaaloa. (2) Ate vani a dan vienti, wa yiti a yig goai a cheng. (3) Wa dan nyin goani a jam-oa, wa jaa paa sira ale nganta, a sue dok, wa pa a de. (4) A ze ka nipooba ale nyin wen a nyiem jam zi a nye dila miena a zaan wa. (5) Vani a dan vienti wa ngmaa cheng. (6) Ba dan din jam zi-a, baa piilim ba yiili-a: [Interruption]

(7)	*Sing ba ngwul-a, sing ba ngwul-a, sing ba ngwul-a!*[303]
(8)	*Ase yeri ba nong ni chum ale jam sing ba ngwul-a!*
(9)	*A sing ba ngwul-a, sing ba ngwula, sing ba ngwul-a!*
(10)	*Ase yeri ba nong ni chum ale jam sing ba ngwul-a!*
(11)	*A pari ba ngwul-a, pari ba ngwul-a, pari ba ngwul-a!*
(12)	*Ase yeri ba nong ni chum ale jam pari ba ngwul-a!*
(13)	*A nyini ba ngwul-a, nyini ba ngwul-a, nyini ba ngwul-a!*
(14)	*Ase yeri ba nong ni chum ale jam nyini ba ngwul-a!*

303) The teller starts each verse, the chorus (the audience) joins in after the teller has sung the first verb. The song describes step by step the process of preparing *saab*, millet porridge, the staple food of the Bulsa.

03.01 Women from the Sky Marry Hunter

BUL-E1445 (ENGLISH TRANSLATION)

(1) Once a man lived in his house; he was a hunter. (2) At daybreak, he [usually] got up and set out for the bush. (3) Whenever he returned from the bush, he found the room filled with millet porridge and [other] things [kinds of food]; he took them and ate them. (4) He did not know that some women from the sky used to come down and prepare all these [things] and place [them down] for him. (5) When day broke, he went [to the bush] again. (6) Whenever they [the women] descended, they began their song:

(7) Climb down[304)] [into the barn] quickly, climb down quickly, climb down quickly!

(8) If you [want] to return to your lover's house tomorrow, climb down quickly!

(9) Climb down quickly, climb down quickly, climb down quickly!

(10) If you [want] to return to your lover's house tomorrow, climb down quickly!

(11) Take them[305)] quickly, take them quickly, take them quickly!

(12) If you [want] to return to your lover's house tomorrow, take them quickly!

(13) Come out quickly, come out quickly, come out quickly!

(14) If you [want] to return to your lover's house tomorrow, come out quickly!

---

304) In the following song, all the steps for preparing food from grains of millet or guinea corn in the Bulsa way are described one after the other. The words 'climb down' refers here to the act of climbing down into the barn where millet or guinea corn is stored.

305) 'Take them quickly', means: Take the panicles of millet from the barn (the conical clay granary in the cattle-yard of the compound) quickly! (Pauline Akankyalabey)

(15) *A cheng ba ngwul-a, cheng ba ngwul-a, cheng ba ngwul-a!*

(16) *Ase yeri ba nong ni chum ale jam cheng ba ngwul-a!*

(17) *A kuri ba ngwul-a, kuri ba ngwul-a, kuri ba ngwul-a!*

(18) *Ase yeri ba nong ni chum ale jam kuri ba ngwul-a!*

(19) *A yali ba ngwul-a, yali ba ngwul-a, yali ba ngwul-a!*

(20) *Ase yeri ba nong ni chum ale jam yali ba ngwul-a!*

(21) *A cheng ba ngwul-a, cheng ba ngwul-a, cheng ba ngwul-a!*

(22) *Ase yeri ba nong ni chum ale jam cheng ba ngwul-a!*

(23) *A jo-a ba ngwul-a, jo-a ba ngwul-a, jo-a ba ngwul-a!*

(24) *Ase yeri ba nong ba chum ale jam jo-a ba ngwul-a!*

(25) *A pisi ba ngwul-a, pisi ba ngwul-a, pisi ba ngwul-a!*

(26) *Ase yeri ba nong ni chum ale jam pisi ba ngwul-a!*

(27) *A num ba ngwul-a, num ba ngwul-a, num ba ngwul-a!*

(15) Go quickly, go quickly, go quickly!

(16) If you [want] to return to your lover's house tomorrow, go quickly!

(17) Pound them[306] quickly, pound them quickly, pound them quickly!

(18) If you [want] to return to your lover's house tomorrow, pound them quickly!

(19) Winnow them[307] quickly, winnow them quickly, winnow them quickly!

(20) If you [want] to return to your lover's house tomorrow, winnow them quickly!

(21) Go quickly, go quickly, go quickly!

(22) If you [want] to return to your lover's house tomorrow, go quickly!

(23) Enter[308] quickly, enter quickly, enter quickly!

(24) If you [want] to return to your lover's house tomorrow, enter quickly!

(25) Pick up[309] quickly, pick up quickly, pick up quickly[310]!

(26) If you [want] to return to your lover's house tomorrow, pick up quickly!

(27) Grind[311] quickly, grind quickly, grind quickly!

---

306) I.e. the panicles or grains of millet or guinea corn.

307) I.e. the grains of millet, by pouring them from one vessel into another one, the wind blowing away the chaff.

308) The word *jo*, 'to enter' here means that the women, on returning from the mortar outside the house, should enter the house or compound again.

309) The word *pisi*, 'to pick up, to collect from the gound' here means that husks which have not been winnowed shall be picked up before grinding the grains of millet.

310) Having pounded and winnowed the millet, the women now have to go through the millet and pick out or separate stones or unpounded stocks or pieces (Pauline Akankyalabey).

311) Grind the millet to produce millet flour.

(28) *Ase yeri ba nong ni chum ale jam num ba ngwul-a!*

(29) *A vaa ba ngwul-a, vaa ba ngwul-a, vaa ba ngwul-a!*

(30) *Ase yeri ba nong ni chum ale jam vaa ba ngwul-a!*

(31) *A nyini ba ngwul-a, nyini ba ngwul-a, nyini ba ngwul-a!*

(32) *Ase yeri ba nong ni chum ale jam nyini ba ngwul-a!*

(33) *A kuri ba ngwul-a, kuri ba ngwul-a, kuri ba ngwul-a!*

(34) *Ase yeri ba nong ni chum ale jam kuri ba ngwul-a!*

(35) *A chiem a wuli, chiem a wuli, chiem a wul-a!*

(36) *Ase yeri ba nong ni chum ale jam chiem a wul-a!*

(37) *A dig ba ngwul-a, dig ba ngwul-a, dig ba ngwul-a!*

(38) *Ase yeri ba nong ni chum ale jam dig ba ngwul-a!*

(28) If you [want] to return to your lover's house tomorrow, grind quickly!

(29) Sweep[312] quickly, sweep quickly, sweep quickly!

(30) If you [want] to return to your lover's house tomorrow, sweep quickly!

(31) Go out quickly, go out quickly, go out quickly!

(32) If you [want] to return to your lover's house tomorrow, go out quickly!

(33) Pound[313] quickly, pound quickly, pound quickly!

(34) If you [want] to return to your lover's house tomorrow, pound quickly!

(35) Light [the fire][314] quickly, light [the fire] quickly, light [the fire] quickly!

(36) If you [want] to return to your lover's house tomorrow, light [the fire] quickly!

(37) Cook[315] it quickly, cook it quickly, cook it quickly!

(38) If you [want] to return to your lover's house tomorrow, cook quickly!

---

312) This refers to the sweeping together of the millet flour 'from the grinding stone. This is normally done by using a special type of broom to gather all the flour into the hole of the grinding stone. It is then collected into a calabash.' (Pauline Akankyalabey).

313) This refers to 'the pounding of the ingredients e.g. groundnuts, dawadawa spice and so on to use in preparing the soup (*jenta*) for the millet porridge.' (Pauline Akankyalabey).

314) 'To prepare the fire to cook the meal.' (Pauline Akankyalabey).

315) 'To put the pot of water on the fire to boil in order to prepare the millet porridge.' (Pauline Akankyalabey).

(39) *A dam ba ngwul-a, dam ba ngwul-a, dam ba ngwul-a!*

(40) *Ase yeri ba nong ni chum ale jam dam ba ngwul-a!*

(41) *A kori ba ngwul-a, kori ba ngwul-a, kori ba ngwul-a!*

(42) *Ase yeri ba nong ni chum ale jam kor' ba ngwul-a!*

(43) *A kpii ba ngwul-a, kpii ba ngwul-a, kpii ba ngwula!*

(44) *Ase yeri ba nong ni chum ale jam kpii ba ngwul-a!*

(45) *A pari ba ngwul-a, pari ba ngwul-a, pari ba ngwula!*

(46) *Ase yeri ba nong ni chum ale jam pari ba ngwul-a!*

(47) *A de ba ngwul-a, de ba ngwul-a, de ba ngwula!*

(48) *Ase yeri ba nong ni chum ale jam de ba ngwul-a!*

(49) *A yiti ba ngwul-a, yiti ba ngwul-a, yiti ba ngwula!*

(39) Stir[316)] it quickly, stir it quickly, stir it quickly!

(40) If you [want] to return to your lover's house tomorrow, stir quickly!

(41) Take it out[317)] quickly, take it out quickly, take it out quickly!

(42) If you [want] to return to your lover's house tomorrow, take it out quickly!

(43) Pour[318)] it quickly, pour it quickly, pour it quickly!

(44) If you [want] to return to your lover's house tomorrow, pour it quickly!

(45) Take it quickly, take it quickly, take it quickly!

(46) If you [want] to return to your lover's house tomorrow, take it quickly!

(47) Eat it quickly, eat it quickly, eat it quickly!

(48) If you [want] to return to your lover's house tomorrow, eat it quickly!

(49) Fly[319)] quickly, fly quickly, fly quickly!

---

316) 'Stirring the millet porridge: When the water is boiling, some of the flour is mixed with cold water and then poured into the boiling water and stirred until it becomes porridge. The porridge is left to boil for some minutes and then some of it is taken out and put into another vessel. The millet flour is then quickly stirred into the boiling porridge which is still on the fire so that it is mixed evenly and that no lumps develop. The porridge in the other container is added and stirred until the desired thickness is obtained.' (Pauline Akankyalabey).

317) *kori* or (Kröger BED) *koori*: 'To take millet porridge out of the cooking pot into eating vessels e.g. calabashes or small earthenware pots used for serving food. From the earthenware pots the porridge is again transferred into a calabash and the pot is used to serve the soup (*jenta*) that goes with the porridge.' (Pauline Akankyalabey).

318) *kpiiri*, *kpii* v.: 'to transfer the millet porridge from an earthenware pot into a calabash.' (Pauline Akankyalabey).

319) *yiti*, v. '1. to get up, [...] to rise, to arise [...] 2. to wake up [...] 3. to leave [...] 4. to fly (up, away, out) [...].' (Kröger BED) - 'In the present case, the verb *yiti* means 'to fly' or 'to go up to the sky' from where they (the women) had come.' (Pauline Akankyalabey).

(50) *Ase yeri ba nong ni chum ale jam yiti ba ngwul-a!*

(51) Ba nue kama dila, alege nidoawa nganta a ngman sung liika noai a ngman vug a zaan. (52) Ba ngmaa yiri kama dila:

(53) *A yiri ba ngwul-a, yiri ba ngwul-a, yiri ba ngwul-a!*

(54) *Ase yeri ba nong ni chum ale jam yiri ba ngwul-a!*

(55) *A kuli ba ngwul-a, kuli ba ngwul-a, kuli ba ngwul-a!*

(56) *Ase yeri ba nong ni chum ale jam kuli ba ngwul-a!*

(57) Ba ngman jue ka ba weni dila. (58) Nuruwa jam a pa de. (59) Vani a dan vienti, nuruwa ngmaa nyin, ba ngman jam zi, ngmaa nye; nuruwa ngman jam a pa de.

(60) Dandidai nuruwa yaa nye a kpier-a, a yaa ga maga, a yaa a nya ba. (61) Ku an beni ya, ba yaam bo siuk, ba jam zi ya. (62) A pai ba buini tiini a tiili du, yii-yiiroawa me yaam a piilim wa yiini:

[song (7-50) repeated[320]]

320) The singer omitted only the verses (25) and (26).

(50) If you [want] to return to your lover's house tomorrow, fly quickly!

(51) They finished like this, having placed the man's food on top[321] of the pot and having covered [it]. (52) They flew up [to the sky] again like this [singing]:

(53) Fly up quickly, fly up quickly, fly up quickly!

(54) If you [want] to return to your lover's house tomorrow, fly up quickly!

(55) Go home quickly, go home quickly, go home quickly!

(56) If you [want] to return to your lover's house tomorrow, go home quickly!

(57) Thus, they went up to the sky[322] again. (58) When the man came [returned to his house], he took [the food] and ate it. (59) At daybreak, the man again went out [to the bush]; they [the women] came down again and did [the same thing] again and the man came [home] again, took the food and ate it.

(60) One day the man found it unbearable, went and hid and watched them. (61) Soon they were again on their way; they came and landed. (62) [As usual] they placed their granary ladder there [against the granary] and the singer also began her song again:

[song (7-50) repeated[323]]

---

321) A pot called *liik* is an 'earthenware vessel with a narrow mouth (generally used for storing liquids)' (Kröger BED); in the present context the *liik* is used to rest a bigger pot, on top of it, containing the food.

322) Lit.: '[...] they went up to their sky there'.

323) The singer omitted only the verses (25) and (26).

(63) Ba ale din nye dila ate ba yiti-a, yeni nyono a jaa jo ain: (64) 'Naa-biik a kan zaab tuntuem-oa!' (65) Ba nya waa saalim kama, wa an maring a kal-a wa nyiini-a. (66) Wa nyiem be jam a nya ngandiintanga a pai a de kama. (67) 'Ti be din maa ka chaab a boro ate ni nye ate maa de, ku ten nala?' (68) Naa-biik be kan zaab tuntuem-oa, abe ba te ate ba maa chaab a bo yeni po.

(69) Nya nipok boka kiri le la; nipok a daam bo ka wen. (70) Ka yaaloa ale ta wa a jam.

(71) Sunsuelini miena ale la.

(63) As they did this and were just about to fly up, the owner of the house[324] came and entered and said: (64) 'A chief's son does not despise[325] ashes[326].' (65) [He said that] they should understand that he was begging them [to remain with him], [for] he did not like living alone[327] [unmarried]. (66) [He said that] whenever he had come [back from the hunt] and found the food [they had prepared], he had taken and eaten [it]. (67) 'Would it not be better if we were living together so that you[328] could cook for me to eat?' (68) Since a chief's son does not refuse ashes, they [the women] should agree to live in the house together.

(69) Look, that is the reason why women are there[329]; formerly women lived in the sky. (70) It was a hunter who brought them [to earth].

(71) That is the whole story.

---

324) Meaning, the hunter as co-owner of the house.

325) *zaabi*, *zaa* or *zaab*, v. '1. to despise, to disdain, to decry (e.g. through envy), to underrate, to feel superior, to consider or regard as insufficient, unsatisfactory or inferior, to be discontented with, to refuse (restr.) [...]' (Kröger BED)

326) 'This expression is to be understood in the context of the use of ashes in Bulsa religious ritual.' (Pauline Akankyalabey) - Further information is required concerning the meaning of this saying.

327) Lit.: '[...] he did not like to sit, to stay alone.'

328) 2nd pers. pl.

329) Lit.: '[...] why a woman is there', i.e. why women now live together with men.

BUL-E0426 (BULI-TEXT)

(1) Kaa nidoaba bata, dakoaksa nyini, ale bo ba yeri po; a yaa le yaa badek a ga kpa talim. (2) Ba nyiem be dan nyini miena ba yeni, ba lig kama.

(3) Ba dan cheng goan-a, ba jaa a paari nwa saab za, nwa saab za. (4) Ba pai de. (5) Daanga miena dila, daanga miena dila.

(6) Dandiḍai-a, yoawa yaa ain waa: (7) 'Ni kan te ti nye wani dila! (8) Daanga miena, taa dạn jaa paari le saamu za-a, alege te ti ze bu nyono-a, alege pai a de la-a, ni te ate ti nya bu nyono!'

(9) Kpagni ain wensie. (10) Ba be dan yir-a, yoawa ale sunsung po denoawa, baa cheng goani ale wa ale sing doa bukuni po. (11) Ba le yiti la, bạn nag nanpaga, a yig goani a cheng. (12) Wa doa bukuni po, ku le ga nag se 'twẹlve' la-a, nipok moaning

03.02 Women from the Sky Marry Three Bachelors

BUL-E0426 (ENGLISH TRANSLATION)

(1) There were three men, all still only[330] bachelors, who lived in their house; they were sure of themselves[331], and went and cleared[332] a bush field. (2) Any time they all left their house, they closed it.

(3) Whenever they went to the bush and when they returned [afterwards], they found that there was millet porridge standing [in the house] for each of them. (4) They took it and ate it. (5) Day after day, this [happened].

(6) Then one day the junior brother said: (7) 'Don't let us behave like this [any more]! (8) Every day when we return, the millet porridge is standing [there], but [although] we do not know to whom it belongs[333], we take it and eat it; let us try and find out to whom it belongs!'

(9) The eldest [brother] said that it was true[334]. (10) [He said that] when they woke up [the next morning], the junior and the middle [brother] should go to the bush, while he [himself] would climb down into the chicken coop [and hide there]. (11) When they got up, they did not dispute [their elder brother's suggestion]; they set out [for the

---

330) *dakoaksa nyini*, lit. 'bachelors only', i.e. without wives.

331) *yaa badek* or *yaali badek*, lit. '[they] liked, loved, wanted themselves': the bachelors wilfully overlooked the fact that they had no wives who are needed for farming, e.g. to bring flour water to the men working on the field in the bush. Pauline Akankyalabey translated *yaa badek* with the adverb 'confidently'; it may also be translated with 'to bluff, to show off'.

332) *kpa* 'to weed, [...] to clear the ground for new crops, to hoe between growing plants, to farm, to do farmwork [...]' (Kröger BED).

333) Lit.: '[...] we do not know its owner' (*nyono*, def. *nyonowa*, pl. *nyam* '1. owner, possessor, holder, bearer, propietor [...])' (Kröger BED). - Pauline Akankyalabey translated it: '[...] who has prepared it.' It may also be translated, 'We do not know whom it is meant for.'

334) I.e. he assented to his junior borther's opinion that they did not know who the 'owners' of the millet porridge were.

'zeng-zeng-a' ale nyin wen jam zi. (13) Wa choa pilim nyin wen jam zi, wa choa pilim jam sing. (14) Nwala ain waa: (15) 'Maa jo nanzuk!' (16) Nwala ain waa: (17) 'Mi be le cheng beli!' (18) Nwala ain: (19) 'Mi me le soa jentanga digka!' (20) Ba dig nue ya. (21) Nwala ain waa: (22) 'Pai fi chorowa ngandiintanga a zaan!' (23) Nwala me pai wa chorowa ngandiintanga a zaan, nwala me pai wa chorowa ngantanga zaan. (24) Ba miena yiti ya, ba me jue wen. (25) Nidoa duag bukuri po nya, wa nya - wa noai maali ya!

(26) Bimbaansa jaa paari saab za. (27) Ba wieni ain: (28) 'Ti moa, wieni, ku ka se-a?' (29) Ain ba kan ngman biisi, nya wani ka togka. (30) Wa yin di ka nyeka se ka

bush]. (12) He [the senior brother] lay in the chicken coop, and when it [the clock] was about to strike twelve[335], a very[336] fair-skinned[337] woman came from the sky and landed [inside the house]. (13) Another [woman] also descended from the sky and yet another one came down. (14) The first one said: (15) 'I shall go into the grinding room [to grind the millet]!' (16) The other one said: (17) 'Then, I will go to the river [and fetch water]!' (18) The third one said: (19) 'And I shall be responsible for the cooking of the soup[338]!' (20) Soon they had finished cooking. (21) The first one said: (22) 'You take your husband's food and keep [it] for him!' (23) One took her husband's food and kept [it] and the other also took her husband's food and kept [it]. (24) Then they all got up and went up to the sky again. (25) The man lay in the hen coop and watched; he watched and - he was speechless[339]!

(26) The boys [his brothers] returned and found the millet porridge ready to eat. (27) They asked [their senior brother]: (28) 'Our senior brother, tell us, what happened?'[340] (29) [The senior brother] said that they shouldn't talk [about it] at all, for the matter was really serious. (30) He [one of the two] asked how serious the matter was. (31) [The elder brother] said they should let [the matter] drop. (32) The middle

---

335) The teller uses the English word 'twelve'; the Buli phrase '*ku le ga nag se* 'twelve' *la* [...]', translated word-for-word, reads: 'it / {particle denoting the past} / go / strike, beat / about, around, approximately / twelve / {particle denoting relative clause} [...]'.

336) *zeng-zeng* colloquial expression, meaning 'very much, greatly, extremely, remarkably'.

337) The (relatively) fair colour of the skin of women corresponds to the ideal of beauty of the Bulsa. The word *moaning* denotes the colour 'red' in a wide sense, including also all shades of colour which we designate with the terms 'brown, yellow, orange, khaki' etc. (cf. Kröger BED).

338) The word *jenta* (pl.) means a 'soup' or 'sauce' which is usually added to the rather tasteless *saab*, or 'millet porridge', the staple food of the Bulsa. The *jenta* contains all sorts of spicy leaves and ingredients such as pepper and salt. Sometimes, pieces of meat and/or fish may be added to the *jenta*.

339) [...] *wa noai maali ya*, lit. 'his mouth was silenced or crushed'; the verb *maali* means '1. to kill a small animal (e.g. an insect) by rubbing one's foot over it, to crush [...], to be crushed [...] 2. to silence (sb.)' (Kröger BED).

340) Lit.: '[...] how was it?'

se la? (31) Ain ba basi. (32) Sunsung po denoawa ain waa: (33) 'Fi daa nidoa! (34) Naa chum cheng goai abe ni ge ate mi war'!' (35) 'Ah, ti chum be le kan wari!'

(36) Vari vienti, kpagni gum yoawa po, ba yig goai a cheng alege a tali sunsung po denoawa. (37) Wa doa, wa doa, bang pi-ale-buyewa nag ya,kpajiaka jam ya; wa noai maali ya. (38) Ba mani saab, ba kooi zaan, ba yiti; wa doa chim.

(39) Ba jaa paa ain: (40) 'N doa, ka se?' (41) Ain wani ka nyeka. (42) Yoawa ain waa: (43) 'Naa daa nidoaba! (44) Naa yaa be dan ka nidoaba-a, wani dek tin soa ka se? (45) Naa chum be cheng-a abe ni ge ate mi wari!' (46) 'Ti chum be ka le beni, ti le taam talim!' (47) Vari vienti ba me yiti a cheng talim.

(48) Biika din gan wa jo bui noai-a, din gaa nye daanika po tuntuemu-a ta yig bukuni po a sing, sing doa. (49) Kpajaasanga jam ya, ba mani saab zaan. (50) Nwa yin: (51) 'Pai fi chorowa chin-moani ta ga zaani, pai fi choro chin-moai ta ga zaan!' (52) Nwa yin: (53) 'Ni nye awuli ate ti nyin!'

one said: (33) 'You aren't really a man! (34) Tomorrow [both of] you will go to the bush and you will allow me to stay [here]!' (35) [The other brothers said:] 'Well then, tomorrow we shall not stay behind!'

(36) The next day the senior brother joined the junior one and they set out for the bush, leaving behind the middle brother. (37) He [the middle brother] lay there; he lay there and on the stroke of 12 o'clock [at noontime] the great one[341)] [the woman from the sky] arrived; he was at once dumbfounded[342)]. (38) They [the women[343)]] prepared the millet porridge, they served[344)] it and placed it [down], [and then] they went up; he [the man] lay there speechless.

(39) They [his brothers] returned and said: (40) 'My friend, what happened?' (41) [He] said that the matter was serious. (42) The junior brother said: (43) '[Both of] you are not men! (44) If you are really men, how serious is this matter[345)] [that you couldn't cope with]? (45) Tomorrow you should go [to the bush] while you let me stay [here]!' (46) 'Tomorrow we shall not delay, we will go along to the bush farm!' (47) At daybreak they [the two elder brothers] got up and went to the bush farm.

(48) As the boy [the man] was about to enter the opening of the chicken coop, he went and fetched some ashes from the fire-place, took the ashes into the chicken coop, and climbed down [into the chicken coop], climbed down and lay [there]. (49) The mighty ones [the women] arrived; they prepared the millet porridge and put it down. (50) One of them said: (51) 'Take your husband's red calabash [with food] and put [it] down, [you also] take your husband's red calabash [with food] and put it down!' (52) Another one said: (53) 'Hurry up and let's go out!'

---

341) *kpajiak*, pl. *kpajaasa* important, big, mighty, great person or thing.

342) Cf. sentence no. (25).

343) The change to the plural is not explained by the teller.

344) *koori*, abbr. *kooi*, 'to ladle or scoop solid food (e.g. millet gruel) from one container (clay vessel, cooking pot) into another (plate, calabash).' (Kröger BED)

345) [...] *wani dek tin soa ka se*? Lit.: '[...] the thing, matter, affair was like what?' The verb *soa* means '1. to own, to possess [...] 5. *soa se* or *soa* si transl. as, like, such as, as much as [...]' (Kröger BED).

(54) Ba le din ga zaan dabiaka po-a, ate ba yiti-a, biik din pobsi tuntuem ale wieni ain: (55) 'Naab kan gaam tintuem-oa!' (56) Ba miena din wari a kali. (57) Biik a din nyin bukuri po a daa nyin. (58) Wa pok din pai saab ta jam zaan wa ning. (59) Wa yaa de, de ale kala a limsi. (60) Kpajaasa jue nue, din jaa paa ain: (61) 'Fi ka nidoa!' (62) Ba din te ba miena ngandiinta; wai miena ale wa pok.

(63) Ba yaa doa, ba boro, ba boro, ba boro. (64) Kpagni powa ain waa: (65) Ba nya wa a yaali ain wa cheng ga nya ka wa ko ale wa ma, abe ba te wa siuk. (66) Ba yin siuk doa. (67) Kpagni be le siag basi wa powa ate wa cheng dila? (68) Wa din yiti din za daa num zom chin, nya wa kpong, a din pai a nyoro.

(69) Wa din za daa pai wa namarik, nya wa liak, nya wa tom, din geri. (70) Baa cheng, nipok-bili moata yeri-a, wa yin waa: (71) 'Ti dan ga moati tamponi chiak-a, mi kowa biak-a ale din yiti chien la-a, kan chali! (72) Fi be dan ngman jo nangkpiengka po-a, bu-duku ale yiti chien ain ku chub fu la-a, kan chali! (73) Fi ngman jo dabiaka po-a, nanjunsanga la a kali fu la-a, kan yiagi! (74) Biaka ka goa-biak, bu-duku gbengni, nanjunganga sie-a!' (75) Wa yin wa wom ya. (76) Wa va wa pok ngaang, wa le din ga moati tamponi-a, ate goa-biaka din ga na-a, biik din pai tom yugi basi ale pai chal-a choa. (77) Nipowa taam ga jo.

(54) When they went and stood in the courtyard and were about to go up [to the sky], the boy blew the ashes and said: (55) 'A chief does not walk over ashes!'[346)] (56) Then all of them stopped and sat down. (57) Then the boy came out of the chicken coop. (58) His wife then took his millet porridge and came and placed it in front of him. (59) He ate and ate, sat down and waited. (60) When the great ones [the elder brothers] had arrived, they said: (61) 'You are really a man!' (62) They [the women] gave all of them food, each from his wife.

(63) They lived on and on. (64) Then the senior brother's wife said: (65) They should understand that she wanted to go and see her father and mother and that they should give her permission [to go]. (66) They said that permission was granted [for her to go]. (67) [But:] would the senior [brother] have allowed his wife to go home like that[347)]? (68) She got up and ground a calabashful of millet flour, [then] she found a guinea-fowl and added it to it[348)].

(69) Then he [the senior brother] took his quiver, looked for his axe, looked for his bow and slung them over his shoulder. (70) They walked on and as they were drawing nearer the girl's [the woman's] home, she said: (71) 'When we get near the rubbish heap[349)] and my father's dog gets up and comes [towards us], don't run away! (72) When you then enter the cattle yard and the billy-goat gets up as if to hit you, don't run away! (73) Again, when you enter the courtyard and the flies there will sit on you, don't drive them away! (74) The dog is a leopard, the billy-goat a lion and the flies are bees!' (75) He said that he had understood. (76) He followed his wife, [but] as soon as he approached the rubbish heap and the leopard growled with anger, the boy [man]

---

346) 'Ashes are used in various Bulsa rituals; they appear to be a symbol of pacification and intercession and even a chief would not fail to recognise their importance' (Pauline Akankyalabey).

347) I.e. according to the customs of the Bulsa, the man would not let his wife go and visit her parents empty-handed.

348) She put it on top of the millet flour in the calabash.

349) A rubbish heap or ash heap (*tampoi*, def. *tamponi*) is in front of every Bulsa compound.

(78) Wa ga paai yeri-a; baa beg wa ain ka boan wari. (79) 'Nya ku ka nyeka!' (80) Sunsung po denoawa ain waa, wa me ben wa kuli kama. (81) Wa me chorowa ain wa le ga basi wa. (82) Wa me pai wa tom, pai wa namarik, pa wa liak a vi wa ngmankpaluk. (83) Ba cheng ga moata yeni-a, wa ain waa: (84) 'Mi kowa biak-a, ale yiti chien la-a, kan chali-a, ale kaa te ka fi tia!'. (85) Wa yin: 'Nguu!' (86) 'Ti be le taam a jo nangkpiengka po la-a, te bu-duku yiti chien la-a, kan chali, ale ku me a nye ka fi tia! (87) Ti danjo paa dabiaka po-a, sienga ale yiti chien la-a, a jaa kal fu la-a, kan yiagi, ale ka nanjungsa.' (88) Wa yin: 'Nguu!' (89) Ba va chaab ga paa doa, goa-biak din ga vaar yiti-a, wa din ga yiti ga lo jambaya pieta ale wa china, wa chali be. (90) Wa jaa a paari, ba yin ka boan wari. (91) Ain wani ka nyeka.

(92) Baangka powa ain waa: wa me le kuli kama. (93) Wa me din yiti za daa gomsi, din pai wa liak ale wa namarika a vi. (94) Baa cheng, a ga moati yeni-a, wa yin: (95) 'Biaka le chien la-a, kan chali, ale ka te ka fi tia. (96) Gbengni me le yiti chien la-a, kan fi chali, ale wa me a te ka fi tia. (97) Fi jo dabiaka po-a, ate nanjunsanga a kali fu la-a, kan yiagi, ale si me a te ka fi tia!' (98) Wa yin: 'Nguu!' (99) Baa cheng, baa cheng, ba le din ga moati yeni-a, goa-biak din ga vaa yiti-a, a din chien ain ka pai biik-a, wa yin: (100) 'N be jam-oa, n be jam-oa!' (101) Wa taam ya. (102) Wa le din ga jo nangkpiengka po-a, bu-duk din ga vaa yiti-a, wa yin: (103) 'N be jam-oa, n be jam-oa!' (104) Wa taam ya. (105) Wa jo a paa dabiaka po-a, sie din yiti lig pum-pum-pum. (106) Wa kala chim.

threw his bow away and took to his heels. (77) The woman passed by and entered [the house].

(78) He [the man] got home and they asked him what the matter was. (79) [He said:] 'It is very serious!' (80) The middle [brother's wife] also said that she wanted to go home. (81) Her husband also said that he would accompany her [home]. (82) He also took his bow, took his quiver, took his axe and slung them on his shoulder. (83) When they came near the house, she said: (84) 'When my father's dog gets up and comes [near you], don't run away, for it only welcomes you!' (85) He said: 'All right!' (86) 'When we go on and enter the cattle yard and the billy-goat gets up and comes [near us], don't run, for it also [means to] welcome you! (87) When we enter the courtyard and the bees get up and come out[350] and sit on you, don't drive them away, for they aren't [really bees] but flies.' (88) He said: 'All right!' (89) He followed her and they arrived at the place, but when the leopard suddenly jumped up, he [the middle brother] retreated [with fright] and fell flat on his back with his calabashes, his face white with fear[351]; he ran away. (90) When he reached home, they asked him what the matter was. (91) He said that the matter was beyond resolution.

(92) The junior brother's wife said she also wanted to go home. (93) He [the junior brother] also got up and made himself ready; he took his axe and quiver and slung them [over his shoulder]. (94) They walked on and as they approached the house she said: (95) 'When the dog comes [near you], don't run, for it will welcome you. (96) When the lion also gets up and comes [towards us], don't run for it also welcomes you. (97) When you enter the courtyard and the flies sit on you, don't drive them away, for they too want to welcome you!' (98) He said: 'All right!' (99) They walked on and on and when they came near the house, the leopard got up and came as if to take [kill] the boy [man]; he [the boy] said: (100) 'Thank you, thank you!'[352] (101) He passed by. (102) As soon as he entered the cattle yard, the billy-goat got up [as if to attack him]; he said: (103) 'Thank you, thank you!' (104) He passed by. (105) As he entered and

---

350) Pauline Akankyalabey translated: '[...] when the bees hover over you.'

351) *jambayala pieta*, 'to lie with the face in the air, the eyes wide open with fear'.

352) *N be jam-oa* means literally: 'May I come!'; it is usually the response to the greeting *'tia!'* which means 'welcome!'.

(107) Ba yaa nye dila a goa ate vari yaa vienti ain ban ba basi biik ate wa kuli. (108) Ba yaa nyini a yig ba naab a ko. (109) Ale doglie doa sampok zuk-a, wa din nyin du a din pasi lo din yin: (110) 'Fin kala, fi kala ain fi kpi kama le kali la! (111) Ba be dan ko naamu-a, kpaatanga le lantanga ate ba ta jo ain ba te fu la, te mi de chag ate n dag fu siukui, fi len fi va siukui ate fi kuli!' (112) Wa yin wa wom ya, wa be kan cheng yalingi. (113) (113) Doglie ain me le doa la be maa nya. (114) Ban beni ya, saab 'weea!', lanta sue bimbili, doglie an ben du, wa me din pasi lo. (115) Biik an din ta ngandiitanga ga wa noai 'kuataa', ain doglie be ngoa. (116) Wa de ain wa nya wa chag kama yogla. (117) Wa yin: (118) 'Fi chag ya?' (119) Wa yin: 'Nguu!'

(120) Dogliewa ain waa: (121) 'Fi nya nipooma ale bo yeni po la; fi nya ba la a niesi chaab dii la; fi be ngman seb fidek powa a gaari alege ka fi moama pooma? (122) Be nya ba be za ain ba pai ka chib ate ba miena kala; ba miena be dan ga kal chimu zuk-a, a nya mi. (123) Mi la duiri ba wai la-a, seb nya le ka moa-kpagni powa le la! (124) Ba le fob mi te mi yiti ga lo la-a, te mi pilim chien la-a, a jaa duiri wai la,

reached the courtyard, the bees flew up, covering the whole place. (106) He sat there still[353].

(107) They [the man and his wife] did that and slept; at daybreak they [the people in the house] said that they had given the boy [man] permission to return home. (108) Then they went out and took [one of] their cows and killed it. (109) Meanwhile, a cat which had been lying on the grass roof [of the house] came out from there, jumped down and said [to the man]: (110) 'Are you not sitting [there]? - you sit there, say: you will certainly die, but you [still] sit there[354]! (111) When they slaughter the cow and bring in the fat and the meat to give [them] to you, give them to me and let me eat till I've had enough, then I will show you which way to pass and go home!' (112) He [the junior brother] said that he had understood and that it [the cat] should not go out of sight. (113) The cat said that it would lie down and wait. (114) They [the people in the house] did not waste time [bringing] the millet porridge, and in very large quantities[355]: the meat filled a clay pot; the cat wasted no time and jumped down. (115) The boy did not taste the food[356], [but] said that the cat should take it. (116) It ate [until at last] it said he [the man] could be sure that it was now really satisfied. (117) He [the man] asked: (118) 'Are you really satisfied?' (119) It said: 'Yes!'

(120) [Then] the cat said: (121) 'You see the women in this house, [and] you see how they resemble each other; how are you going to identify your own wife, let alone the wives of your elder brothers? (122) Look, they are going to take a big log[357] and make all of them [the women] sit [on it for you to identify them]; when they have all gone to sit on the log, you just watch me. (123) The one I shall brush slightly is your eldest brother's wife! (124) They will hit me and I shall get up and fall over, and [when] I come again, the one I shall brush slightly against is the middle brother's wife! (125)

---

353) I.e. he ignored them [the flies or bees].

354) With this somewhat anacoluthic sentence the cat means to say that the man sitting in the house or by the house will die if he does not know how to find his wife and his brother's wives out of God's daughters who all look alike.

355) *weea!* interj. 'so plentiful, such a lot, so many!'

356) Lit.: 'The boy did not (*kuataa*, Hausa: 'never') take the food to his mouth'.

357) *chib*, def. *chimu*, pl. *chibsa* 'big log (beam) for the roof of a room with a flat ceiling' (Kröger BED).

sunsungka po denoawa powa ale la! (125) Ba le pilim fob mi a yig chigsi nangaang la, a limsi mu-a? (126) N le jaa a duiri wai la, fidek powa ale la!' (127) Wa wieni ain wa wom ya.

(128) Ba din te nipooma miena a din so din jaari. (129) Ba din pai chib din dueni se dela ale mampani la. (130) Naawen pooba yo, wa lieba yo, ba miena din kali linewa ga saari. (131) Biika nyini za, wa ngman ze ngan-moansanga a gaari. (132) Doglie paai nue, din gaa duiri kpagni powa, wa yin:(133) 'Mi moawa powa ale nna!' (134) Ba din yig doglie a fob, yug basi nakpiak. (135) Ba yin wa dag wa sunsung po powa ngman-a. (136) Wa yin wa chiena. (137) Doglie din jam gaa duiri wala ngman-a. (138) Wa wieni ain: (139) 'Wala me powa ale nna!' (140) Ba wieni ain: (141) 'Jaamu nna!', ba yig ta jo lig. (142) Ba yin: (143) 'Dag fidek powa!' (144) Ain wa le dag. (145) Doglie yaan pai nue, a din gaa duiri. (146) Wa yin wadek powa yaa le nna yogla. (147) Ba yin ba nue ya, ba be yiti. (148) Ate ba yaa jo a basi ba, ate ba yaa a wieni ain baa kul.

They will hit me again and take me and drop me at the back of the house, [but] will you wait for me? (126) I shall come and the one I brush slightly against, is your own wife!' (127) He [the boy] said he had understood.

(128) Then they made all the women wash themselves and dress up. (129) Then they took a log [measuring] from here to the main road[358] and put it down [for them to sit on it]. (130) Regardless of whether they were God's wives or his daughters, they all sat [on the log] in a line[359] from one end to the other. (131) The boy came out and stood there; he did not know how to distinguish between [all] the fair-skinned women[360]. (132) When the cat had arrived, it went and brushed slightly against the senior brother's wife, and he [the boy] said: (133) 'This is my eldest brother's wife!' (134) They got hold of the cat, beat it and threw it aside. (135) They told him to show [them] the wife of the middle brother. (136) He said that he was going [to do that][361]. (137) Then the cat came and brushed against the other one. (138) He said: (139) 'That is the wife of [my] other [brother]!' (140) They [the people of the house] said: (141) 'This thing [cat]!', they [should] get hold of it and lock it up. (142) They [again] said [to the boy]: (143) 'Show [us] your own wife!' (144) He said that he would show [her]. (145) When the cat had come again, it went and brushed against [the woman]. (146) He said that this was now his own wife. (147) They said that they had finished and that they [the women] should get up. (148) They then went in and released them [the man and his wives], and then they said that they should go home.

---

358) Pauline Akankyalabey: 'The length of the log is approximately the distance from the house where the storytelling is taking place to the main road.'

359) The teller uses the English word 'line' with the definite suffix *-wa*.

360) Lit.: 'the red things' - Pauline Akankyalabey translated this sentence: ' [...] there were so many fair-skinned women that he hadn't the least idea how to identify them.'

361) Pauline Akankyalabey translated this sentence: 'He said that they should wait a moment.'

(149) Ate kpagni powa, ale susung po denoawa powa ain baa yaali ain ba va wen-biri yeri a puusi ba ngesoa, ale bo dula, ga paari ate wa pai nur-biik lam a dig jenta ate bala a de.

(150) Dila ale soa ate sakpak bo teng zuk pieloa me boro. (151) Dan kan daa ka ba le moab dula la nying sakpak te ka teng zuk-a.

(152) Mi sunsuelini miena kpegtalegi.

(153)	*Ayaaloa pok ale duok.*
(154)	*Nangaang zaa ta puuk.*
(155)	*Daa biag chum le vonung.*
(156)	*Kakaba nangbain chek-chek.*
(157)	*Ase ka cheng Nabiak pinanga.*
(158)	*Noai se kantelik biik.*

(149) Then the wives of the senior and the middle brothers said that they wanted to pass by Sun's[362] house in order to greet their maternal uncle[363] who lived there; they went and arrived [there] and he [their mother's brother] took human[364] meat and cooked soup for them and they ate [it].

(150) That is why there are witches[365] as well as innocent persons[366] on earth. (151) Had they not deviated [at Sun's house] there would not be any witches on earth.

(152) All of my story comes to an end [here][367].

(153) Hunter's wife with a gun.
(154) The millet behind the house is pregnant [with fruit].
(155) It will give birth tommorrow or the day after tomorrow.
(156) Kakaba's[368] sharp, sharp mouth.
(157) As if it had gone to the Nabiak hills[369].
(158) A mouth like that of a baby mouse's.

---

362) *wen-biri*, '(*wen* sun, *biri* seed), def. *wen-bini*, no pl., sun, sunshine' (Kröger BED).

363) *ngesoa*, 'spec. maternal relative, e.g.: mother's father, mother's father's brother, mother's brother; maternal uncle [...] *ngesoa yeri* [...] mother's (parental) compound' (Kröger BED). In the latter sense, this would mean that the women, married to the men on earth, were the daughters of the Sky (God), their father, and the Sun, their mother.

364) *nur-biik,* lit. 'son of man', 'human being, human (n.) [...]' (Kröger BED).

365) *sakpak,* 'witch, wizard, magician' (Kröger BED). - The teller uses the singular in this and the following sentence.

366) *pieloa*, def. *pieloawa*, pl. *pieliba*, 'plain, innocent, sincere, candid, frank person (used for somebody who is not suspected of being a witch or wizard)' (Kröger BED).

367) The end of the story is marked by the nonsensical sentences which follow. This is a pattern frequently used by Bulsa storytellers.

368) Kakaba is the son of Kakariba, both are names not in Buli but in Twi (Pauline Akankyalabey). No further information on them is available.

369) The location of these hills is unknown; they may exist only in fantasy (Pauline Akankyalabey).

(159) *Noai se baanoa kayak.*

(160) *Chikperi kem se piuk tankomi.*

(161) *Ase kanziak moari yoari kpai.*

(162) *Ayiba, tangbim!*

(159) A mouth like a soothsayer's rattle[370].

(160) The jaw as hard and strong as a hyena's groin.

(161) Like a wart growing on a penis' occiput.

(162) *Ayiba - tangbim!*

370) *kayak,* 'rattle made of a holow calabash and filled with small stones and/or baobab seeds, used e.g. by the diviner' (Kröger BED).

BUL-E0182 (BULI TEXT)

(1) Kaa nuruba bata, ale maa chaab bo ba yeri po. (2) Batawa dila, ba wa-wai ka nipok-a. (3) Ba yaa nyiem nyin cheng goai, a ga kpa, kpa ba jaa paari yeri ale ba dig ngan-diinta a zaani. (4) Ba miena batawa dila, fi chin-moan, fi chin-moan; wai buudi miena ale wa kalik jigi, wa kalik jigi.

(5) Ba yaa a nye dila, dandidai ba yaa wieni ain kpagni wari yeri a nya ja-buui alaa nye ngan-diintanga dila la. (6) Kpagni yaa wari yeri, a yaa doa bukuri po. (7) Wa ale doa bukuni po la, nipooba bata, yaa va chaab nyin wen jam zi. (8) Ba le jam paari zi la, ate wanyi a cheng beli, wanyi jo nangzuk, wanyi boro a nari samoansa. (9) Ate ba nye dila, a nye ba ngan-diintanga ga nueri, a de ba me dek ngandiitanga ga nueri. (10) A pai chin-moananga a wieni ain: (11) 'Oh, yaa te n pai n chorowa saamu ta ga zaan-a!' (12) Ba nye dila ta ga zaani; fi zaana jigi, fi zaana jigi alege yiti ga zaani dabiaka sunsung a bob chaab ngman pilim yiti a jueli wen.

(13) Baa nye dila alege ate nuruwa doa a nya. (14) Ba nyin goaini jam, jam paari ate wa pai wieni wa ale wari yeri ate ku cheng dii la. (15) Sunsungpo denowa a wieni ain waa, wa ka beruk 'paa', ate wa basi ate ba ngman chengi? (16) Ain wa chum ale wari. (17) Vari vienti ate kpagni ale baangka yiti zaa cheng alege ate sunsungpo denowa

03.03 Women from the Sky Marry Three Brothers

BUL-E0182 (ENGLISH TRANSLATION)

(1) Once there were three men who lived together in their house. (2) Of these three none of them had a wife. (3) They used to go to the bush and farm and farm and whenever they [returned] and arrived back at their house, [they found that] they [someone] had prepared some food and put it down [for them]. (4) Each of the three had his separate calabash of food, and each of them had his own place to sit [and eat][371)].

(5) They went on doing this, until one day they decided that the eldest of them should stay at home and see what sort of thing it was [that came] to prepare the food like that. (6) The eldest [of the three men] remained at home, lying down [hiding] in a chicken coop. (7) While he was lying in the chicken coop three women came down from the sky together. (8) As soon as they had landed, one of them went to the river [to fetch water], another one went into the grinding room [to grind the millet], while another one was washing the [dirty] pots. (9) They did this and when they had finished preparing the food, they ate their own [share of] the food. (10) Then they took the calabashes [of food] saying: (11) 'Oh, let me take my husband's food and put it down!' (12) They did that and went and put it [the food] down, each at a place of her own choice[372)], and then they went to the middle of the courtyard, held one another tightly and again went up to the sky.

(13) While they [the women] did all this, the man lay watching. (14) When the others returned from the bush, he told them what had happened while he was at home. (15) The middle one told him [the eldest] that he was a real fool: why did he let them go away? (16) He [the middle one] said that he would remain at home the next day. (17) The next day, the senior and the junior [brother], got up and went [to the bush]

---

371) Lit.: 'All the three there, your [2nd pers. sing.] red calabash, your red calabash; everybody of their whole lineage [= each of them] had his sitting place, his sitting place.'

372) Lit.: '[...] at your putting down place, at your putting down place [...]'.

zaa wari. (18) Wa ale wari dila la, ba jam, ba yaam bo ba tuimanga po. (19) Ba tom nueri, a nye ba ja-buudi miena nueri, yiti ga zaani dabiaka sunsung a bob chaab, ba laa taam la, alege ate wa me doa. (20) Ate ba nyin goaini jam beg ate wa ain: (21) 'Oh, wani pagra kama!'

(22) Vani vienti, ate baangka wieni ain wa ale wari. (23) Ba ta baangka a le ain: (24) 'Tama ale tin chim kpaga, a nye wani kpieri, ka fi alen fi nye boa?' (25) Wa wieni ain dan ka di, wa be le wari; ba cheng be ba ngman jam le. (26) Ba nye-nye ka dila a cheng goaini alege basi wa. (27) Ate wa nye wa tuntuem ta jo doa. (28) Ba nyin du jam ya, jam boro a tom ba tuimanga. (29) Ba tom, tom ba tuimanga miena ga nueri, a yaa le yiti ga ba zaani la, wa vaa nyin, pai tuntuemu lonsi ale wieni ain ba kan ngman ga jigi ya. (30) Ba basi ate ba miena maa chaab a boro; nipooba sagi-e, nipooba wari ya. (31) Wa ga pai wa saab a de alege kala. (32) Nipooma miena dila, ba miena dila, ba a niesi ka chaab. (33) Fi dan ga nya nwa fi yin nwa, fin nya nwa fi yin nwa. (34) Ba nyin goaini jam ya, ba ale din jaa paari ale yeni po a biisi 'vuna, vuna, vuna', ba ngman ze joka. (35) Biik yig kusung a nyin, nyini a paari ale ba wari za. (36) Ain ka boa wari, ba jo. (37) Ba yig dok a jo, ba jo a paari nipooba - geri! (38) Ba de ba ngan-diintanga ate ba maa chaab boro.

while the middle one remained at home. (18) While he was at home, they [the women again] came and worked as usual. (19) They finished working, and when they had done everything that was to be done, [they] went and stood in the middle of the courtyard, held each other tightly and passed by[373], while he [the middle brother] lay [in his hiding place]. (20) When they [the others] returned from the bush, they asked him [what had happened] and he said: (21) 'Oh, it is a difficult matter!'

(22) The next day, the junior brother said that he would remain [at home]. (23) They [the other two brothers] insulted the junior [brother] saying: (24) 'We have grown up to be elders, but [even] we failed completely to manage the affair, so what will you be able to do?' (25) He told them that in view of what [they had said], he would stay behind; they should go and when they returned [to find that he had not been successful] then they [his brothers] could continue to insult him. (26) They went on like this and finally went to the bush leaving the [junior brother] at home. (27) He fetched some ashes, took them [with him into his hiding place] and lay down. (28) [Soon] they [the women] came out [of the sky] and then they started doing their work. (29) They worked and worked and when they had finished all their work, they went and stood [in the middle of the courtyard]; [then] he [the junior brother] came out [of the chicken coop], scattered the ashes and told them not go away again. (30) He suggested they all live together; the women agreed and stayed. (31) He went and took his millet porridge and ate [it]; then he sat and waited [for his brothers' return]. (32) They [the three women] were all alike, they were all alike, they resembled each other. (33) [The resemblance was so close] that if you saw one of them, you would say it was the other one and when you saw the other one, you would say it was [the first] one. (34) They [the two brothers] had come back from the bush, and when they arrived, they heard [people] talking '*vuna, vuna, vuna*'[374] within the house, so they didn't dare to enter. (35) The boy went outside to the *kusung*[375], [he] went out and met them; they remained standing. (36) He asked [them] what the matter was [and told them] to enter [the house]. (37) They

---

373) I.e. went up into the sky again.

374) Noise made by several people talking at the same time.

375) Shelter in front of the house; see glossary.

(39) Ku yaa paari ning, kpagni yaa yiti wieni ain wa a yaali ain ka wa kuli ga nya yeri. (40) Ba din yiti zaa gomsi ba ale a gomsi dii a basi nipok ate waa kuli la. (41) Ate wa chorowa yiti za ta waa kuli. (42) Ba daa cheng din ga paari, din ga moati yeni, tamponi a nye ase ka yeni nna. (43) Ba ale din ga paari, wierik din kpesi-kpesi nyin tamponi po a din na 'chung!' (44) Anidoa yiti ga zi alege tali nipok. (45) Nipowa a cheng ga jo.

(46) Ba kala ale wa jaa jo. (47) Ain: 'Nipowa, fi pai wa basi ka be? (48) Fi cheng, fan paari du ale pilim a ngmani?' (49) Ain: 'N doa, wani, di ka nyeka jigi ya!'

(50) Sunsungpo denowa me, wa me yiti, dila dek-dek-a. (51) Baangka yaam yiti ya, a din gomsi wa jaab miena, a yiti va. (52) Wa yaa cheng ate wa powa ya, wieni wa ain

went inside [the compound] to the *dok*[376], they entered and met the women - upon my word[377]! (38) They ate their food and then they lived together.

(39) After some time had passed, the senior [woman] got up and said that she wanted to go and visit [her parents] at home. (40) They [her husband and his brothers] got up and made all the preparations necessary when a woman gets permission to go home[378]. (41) Then her husband got up to accompany her home. (42) They went on and soon they arrived and came near to the house; the rubbish heap lay just a short distance away[379]. (43) As soon as they got there, a leopard suddenly sprang out of the rubbish heap with all its strength and growled loudly. (44) The man[380] turned and took to his heels leaving the woman alone. (45) The woman walked on and entered [the house].

(46) They [the other two brothers] were sitting down when he [the senior brother] came [back] and entered [the house]. (47) They asked: 'Where did you leave the woman? (48) You [only just] went [away with her], you haven't even arrived there, why have you [already] come back?' (49) He replied: 'My friend, this matter - nothing can be done about it!'

(50) The middle [brother] also got up [and] the same thing [happened to him]. (51) Then it was the turn of the junior one; he got up and prepared all his things[381] and then he got up and followed [his wife]. (52) While they were going to her father, [his

---

376) *dok*, def. *doku*, pl. *diina*, room or set of rooms; see glossary.

377) The interjection *'geri!'* expresses astonishment, especially when one meets someone or when one comes across something unexpectedly.

378) Visiting her parents for the first time after her marriage.

379) 'The distance between the rubbish heap and the couple was like that between the place where the storyteller is sitting [probably in the *kusung*] and the house' (Pauline Akankyalabey).

380) The teller uses the personalized form *A-nidoa*; the prefix *A-* 'marks a human proper name; it can be prefixed to all parts of speech, sometimes to a whole sentence' (Kröger BED). According to Ms. Pauline Akankyalabey, *Anidoa* may be translated as 'Mr. X'.

381) I. e. everything that he needed for his journey and for the visit of his parents-in-law.

waa, ain ba laa cheng la, ba le ga paari tamponi ate jaamu a na la, wa nya ka wa kowa ba-duok. (53) Ba ale ga paari kusungku po ate jaamu a naa la, wa nya ka wa toa kpagni ale la. (54) Ba ale ga jo nangkpiengka po ate goa-naamu za ate bu nyingka a gog misa-misa wa la, wa nya ka wa toa baangka ale la. (55) Ba ale ga jo dabiaka po ate ba-duoku doa a moag ninanga a soa nna la, wa nya ka wa kowa ale la. (56) Ba ale ga jo dalongku po, ate waab kpiomu sueri dalongku la, wa nya ka wa mawa ale la. (57) Biik yin wa wom ya.

(58) Ba le din ga paari ate wierika din na nyini-a, wa wieni ain 'wa be kal-e, wa be kal-e!' (59) Ka ngman pilim ga taam a jo ka goluku po. (60) Ba yig nansiung a paari. (61) Ba le din ga paari ate gbengni naa nyin kusung po nyin-a, a kala a lieli nyi--nyiengsa, wa yin: 'wa be kal-e, wa be kali!' (62) Ba taam a jo, jo gaa paari nangkpieng po ate goa-naab fusi-a, wa yin 'wa be za, wa be za!', a gaam taam a jo. (63) Wa jo ga paari biak ale kasiyam moag nina nnala doa a nya wa, a din vaari yiti nienti nna 'kpababababa', wa yin: 'wa be za kama, wa be za kama!', a taam a jo. (64) Nipowa tuili wa koalima zaani, a yig dalong po a jo; wa sang vaa jo. (65) Wa gaa paari ale waamu kasiyam tuesi doku miena-miena, wa wieni ain: 'wa be doa kama, wa be doa kama!', a gurim a kali. (66) Ku an bola beni ya, fi ze waamu ale va ka tengsi-ngai doku po.

wife] told him that when they reached the rubbish heap, he should realize that the thing that would growl was [only] her father's male dog. (53) When they reached the *kusung*, he should realize that the thing that would growl was her eldest brother. (54) When they entered the cattle yard, the bush cow that stood [there] with its body shaking would be her junior brother. (55) When they entered the courtyard[382] [he would see] a male dog with its eyes wide open[383] and he should realize that this was her father. (56) When they entered the outer room[384] [he would see] a big snake (python) which filled [all of] the outer room; he should realize that this was her mother. (57) The boy said that he had understood her.

(58) When they got there and the leopard sprang out [from the rubbish heap] growling, he [the man] said, 'good day, good day to you[385]!' (59) It turned back, went and entered its hole. (60) They got closer to the entrance. (61) When they arrived there, a lion shot out of the *kusung* with a loud roar, and then sat licking its paws; he [the man greeted] it by saying, 'good day to you, good day!' (62) They passed by and entered, arriving in the cattle yard where the bush cow was standing, swollen [with anger][386]; he [the man] said, 'good day, good day!'[387] and passed by and entered [the *dok*]. (63) He entered and found a dog lying down staring at him with its eyes wide open, and suddenly it stood up and stretched itself [to its full length]; he [the man] said, 'good day, good day!' and passed by and entered [the outer room]. (64) The woman put down her load[388] and entered the outer room; he followed her inside. (65) He entered and found that the snake had in fact occupied the whole room and he said, 'good day, good

---

382) *dabiak*, courtyard, see glossary.

383) The verb *moagi* means literally '(only of the sun) to be up, to have risen (high), to be high in the sky, to shine brightly, to be hot, to burn' (Kröger BED). The teller in his figure of speech compares the dog's eyes with the shining sun.

384) *dalong*, 'outer room', see glossary.

385) Lit.: 'He should be sitting!' The teller uses reported speech which was put here into inverted commas.

386) *fuusi*, v. '1. to inflate, to blow up, to swell (also with anger), to be inflated, blown up, swollen [...] 2. to grow angry, to explode with anger [...]' (Kröger BED).

387) Lit.: 'He should be standing', another greeting formula of the Bulsa.

388) Probably the gifts she had brought from her husband's house.

(67) Wa ale din gan wa kali la, wa nya ka nuru moanik ale yi tangkalung a jo jam nye wa tia. (68) Biik a pilim paai sang se dila la, a yiti jaa nye wa tia. (69) Wa nya ka nuru moanik tanjangi ale yi tangkalung ate ku a pisi teng, nya wa tiengsa, a yiti jam nye wa tia. (70) Wa kala, wa nya ka nipok ale kasiyam kpak, jaa nye wa tia a ta nyiam jaa te wa. (71) Ate wa puusi ba, a pai wa nangchelinsa a tog. (72) Ate wa yaa goa.

(73) Doglie be le bo yeni po, wa ale doa gbong la, ba nye ngan-diintanga a dig lanta, nur-biik lanta ti toga, goai-dungsa lanta ti toga. (74) Doglie bo yeni po; ba le boro a dig ngan-diintanga la, dogliewa yaa jueli, a jue wieni wa ain waa, wa daa yaali ain wa nya wadek a kuli, ba dan nye ngan-diintanga wa basi ate wa de chag. (75) Wa ale sag wa siuk ate wa chum kuli. (76) Ain di da wari ya. (77) Ba dig ngan-diinta nueri, dogliewa

day[389]!', folded [his legs] and sat down. (66) After a short while, one did not know to which part of the room the snake had gone[390].

(67) As he was about to sit down, he saw a fair-skinned man wearing a leather apron[391], who came in and welcomed him. (68) Next a boy followed in the same manner; he also came and welcomed him. (69) [Then] he [the junior brother] saw a huge fair-skinned man with a big beard who was wearing a leather apron which swept the ground; he [also] came and greeted him. (70) He remained seated and [soon] he saw a very old woman who came and welcomed him and who went and brought him [millet] water[392]. (71) He greeted them all and told them the reason why he had come. (72) Then he wanted to sleep[393].

(73) There was a cat in the house and while he [the junior brother] was lying on the platform roof[394], they [his in-laws] prepared food and cooked some meat - human meat on the one side, and meat of wild animals[395] on the other side[396]. (74) There was a cat in the house; while they were preparing the food, the cat climbed [onto the platform roof] and told him [the junior brother] that if he wanted to return home without much trouble[397], he should allow him [the cat] to eat to his satisfaction when the food was ready. (75) He [the cat] would show him the way to return home [safely] the next day. (76) He [the man] said this was no problem. (77) When they had finished cooking the food, the cat told him that when they brought the food and put it down, he

---

389) Lit.: 'He should lie down, he should lie down by all means!'

390) I.e. the snake had vanished.

391) *tangkalung* (< *tang* or *teng*, 'earth, soil, ground' and *kali* 'to sit'), 'leather apron (often goat-skin, worn only by men)' (Kröger BED), worn on the side or on the backside, used to sit upon the ground.

392) To give water mixed with millet flour is the customary way of welcoming a stranger among the Bulsa.

393) I.e. he decided to spend the night with his in-laws.

394) This roof is frequently used for sleeping in the night, especially in the hot season.

395) *goai-dungsa*, lit. 'bush animals', wild animals of the bush.

396) I.e. each kind of meat was cooked separately.

397) Lit.: '[...] if he wanted to see himself and go home [...]'.

yaa wieni wa ain ba le ta ngan-diintanga a jam zaani ate wa a duiiri ngan-diin tii la, wa de ngan-diin tila. (78) Wa ale kan duiiri tii la, wa kan pai nisa a tiri. (79) Wa wieni ain wa wom ya.

(80) Ate ba ta ngan-diintanga jueli, nya niinga lantanga, nya nur-biik lantanga, nya nur-biik jentanga, nya niinga jentanga. (81) Wa tuesi nyiamu paizaani wa ning alege kala. (82) Dogliewa a jam jueli a nye 'ngiaun!' a ga duiiri lantanga. (83) Wa pai tila a zaani wa ning. (84) Wa nye 'ngiaun!' a ga duiiri saamu, wa pai bula zaani wa ning ale pai nbala zaani nakpiak. (85) Wa din yieri lantanga din ta ga dueni - pugli! (86) Doglie din va, doglie din va, doglie din va a ga chag, a yiti zi nan-gaang, ale tali lantanga dueni. (87) Wa dan kan chag wa tali dueni? (88) Alege ate wa yaa taati ngan-diintanga yogla. (89) Wa de ngan-diintanga nueri, ba jue pai chinanga. (90) Ba jueli a paari nbala za alege wa de nbala. (91) Ain: 'Ah, nurwa nna, wa yaa be ka se-a? (92) Ah, di da wari ya, vari kan vienti?'

should only eat the food that he [the cat] would brush against slightly. (78) He [the man] should not touch the food which he [the cat] had not brushed against. (79) He [the man] said that he had understood.

(80) They [the people in the house] took the food up [to the platform roof]; behold: [in one dish] beef[398)] [cow meat], behold: [in another dish] human meat, behold: the soup [prepared from] human meat and behold: the soup [prepared from] beef[399)]! (81) He took the water[400)], put it in front of him and [went on] sitting [and waited]. (82) The cat came climbing up [to the platform roof] and cried 'miaow![401)]', then it went and brushed against the [dish with the] meat. (83) He [the man] took that [bowl of] meat and placed it in front of him. (84) It [again] cried 'miaow!' and brushed against the [vessel with the] millet porridge; he took that also and placed it in front of him and took the others [the cat hadn't touched] and placed them aside. (85) He [the man] then took out [some of the] meat and piled it all up like a heap [for the cat to eat]. (86) The cat then went and went and went [and ate the meat], until it was satisfied; then it got up and jumped outside the house leaving the rest of the meat [to the man]. (87) If it [the cat] were not satisfied, would it have left some of the meat? (88) Then he [the man] started eating the food. (89) When he had finished eating the food, they [the people in the house] climbed up to take the calabash bowls away. (90) When they had climbed up, they discovered that some [of the dishes] were standing [untouched], whereas he had eaten from some of the others. (91) They said: 'Ah, what sort of man is this? (92) Anyway, it doesn't matter - will there not be a daybreak?[402)]'

---

398) This is not in keeping with what the teller said before, viz. that the people cooked the meat of wild bush animals (see sentence no. 73).

399) Lit.: 'soup or sauce of a [= prepared from] human being' and 'soup or sauce of [= prepared from] cows'. The soup or sauce (*jenta*) is eaten together with the millet porridge (*saab*), the staple food of the Bulsa.

400) The water was given to him for letting him wash his hands before eating his meal.

401) In Buli, the cats mew '*ngiaun!*'.

402) I.e. the people in the sky are confident that the man, having avoided to eat the human flesh, will be defeated the next day.

(93) Dogliewa ngman pilim jam, ain: (94) 'Vari alaa vienti ate ba pai chimu ta nyini a dueni, ate nipooma miena maa chaab kali la, n laa duiiri wai la, nya ka fi moa kpagni powa ale la. (95) Wai ate maa duiiri la, nwala powa ale la. (96) Wai ale pai sang ngaangka la, fidek powa le la!' (97) Biik yin 'nguung!', wa wom ya.

(98) Vari vienti, wa yiti puusi banti. (99) Ba gomsi, ba laa gomsi dii a basi nipooba te ba goa ba ko yie a kuli la. (100) Ba gomsi dila miena nueri, a pai chib ta nyin dueni, chimu zaani dela a nya felik tiimu. (101) Ate nipooba nyin pati chib zuk-a, ba dan yin fi nya nyawade ka nna, fi velim - ba miena bunyi. (102) Ate ba ta ba a nyin kali a wieni ain nipooma be le la ba kala, wadek be le ta wa pooma jam. (103) Wa be ga yieri wa pooma ba po, ate ba dan yin ba te wa siuk, be ba te wa siuk. (104) Nurwa din ga zaani de a din tabri noai, a nya ta taam ga tuiiri. (105) Wa nye dila alege ate dogliewa me za. (106) Dogliewa nyiem din ga nye 'ngiaun!' a din ga jo nipooma po, wa din ga duiiri nwa nangsa din chali ga va nna taam cheng. (107) Nurwa din diem za - kaa-o!, zaan-zaan

(93) The cat came back again and said to him: (94) 'When day breaks, they will take out a big log[403] and make all the women sit together on the log: the first woman I will brush against, look, this is your eldest brother's wife! (95) The [next] one I shall brush against is the wife of your other brother. (96) The one woman who comes last [whom I will brush against] is your own wife!' (97) The boy said 'yes!', he had understood.

(98) At daybreak, he [the man] got up and greeted them and said goodbye. (99) They prepared [all] that [is customary] when women leave who have stayed in their father's house[404] and return home [to their husbands]. (100) When they had finished preparing all that, they took a log as long as the distance from here[405] to that niim[406] tree over there and put it down. (101) And [all] the women came out, spreading [in a row] on the log, [each resembling the other so much that] if one said he could distinguish between any two of them, he would be telling a lie; they all [looked like] one and the same. (102) They brought them [the women] and made them sit outside and then told him that [on the log] the women were sitting there and that he himself had brought his wives. (103) He [the man] should go and identify his wives; if [everything is in order] they would give him permission [to go], [i.e.] they would give him permission [to return home with them]. (104) The man went and stood aside, and with an air of disbelief[407] he viewed the scene from one end to the other. (105) While he was doing this, the cat was also standing nearby. (106) Then the cat cried 'miaow!', and entering the midst of the women, brushed against the legs of one of them and then ran and passed by. (107) The man was still standing and reflecting, he stood for a while

---

403) *chib*, def. *chimu*, 'big log (beam) for the roof of a room with a flat ceiling' (Kröger BED).

404) Lit.: '[who] have slept in their father's [= parents'] houses'.

405) I.e. the place where the teller is sitting.

406) *fel-tiib* or *felik tiib*, '(lit. 'White Man's tree') nim tree (Azadirachta indica)' (Kröger BED), English also neem or niim.

407) *Wa tabri noai*, lit: 'He put his hand to his mouth.' Idiomatically this means to view a situation with disbelief, astonishment etc., but also with admiration.

cheng ga yieri walala. (108) Dogliewa din cheng jam ga duiiri nwa, wa ga yieri wala. (109) Dii laa yin ku saari butawa la, ba yig dogliewa yug basi nan-gaang. (110) Dogliewa din zaani dula, a daa chali, wa le seb nya ba yaali ain ba yig ku kaasi la, dogliewa daa chali kpari-kpari-kpari: 'ngiaun!!' (111) Ku nueri ya, wa ga laa yieri wa lala.

(112) Wa pooma batawa le la, ba jo za gomsi pai a te wa. (113) Ba kala ale wa ta ba jaa jo. (114) Ate wa ta ba jam, ate ba miena yaa maa chaab boro.

(115) Di ale soa ate nipok bo teng po. (116) Nyiemwa, ka nurdoaba nyini le boro. (117) Nipooba daam nyin ka wen jaa nye ngan-diinta a te nur-biik. (118) Di le soa te nipooba bo teng po yogla. (119) Dila be le soa te ba wieni ain baang dan poom ka didiiya, wa ta sui pagrik kama gaam jaabuudi miena wu.

(120) Mi sunsuelini kpegtalegi.

and then went and took out that particular [woman]. (108) The cat again went and brushed against another [woman] and he [the man] went and took out that [woman] also]. (109) When it came to the third time, they caught the cat and threw it outside the house. (110) The cat stood there [outside the house] and as it became afraid, knowing very well that they [the people] wanted to spoil it[408)], the cat ran fast-fast-fast [and cried]: 'miaow!!' (111) That was the end; the man went and took out that woman too.

(112) His three wives[409)] were there, and they [the people] made the necessary preparations [for them to return home] and gave them [his wives] to him. (113) They [his brothers] were sitting [at home] when he brought them and they all entered [the house]. (114) He [the man] brought the women and then they all lived together.

(115) That is how women came to live on earth. (116) In the past there existed only men. (117) Formerly, the women used to come from the sky and prepare food to give it to mankind. (118) That is how women live on earth at present. (119) It is also for this reason that they often say that a younger person may be anything, but certainly he has a stronger heart than any other thing [on earth].

(120) That is the end of my story.

---

408) Viz. the plans of the cat and the man.

409) I.e. his wife and the wives of his two brothers. The three brothers are regarded as a social unit, but this does not mean that the Bulsa practice fraternal polyandry or a kind of Punalua marriage. On the contrary, they abhor promiscuity within the nuclear and the extended family, and if such cases occur, severe consequences ensue for all parties involved.

BUL-E0503 (BULI TEXT)

(1) Ka nur ale wa ma ale wa ko ale bo ba yeri po.

(2) Nurwa yaa ta nganta nna yeg-yega ale ka nipok-oa. (3) Wa kowa ale mawa nye wa kpieri ain wa faari nipok alege ate wa zeri. (4) Wa nyiem dan jueli goai, wa ta daata jam te wa mawa. (5) Wa dan wom ain gokta bo sinsii, wa cheng kama.

(6) Dai-di-ndi-dai ate wa jueli goai a yaa chiena, wa yaa boro a yaali daata ain wa ta jam te wa mawa, wa yaa nya da-korik a za ate wa gaa nag. (7) Wa le nag la, nipok kauk a yaa nyin du, jam zi a yueni biika ain wa pa wa ate ba kuli biika yeni. (8) Ate biik yueni ain ba gai a nye se, ate nipok kauku yueni ain ba gai ate wa chim wa pok. (9) Biik yaa deri kaari; biika ale kaari nueri la, nipok kauku me kaari a yueni ain: 'Pa mu, yoo!' (10) Biika yaa zeri ate nipok kauku yueni ain wa be kpi ate biika kpi. (11) Wa ngman yueni ain wa yiti ate wa yiti. (12) Ate nipowa yueni ain wa pa wa ate ba kuli ate biika pa wa a ta kuli.

(13) Wa le kuli la, wa mawa ale kowa yaa beg wa ain boan wari? - ate wa yueni ain ka wa pok ale la ale an yueni ku kiri miena. (14) Biika mawa ale wa kowa yaa yueni ain ba kan faari nipooba ate wa, ate wa zeri ale gai a ta nipok kauk a jam ba yeri po! (15) Ba nyiem dan man saab, nipok kauku yueni ain wa ngmari a nyo wa noai po ate wa de, ate biika yueni ain wa ngmari nyo be-e? (16) Ate wa yueni ain kauku po.

03.04 Half-Woman (God's Daughter) Marries Bachelor

BUL-E0503 (ENGLISH TRANSLATION)

(1) There was a man and his mother and his father and they were [living together] in their house.

(2) The man had very many riches, but no wife. (3) His father and mother tried in vain to make him marry a woman, but he refused. (4) He used to go to the bush in order to collect firewood for his mother. (5) Whenever he heard that there was dancing somewhere, he would go there.

(6) One day when he had gone to the bush and when he was fetching firewood in order to take it to his mother, he saw a dead tree standing and he went to cut it [down]. (7) As he was cutting the wood, half a woman came out [of it] there, jumped down and told the boy that he should take her [with him], and that they should go home to the boy's [son's] house. (8) Then the boy [son] asked what they would do when they went [got] there, whereupon the half-woman said that they would go [to his home] and she would become his wife. (9) The boy [son] then all of a sudden cried and when the boy [son] had finished crying the half-woman also cried and said: 'Do take me!' (10) The boy [son] refused; but then the half-woman said that he should drop dead, and the boy [son] died. (11) Then she said that he should get up, and he got up. (12) The woman said that he should take her home, and the boy [son] took her home.

(13) When he had come home, his mother and father asked him what the matter was, and he said that this was his wife but he did not tell them the whole story [reason, origin] behind it. (14) The boy's mother and his father then said that they had not been able to marry him to [ordinary] women, because he [had] refused, but then he went and brought a half-woman into their house. (15) Whenever they cooked *saab*[410], the half-woman said that he should take out some and put it into her mouth for her to eat, and the boy would ask her: if he took out [the *saab*], where should he place it? (16) Then she said: 'Into the half [of her mouth].' (17) Then the boy took [some *saab*] and placed

---

[410] See glossary.

(17) Ate biika yaa ngmari a dueni kauku po. (18) Nurwai miena dan jam, ate ba yueni ain ka biika pok ale la, ba mien'a kaari kama, ain boan ale soa ale biika basi nipok mangsanga soa nna ale ga a faari ja-kaukude? (19) Biika vaanchaab a yaa ta wa a la.

(20) Wa kowa ale wa mawa yaa yueni ain wa bu dan kan ta wa powa ga a te, wa be nyini ba yeri po a yaali jigi. (21) Nipok kauku yaa yueni ain wa kan yaali ain wa yiag wa nyama ba yeni po ate ba nyini, abe wa pa wa ta cheng sinsii ate wa nya wa la. (22) Biik yaa deri poli ain wa yueni kama ain wa ta wa ga pasi abe wa ngman jam.

(23) Biika ale ta wa ga paari dula jigni la, wa yaa nya kpatuok yeri ale di za. (24) Nipok kauku yaa yueni biika ain wa viti kpatuoku, ate wa viti gaa nya ale vorub kpiem doa. (25) Nipowa yaa yueni biika ain wa sing ate wa kan siagi. (26) Ate nipowa yueni ain wa bu kpi ate wa kpi. (27) Ate wa ngman yueni ain wa yiti, ate wa yiti.

(28) Wa le yiti la, wa yaa yueni ain wa sing ate wa sing cheng gaa paari ate yeri kpein a za. (29) Ate nipowa yaa yueni ain wa kanla kusungku ate wa jo dok abe wa nyini. (30) Ase ka nipowa ko yeri ale la. (31) Nurwa yaa kal' la, ate biik nyini yueni wa ain wa powa a wu wa, ate wa yiti jo. (32) Wa ale jo la, ba ngari nyiam ate wa ate wa so. (33) Ate ba pa garuk nalinsa te wa ate wa jo-a.

(34) Wa powa yeni ka Naawen yeri. (35) Wa ale jo wa gatanga nueri la, ba yaa beg wa ain ka boan ate waa yaali? (36) Ate wa yueni ain ka wa pok ale yueni ain ba kuli wa

it into the half [of her mouth]. (18) When all the people came [to the boy's house] and they were told that this was the boy's wife, they would cry out, asking why the boy had sent away the proper women and gone to marry this half-thing? (19) The boy's [son's] fellows then made fun of him and laughed at him.

(20) His father and his mother then told him that if he did not take his wife away, he should leave their house and look for a [another] place. (21) The half-woman then said that she did not want to drive away his 'owners'[411] from their house, so that they would have to leave; therefore he should take her to the place where he had found her. (22) The boy then thought that she had said that he should go with her and separate from her there [at the place where he had found her] and that he would then come [back] again.

(23) When the boy had arrived with her at that place, he saw a house [in the shape of] a termite hill standing there. (24) The half-woman then told the boy that he should remove the termite hill by force, and when he had removed it, he saw that there was a big hole [under it]. (25) Then the woman told the boy that he should go down, but he did not agree. (26) Then the woman said that he should drop dead, and he died. (27) Then she said again that he should get up, and he got up.

(28) When he had got up, she said that he should go down and he went down and went and arrived at a [place where] a big house stood. (29) Then the woman said that he should keep sitting in the *kusung*[412] and that she would enter a room and then come out again. (30) This was the woman's father's house. (31) As the man was sitting there, a child came out [of the house] telling him that his wife was calling him, and he got up and entered [the house]. (32) When he entered, they [the people in the compound] fetched water for him and he washed himself. (33) Then they gave him nice clothes, and he put them on.

(34) The house of his wife was the house of God. (35) When he had put on his clothes, he was asked what he wanted. (36) Then he said that it was his wife who had

---

411) '...*wa kan yaali ain wa yiag wa nyama*', lit. 'she did not want to drive away his owners'. *Nyama* (sing. *nyono*) are the 'owners' in the sense of elders or parents who are responsible for their juniors, in this case for their son. The half-woman abstained from chasing away her husband's parents, although it would have been in her powers to throw them out of their house.

412) See glossary.

yeni ate wa yaa ta wa jam. (37) Dii nying la wa powa daa wuuta po denoa, wa ta yeri kama. (38) Wa bu va wa jam ain wa nya ka wa yeni. (39) Ba yaa beg wa ain wa dan nya wa powa, wa seb wa ya? (40) Ate wa yueni ain: 'Eee!' (41) Ba yueni ain wa be nyiem a nya ase wa; wa nya wa powa ya, ate wa nyiem gisi kpieri, alege nipok naling kala, wa kan siag wa cheng paari wa jigni. (42) A chali nipowa yogsum ase ka wa powa ale tagri kal. (43) Wa yaa nyiem gisi kpieri la, a yaa yueni ain wan nya wa powa. (44) Ate Naawen yaa deri dag nipok nalingkai ale kala la, sag wa ain wa powa ale la, ale yueni wa ain wa ka wa lie, wa bu daa nipok kauk-oa. (45) Ka wa ale kaa siag ain wa faari nipok, ku ale soa ate wa poom basi ate wa nye dila ain wa faari wa.

(46) Abe wa gomsi ate wa ta wa powa a kuli, biik sui yaa pienti yeg-yega dii nying la wa powa ale chim pumi ale nala la. (47) Wa yaa yueni ain ba tom nur ate wa ga yueni wa kowa ain wa le wa powa chiena. (48) Ba yaa chiena abe ba gomsi a tu wa. (49) Biik ko a yaa nyiem yueni nisoma ain wa biika alaa tom yueni ain wa le wa powa chiena. (50) Wa bu kan yaali wa le nipok kauk wa yeri po. (51) Nisoma yaa tigsi chaab jam kal biik ko yeri po. (52) Ba yaa kala la, ba yaa a beg chaab ain daa biikai ale ta nipok kauku la ya-a? - ate ba yueni ain: 'Eee!' (53) Ba yaa yueni ain wa kan ta nipok kauk ngmaa jam ba teng po.

said that they should go to her house and he had brought her [here]. (37) [He now had seen that] his wife was not someone from the grass[413], because she really had a house. (38) He had followed her and had come to see her house. (39) Then they asked him that if he saw his wife, would he recognize her? (40) And he said: 'Yes!' (41) They said that he should go around and look for her; then he looked for her and he went round and searched in vain, but a beautiful woman was sitting [there], yet he did not dare to go near her[414]. (42) He feared the woman who was his wife; she had changed and was sitting [there]. (43) When he had roamed about and searched [for her] in vain, he said that he could not find his wife. (44) God then suddenly pointed to the beautiful woman sitting there and revealed to him that this was his wife, and he [= God] told him that she was his daughter and that she was not a half-woman. (45) As he [the man] did not agree to marry a [proper] woman, that is why he made her do this[415] so that he would marry her.

(46) [God said] that he should get ready to take his wife home, and the boy[416] [young man] was very happy because his wife had become whole and beautiful. (47) Then he said that they should send someone [to his father's house] who should go and tell his father that he and his wife were coming. (48) Then they went [and told his father that his son and his son's wife were coming and] that they should prepare themselves to meet him. (49) The boy's [young man's] father then went round telling the elders [of his clan] that his son had sent [someone] saying that he and his wife were coming. (50) He did not like [to have] him and his half-wife in his house. (51) The elders then gathered and came to sit in the house of the boy's [young man's] father. (52)

---

413) I.e. he had seen that she was not someone from the 'bush', a homeless creature. This is an allusion to the fact that at the beginning of the story, it was said that he had found her in the bush. If someone is found 'in the bush' or literally 'in the grass' (*wuuta po*), i.e. as a being without parents and a proper home, he or she is regarded with utmost suspicion and contempt. A woman, whom a suitor meets in the market, is also considered as a creature 'from the bush', as long as he has not met her parents in her house. The passage in this story refers to the wooing customs of the Bulsa (cf. Kröger 1978: 258ff. esp.p. 264).

414) He did not recognize her as his wife.

415) I.e. appear in the shape of a half-woman.

416) See glossary under the word *biik*.

(54) Biika ale wa powa ale gomsi nueri la, Naawen yaa yiti pa nipok-laasa pisineuk ain ba va kuli ga tom te wa powa ale pa nurba kook ale ba pooba ain ba ga a kpa ate wa. (55) A pa wusuma pisiye a te wa ain wa te gaa do-a. (56) Ate pa nurba pisiye ain ba gaa nya wusumanga zuk. (57)[417].

(58) Naawen yaa basi ate ngan-nagrisa a ta ba kuli. (59) Ba ale bo sagni po chiena la, biika kowa a yaa wom ngantanga alaa nag la. (60) Tengka nawa me wom a yaa yueni ain ka be naab ale chiena? (61) Ate ba yueni wa ain ba ze. (62) Ba ale chien la, wusuma pisiye a yaa dining a jam a paari ale biika kowa ale nurba kal kusung ate ba yueni ain ka wa biika ale chiena. (63) Tengka naawa ale wom ain nurma biika ale chien la, wa yaa yueni ain baa velim kama dii nying la biika daam ka ngantangade, wa nya ba ka be? (64) Dila nying la wa nye ain wa gaam wa kama, ain wa nye ain wa tuesi wa naam.

(65) Biika ale jam paari la, wa yaa dag wa powa a sag wa kowa. (66) Wa kowa yaa yueni ain wa jo dok ate wa yueni ain wan poom ngmaa yaali wa yeni po boka. (67) Wa yaa deri pa kpa-jein a fobi mobi ate beli a deri doa, ale ngman pa tan-gum a lonsi

[417] This sentence is missing in the Buli text, cf. the English translation.

While they were sitting, they asked one another: 'Was it not that boy [young man] with the half-woman?' - and they said: 'Yes!' (53) Then they said that he [the young man's father] should not have the half-woman again on their land[418] [= in their village].

(54) When the boy [young man] and his wife had finished their preparations, God got up, took ninety girls, who should follow them home and work for his wife, and he took one hundred men and their wives saying that they should go and farm for him. (55) And he took twenty horses, gave them to him saying that he should take them and ride them. (56) And he took twenty people who should go and look after the horses. <(57)[419] The last thing he gave them was an egg and a clod of earth (loam) to take home; and [God said] that if he does not want to stay with the [his] father, he should drop the clod of earth (loam) on the land on which he wants to settle, and the egg too, in front of the house.>

(58) God then ordered some drummers to take them home. (59) As they were in the bush coming, the boy's [young man's] father heard how the drums[420] were being beaten. (60) The chief of the village also heard [it] and said: 'What chief is there coming?' (61) And they said to him that they did not know. (62) As they were coming, the twenty horses arrived first and the boy's [young man's] father and [some] men sat in the *kusung* and they said that it was his son coming. (63) When the chief of the village heard that the man's son was coming, he told them that they were telling lies because as the boy [young man] formerly did not have these things[421], where did he get them? (64) Obviously he tried to be greater than him and he attempted to usurp his chieftaincy.

(65) When the boy [young man] had arrived, he showed his wife to his father. (66) His father then said that he should go into a room [of his house], but he [the boy] said that he no longer wanted to live in his house. (67) Then he quickly took a hen's egg and cracked it [on the ground in front of the house] and suddenly a river was stretching

---

418) See glossary under the word *teng*.

419) This sentence is missing in the Buli text; it appears only in the English translation written down by Mr.Godfrey Achaw.

420) '... *ngantanga alaa nag la*', lit. 'things were beaten'.

421) *nganta*, sing. *jaab*, in the sense of 'possessions, riches', see glossary under the word '*jaab*'.

ate yeri kpein a deri za. (68) Diina miena a boro magsi wa ngang-viiroma ale pooma boka.

(69) Nurma miena a yaa deri a yaali ain biika ate chim ba naab. (70) Ba yaa yueni chaab ain ba jinla ale diem nya naab. (71) Tengka naawa ale za la, ba yaa deri yiti tag wa zu-toka a vug biika zuk po ale yiag ba naawa ain wa cheng du.

(72) Naab yaa kuli gai kala ate wa sui a puuri. (73) Wa yaali ain biika powa ate chim ka wa pok. (74) Nur miena ale bo tengka po la, a yaali ain ba ate goa ale biika powa. (75) Naawa yaa a poli, wa ale wa nye dii a ko biika be wa ta wa powa la. (76) Biika kowa wa-dek a yaali ain wa ate goa ale wa biika powa. (77) Naawa yaa yiti wi tengka miena ate ba jam. (78) Ba ale jam la, wa yaa yueni ain ka wa daam ale ba naab. (79), (80)[422] *(81) Naawa yaa nye dila a basi ate ba yaali daata a ta jam dueni. (82) Wa yaa moag bolim a ju daatanga, ale yueni nurma ain ba daa wom wa noai, ba bob biika lonsi bolimu po ate nurma a sum bob biika a lonsi bolimu po. (83) Ate bu de wa a kabi.*

(84) Naawa yaa deri gai gbaari biika powa. (85) Nipowa yaa yueni biika mawa ain wa daa yaali wa biika wa maari lo bolimu po a kpi. (86) Biika mawa a yaa tuag ain wa lo du a ngman jam a kal. (87) Nipowa ngman yueni wa kowa ain wa daa yaali wa biika, wa maari lo bolimu po a kpi ate wa me tuag ain wa lo du a ngman jam a kali.

---

[422] These sentences appear in the English translation of Mr.Godfrey Achaw, but they are missing in the Buli text.

here and again he took a ball of clay, let it drop and all of a sudden a big house stood [there]. (68) There were sufficient rooms for his followers and [their] wives to live in.

(69) All the people then suddenly wanted the boy [young man] to become their chief. (70) Then they said to each other that only now they had seen [=got] a chief. (71) As the [former] chief of the village was standing there, they exchanged his [the former chief's] cap; they put it on the head of the boy and drove their chief away telling him that he should quit.

(72) The [former] chief then went home, sat down and he was annoyed[423]. (73) He desired that the boy's [young man's] wife should become his wife. (74) All the men who were in the village wanted to go and sleep with the boy's [young man's] wife. (75) The chief then was plotting to find means and ways to kill the boy [young man] so that he could have his wife. (76) Even the boy's [young man's] father wanted to go to bed with his son's wife. (77) The chief got up and called all [the people of his] village that they should come. (78) When they had come, he told them that formerly he had been their chief <(79)[424] ... before that boy came and that he did not know why they wanted to sack him, although he had not wronged them. (80) Since everyone wanted to go to bed with the boy's wife because of her beauty, they supported the chief.> (81) The chief did [= said] this and let them bring firewood and put it down. (82) Then he fetched fire and lit the wood and told the people that if they supported him[425], they should bind the boy and throw him into the fire; and the men really bound the boy and threw him into the fire. (83) And it devoured him and burnt him [to ashes].

(84) Then the chief hurried and embraced the boy's [young man's] wife. (85) The woman then said to the boy's [young man's] mother that if she loved her child, she would also throw herself into the fire and die. (86) The boy's [young man's] mother then went near [the fire] to throw herself into it, but then came back and sat down. (87) The woman again said to his father that if he loved his child, he would also throw

---

[423] *Wa sui puuri*, lit. 'his heart (*sui*) was overflowing (*puuri*)', he was 'angry, annoyed, sad, scornful' (cf. Kröger, BED). Mr. G. Achaw translated: '[...] he was in low spirits'.

[424] The sentences (79) and (80) appear in the English translation of Mr. Godfrey Achaw, but are missing in the Buli text.

[425] Lit.: 'if they listened to his mouth.'

(88) Nipowa dek a yaa yiti pa wa chin tunung[426] *a gaa lo bolimu po a ngari tintuemu a yali ale a yueni ain: (89) 'N-dek nong-oa, yiti ate ti jo!' (90) Ate biika yiti ate wa ale wa powa taam jo alege ate nurma kal kusungku po.*

(91) Ka dila ale soa ate ba yueni ain nipok a yaali wa chorowa a gaam wa chorowa nyama la.

(92) Ka dila ale soa ate ba pa ching paala a tom kisuk tuima la.

426) The word *tunung* is unknown to Mrs. Margaret Lariba Arnheim. According to Kröger BED it means 'leaf of a calabash plant', but this does not make sense in the present context.

himself into the fire and die, but he also went near [the fire] to throw himself into it, returned and sat down.

(88) The woman herself then got up, took a new calabash, went and threw herself into the fire, gathered the ashes [with the calabash] and spilled them saying: (89) 'My beloved one, get up and let us go into [our house]!' (90) And the boy [young man] arose and he and his wife went and walked hand in hand into [their house], while the people were sitting in the *kusung* [shelter].

(91) This is the reason why it is said that a woman loves her husband more than the husband's parents (lit. owners) do.

(92) This is the reason why one takes new calabashes to perform rituals[427].

---

427) Lit.: '... to work the works of forbidden, tabooed, sacred things.'

BUL-E0514 (BULI TEXT)

(1) Naab ale ta wa lie ate wa nala ga gaam taam. (2) Nurba miena yaa cheng yaali wa a kpieri.

(3) Naawa yaa yueni wa liewa ain wa nya. (4) Wa kan yaali ain wa fe wa ate wa yali, ate wa chum dadiira yueni ain wa fe wa kama ate wa yali. (5) Alege wa ale ta diila ain wa yueni wa la, ka wa kan ngman biisi ale nuro; wa dan biisi ale nur', wa chorowa ale la.

(6) Naawen yaa chim gami; wa nyingka miena a nyin ziim, a jam liewa po. (7) Wa ale jam la, wa jaa paari ale liewa kowa bo ka goai a bori za. (8) Wa ale jam la, wa jaa paari ale liewa kalu, wa yaa deri ga pa nipowa a kal' wa nangsa zuk a tiri wa nyingka miena, alege liewa kali, wa kan biisi.

(9) Gamini ale nye dila a kpieri la, wa yiti ga a nya ale ba-bisa doa. (10) Wa yaa pa ba-bisanga ale beg liewa ain naab-biisimu bo ka be ate wa pa mog baasanga? (11) Liewa sina. (12) Gamini yaa gisi nya naab-biisimu a yaa nye naab-biisimu ale saamu nyo wa noai po a chaam ne ale pa noai koruk a pa tug baasanga bitak-fiisanga po a mogi. (13) Liewa yaa chiib kperi a yueni ain wa kaa nye dila, wa ale ko baasanga. (14) Wa dan ko baasanga, ate ba jam, wa le yueni ka boa?

(15) Gamini yaa deri yiti a gogi ain wa jinla faari nipok. (16) Gamini ale yueni dila la, liewa yaa a kum. (17) Duero dan jaa, gamini nyiem ale yueni ain ka wa pok abe ba nyin kuli.

03.05 Leper (God) Marries Chief's Daughter

BUL-E0514 (ENGLISH TRANSLATION)

(1) A chief had a daughter who was so very beautiful, that she surpassed all [others]. (2) All men came to woo her, but they failed [in marrying her].

(3) The chief then said to his daughter that he understood (lit. that he saw). (4) He would not like to force her to marry, so that she might one day say that she had, in fact, been forced to marry. (5) But what he had to tell her was that she should not speak again with any man; if she did speak with a man, he [this man] would become her husband.

(6) God then turned himself into a leper; blood oozed from his whole body, and he came to the [chief's] daughter. (7) When he came, it so happened that the girl's father was in the bush [on a bush farm] sowing his millet. (8) When he [the leper] came, he found the girl sitting; he quickly went and took the woman and made her sit on his legs and touched all [parts of] her body, but the daughter sat and did not say anything.

(9) When the leper did this, but failed [to make the chief's daughter talk], he got up and saw [some] puppies lying [near him]. (10) He took the puppies and asked the girl where there was milk, so that he might feed the puppies. (11) The girl kept silent. (12) The leper then discovered [some] cow's milk[428)], took the cow's milk together with some *saab*[429)] into his mouth, chewed and swallowed it and put his empty mouth on to the little anuses of the dogs, [pretending] to feed them. (13) The daughter lost her self-control and told him that he should not do this [or else] he would kill the dogs. (14) If he killed the dogs and they [people] came, what would she say?

(15) The leper quickly jumped up and danced [with joy] saying that today he [would] marry a woman. (16) When the leper had said this, the daughter [started to] cry. (17) Whenever a suitor came [after that], the leper would say that she was his wife and that they [the suitors] should go home.

---

428) *gisi*, v. 'to search (for), to seek (for), to look (for) [...] *gisi nya* (lit. to search and see) to detect, to find out, to discover' (Kröger BED).

429) See glossary.

(18) Naawa yaa nyin goaini a jaa paari ale wa liewa kum butim. (19) Wa yaa beg wa ain ka boa ate wa kumu? (20) Ate liewa yaa yueni ku ale nye diila. (21) Ate naawa yaa yueni ain wa nya ka wa chorowa ale la, abe wa gomsi ate ba kuli. (22) Naawa ale yueni dila la, liewa yaa ngmasi kum. (23) Ba yaa basi ate wa va gamini a kuli.

(24) Wa ale va gamini kuli la, wa nyiem dan mani saab, wa nyiem zaani ka binta ale sinsam a nyoro a te gamini de. (25) Wa dan nyin a cheng yaba, gamini te wa ligra boorik ate wa ta cheng ga te liewa ko dok-dema. (26) Liewa nyiem dan tuag jigi, wa nye bogta sa kinkangni ate gamini daa yaali ain wa nyini, wa sati lo. (27) Ba nyiem dan cheng yaba ate nipowa a zaa biisi ale nuro, gamini a jam yig wa nisa ale yueni ain: (28) 'N nongo-a, ti kan kuli, yaa fi an diem da fi nganta nue ya-a?' (29) Gamini kasima nye nipowa ka dila ase ba nyin bo nurba sunsung.

(30) Ba yaa boro ate liewa kowa yaa kpi ate wa nyin kum a cheng ale nye bogta taari kingkangni. (31) Gamini yaa a yaali ain wa nyin cheng wa ngachobwa kuumu, wa nyiem ga yaali ain wa jue kingkangni, wa pasi lo. (32) Wa yaa walisi a ga jueli a nyin cheng kuumu a yaa ga a kum ain:

(18) The chief then came [back] from the bush and when he arrived [at his home], [he found] his daughter weeping and totally confused. (19) He asked her why she was weeping? (20) And the daughter told him what had happened. (21) The chief then said that he saw her husband there[430] and that she should get ready so that they [she and her husband] might go home. (22) After the chief had said this, his daughter cried even more. (23) She was then made to follow the leper home.

(24) After she had followed the leper home, whenever she prepared *saab*, she would shit and piss [into the *saab*] and give it to the leper to eat. (25) Whenever she went out to the market, the leper gave her a bag full of money which she should send to her, the [chief's] daughter's paternal relatives. (26) Whenever the daughter was going out, she prepared *bogta*[431] and smeared it on the *kingkangi*-wall[432], so that when the leper wanted to go out, he would slip and fall down. (27) Any time they went to the market and the woman stood talking with somebody, the leper would come and hold her hand, saying: (28) 'My darling, should we not go home or have you not yet bought all your things?' (29) The leper used to do this to the woman whenever they went out among people.

(30) Thus they were living, when [one day] the woman's father died and before she went out to mourn [at her father's house], she prepared *bogta* and smeared it on the *kingkangi*-wall. (31) When the leper wanted to go to his father-in-law's funeral and he wanted to climb over the *kingkangi*-wall, he fell down. (32) Finally he succeeded in climbing over [the wall] and he went out to the funeral, and was mourning[433]:

430) I.e. that the leper was her husband.

431) A slimy vegetable soup.

432) A wall one has to climb over to get into or out of the *dabiak*, the private yard, cf. Schott 1970: 15-16.

433) Singing the following funeral dirge. For the meanings of the Buli word *kum* see glossary.

(33) 'Ayaali-nalimu, fi noai wari ale boa?

(34) Ayaali-nalimu, fi liewa dek a zaani binta ate n de.

(35) Ayaali-nalimu, fi liewa dek a sam sinsam ate n nyu.

(36) Ayaali-nalimu, fi liewa dek ale saam bogta fatim kingangi ate n lo.

(37) Ayaali-nalimu, fi noai wari ale boa?'

(38) Kikiruku [gamini] a yaa nye dila, a nyin kal' kusung. (39) Wa yaa kali, kali, yueni ain: (40) 'Te n jo maar nya n powa ko abe n ge ate ba gu wa!' (41) Nurba bagela yaa zeri ain wa kan jo, bagela yueni ain ba basi ate wa jo. (42) Bai ale yueni ain ba basi ate wa jo la, a gaam bai ale yueni ain ba kan te wa jo la. (43) Ba yaa basi ate wa jo. (44) Wa ale jo la, a jo a paari ale ba yaali ain ba gu wa, ate wa yueni ain ba kan gu wa, ate wa yueni wa wari abe wa ge ate ba gu wa.

(45) Wa yaa ga paar ta wa juik a kpaasi nag wa ate wa yiti. (46) Wa yueni naawa wa liewa ale nye wa diila, ale yueni naawa me ain wa nya wa daa gami ya, wa ká Naawen; beka wa liewa ale kan siag a yali la ale soa ate wa nye dila. (47) Wa yueni dila ale deri chim nur mang a pa wa juiku a te naawa ale yueni ain nur a dan kpi, wa pa ta ga nag yiti, abe wa nya juiku kan jo dok-oa.

(33) 'Lover-of-beauty[434], what have you got to say?
(34) Lover-of-beauty, your own daughter shit and I ate.
(35) Lover-of-beauty, your own daughter pissed and I drank.
(36) Lover-of-beauty, your own daughter smeared *bogta* and made the *kingkangi* slippery and I fell down.
(37) Lover-of-beauty, what have you got to say?'

(38) The *kikiruk*[435] [the leper, i.e. God] did this and came out [of the house of mourning] and sat down in the *kusung*[436]. (39) He was sitting for a while and said: (40) 'Let me go in [to the room where the body was] so that I may also see my wife's father before I leave and he is buried!' (41) Some of the people objected saying that he should not go in, others said that they should let him enter. (42) Those who said that they should let him enter, outnumbered those who said that they should not let him go in. (43) Thereupon they allowed him to go in. (44) When he had gone in and entered and arrived [at the chief's corpse], they were about to bury him [the chief], but he said that they should not bury him so that he could say something before he left and they buried him [the chief].

(45) When he got here, he held his tail[437] and struck the chief [with it] and he arose [from the dead]. (46) He told the chief what his daughter had done to him, and he also told the chief that he should no longer see him as a leper - he was God; it was because his daughter was not willing to marry that he had done this[438]. (47) After he had said this, he suddenly changed into a real man and took his tail, gave it to the chief and said that if anyone died, he should take it, go and strike [the corpse] and make him rise, but he should see to it that the tail was not taken into a room [inside the house].

---

434) The personal name *Ayaali-nalimu* referring to the dead chief, is composed of the following lexemes: *A-*, prefix denoting personal names; *yaali*, v. 'to like, to love'; n. *nalim*, def. *nalimu*, 'goodness, kindness, beauty, glory' (Kröger BED).

435) Ogre, monster, man with supernatural powers; here: the leper, but really *Naawen*, God.

436) Shelter before the house, cf. glossary.

437) The tail of a cow or horse is regarded as a sign of authority.

438) I.e. he had changed his appearance and transformed into a leper.

(48) Wa yaa tara wa powa kuli. (49) Wa ale kuli la, kun beni ya, naawa powa wanyi ko yaa kpi ate ba jam yueni alege ate naawa dek a bo goai. (50) Nipowa a yaa nyin yieri juiku kusungku a ta cheng ga nag wa kowa yiti. (51) Wa kowa yaa yueni ain wa be kan ngman ta juiku kuli; wa basi ate wa daritara ate nur' dan kpi ba yienga abe wa ta ga nag yiti. (52) Naawa powa yaa pa juiku basi te wa kowa ale cheng kuli.

(53) Nurwa yaa pa juiku a ta jo su dala nina ate tiimu a deri kaasi. (54) Ka wa ale pa juiku a su dalinga nina ale soa ate nur dan kpi, ban ngman bag nag wa yiti, ale ba daam nyiem nag nurma yiti kama ase ba nin kpi. (55) Beka dila ale soa ate ba kan de tiim ale nipok la.

(48) Then he took his wife home. (49) Not long after he had left home, the father of one of the chief's wives died and when they came to announce [the death of the chief's father-in-law], the chief himself was in the bush. (50) The woman[439] then came out [of the house], took the tail out of the *kusung*, went away and struck her father who rose [from the dead]. (51) Her father then said that she should not take the tail home [to her husband'shouse]; she should let him have it at once so that if someone died in their 'houses', he could go, strike [him] and make him rise [from the dead]. (52) The chief's wife then took the tail and left it with her father and went home.

(53) The man took the tail, went into [a room] and put it on a ceiling [into the wooden rafters] where the medicine[440] was immediately spoilt. (54) It is because of him who took the tail and put it on the ceiling, that if someone dies, one cannot again strike [him] and make him rise [from the dead] as in former times, when they struck people and made them truly rise [from the dead] after they had died. (55) Because of this they [also] don't take (lit. eat) medicine in the presence of women.

---

439) Whose father had died.

440) I.e. the magical power of the tail.

APPENDICES

I. CLASSIFICATION OF GENRES AND THEMES OF BULSA FOLKTALES

A ANIMAL TALES

AA Animals among Themselves
AM Animals and Men
AN Animals and Natural Phenomena
AS Animals and Supernatural Beings
AT Animal 'Totems'

B TALES ABOUT (PARTS OF) THE HUMAN BODY

BS Tales about Sex

F FORMULA TALES

FC Cumulative (Chain) Tales

H HUMOROUS TALES, JOKES AND ANECDOTES

L LEGENDS

LM Legendary Tales about Men
LP Legendary Tales about Places (Villages), cf. SV

M MEN AND THEIR SOCIAL RELATIONS

MA Tales about Modern Affairs (Government, Schools, Mission, Traffic and Trade etc.)
MC Tales about Chiefs (Buli: *nààb*)
- **MCch** - Chief's children
- **MCda** - Chief's daughter
- **MCso** - Chief's son
- **MCwi** - Chief's wife (wives)

MD Tales about Slaves, the Poor and Other Deprived (Underprivileged) People
ME Tales about (Other) Ethnic Groups and Strangers
MF Tales about Friends and Friendship
MH Tales about Handicapped Persons (Lame, Blind etc.)
ML Tales about Relatives-in-Law

MM Tales about Marriage, Husband and Wife
MN Tales about Courtship and Wooing
MO Tales about Orphans
MP Tales about Parents and their Children
MS Tales about Siblings
MT Tales about Twins
MW Tales about (Co-) Wives

P TALES ABOUT PLANTS

R RIDDLE STORIES

RD Dilemma Tales

S TALES OF THE SUPERNATURAL

SA Tales of Supernatural Animals
SB Tales of God (Buli: *Naawen*)
SC Tales of Diviners (Soothsayers) (Buli: *baano*)
SD Tales of Death (Buli: *kum*) and the Dead (Buli: *kpilima*)
SF Tales about Funerals (Buli: *kuub*) and Other Mortuary Customs
SG Tales of 'Ghosts' (Buli: *kok*)
SH Tales of Supernatural Husbands
SJ Tales of Supernatural Things (Buli: *jaab*)
SM Tales of 'Strong' Men (with Supernatural or Magic Powers)
SO Tales of Ogres, Fairies etc. (Buli: *kikiruk* or *chichiruk*)
SR Tales of Supernatural Rivers
SS Tales of (Nature) 'Spirits' (Buli: *kikirisa* or *chichirisa*)
ST Tales of Supernatural Trees
SU Tales of Supernatural Places and 'Shrines' (Buli: *tanggbain*)
SV Tales of Supernatural 'Villages' (Buli: *teng*) cf. LP
SW Tales of Supernatural Women or Wives
SX Tales of Witches (Wizzards) or Sorcerers (Buli: *sakpak*)

W TALES OF THE WISE AND THE FOOLISH

WF Tales about the Foolish
WM Tales of Wisdom and Moral(s)
WT Tales of Tricksters, Liars and Thieves

Y MYTHOLOGICAL TALES

II. DATA SCHEME

01.	Seminar für Völkerkunde, Universität Münster Studtstrasse 32, D-4400 Münster, Germany Tel. 0251 - 83 45 75		
02.	Date[441]	03. Editor[442]	04. Code-No.
05.	Title		
06.	Language, orig.	07. Ling. Assignment	08.Translations[443]
09.	Source (Manuscript[444] or Publication)		
10.	Other Publications of the Tale		
11.	Place of Recording		12. Date of Record.
13.	Recorded by		14. Tape/ Cassette
15.	Remarks[445]		
16.1	Name of the Teller		
16.2	Social Status of the Teller		
16.3	Profession of the Teller		
16.4	Education of the Teller		
17.	Age		18. Sex
19.1	Place of Birth		
19.2	Place(s) of Residence		
20.	Ethnic Group	21. Native Language	22. Ling. Assignment

---

441) Enter date of last entry, please!

442) Abbreviation of the name of the last collaborator at the end.

443) Language(s) in which translations are available.

444) Place where manuscript is kept (MS-SfV: Münster, Seminar für Völkerkunde).

445) Concerning the 'biology' of the tale; concerning the content cf. no. 30.

23.1.1 Theme of the Tale: 'Internal' Classifications — 23.1.2 Type of the Tale:

23.2 Classification Following Aarne and Thompson 1961 and/or Other Indices

23.3 Similar Tales

23.3.1 - of the Same — 23.3.2 - of Other Ethnic Groups

23.4 Structural Type(s)[446)]

23.5 Genre Categories

23.5.1 - Indigenous ('Emic') — 23.5.2 - Scientific ('Etic')

24.1 Key Words Referring to the Structure of the Tale

24.2 Key Words Referring to the Contents of the Tale

25. Motifs (Mot Nos. According to Stith Thompson: Motif-Index, 1955-58)

26. Abstract

27.1 Explicitly Formulated Messages or Morals

27.2 Implicit Messages or Morals

28. Text in the African Language

29. Translation

30. Comments on the Structure, Morphology and Contents of the Tale

---

446) LH: Lee Haring: Malagasy Tale Index, FFC 231, Helsinki 1982.

III. NOTES AND ANNOTATIONS

04. **BUL-E0008**

05. Chief orders his people to kill all newborn girls and to bring up boys only. When a daughter is born to him, he hides her. When she is discovered, his people want to kill her, too, but she is saved by a woman coming from the sky (God).

06. Buli 07. Gur 08. English
09. Ms: MS-SfV
10.
11. Gbedembilisi, Amangkoa-yeri 12. 26. 02. 89
13. Rüdiger Schott 14.C-BUL-Lit 127/2

15. From the journal of R. Schott: ' ... Together with James Agalic, I went by car to the village of Gbedembilisi ('Little Gbedem'), about 65 km from Sandema in the south of the Bulsa district. ... We called on the Chief of the village and James Agalic explained to him the purpose of our visit. One of his elders remarked that in his youth, it was customary to tell stories after the evening meal. Nowadays, this custom is no longer practiced. (Instead I heard the sounds of a wireless set from the Chief's compound.)

Around 19.45 hours about 30 people had assembled for a round of storytelling. In the course of the evening the crowd of listeners swelled, but then it decreased again - probably because the tellers' storytelling was rather poor. One female teller got stuck in the midst of the tale - this I have hardly ever witnessed before. Another female teller, being blind, but very energetic, cut the other tellers short several times and went on to tell the story herself - this, according to James Agalic, is one way in which Bulsa storytellers may criticize other storytellers. The audience was restless and somehow not attentive; particularly the children disturbed the round by talking - in spite of James Agalic's angry exhortations: '*Ni be goori!*' (Be quiet!) As James told me in the car later on, the female storytellers - they told almost all of the 18 stories - were tired from visiting the market in Fumbisi and the long walk on foot there and back again. The round of storytelling ended around 22 hours ...'

16.1 Asibi Jinaansi
16.2
16.3 housewife
16.4 illiterate
17. c. 55 18. female
19.1 Kunkoak, Atiim-yeri
19.2 Gbedembilisi-Amangkoa-yeri, Naa-yeri
20. Bulsa 21. Buli 22. Gur

23.1.1 MCda, SB, SD, SW
23.1.2 All girls must be killed (sacrificed).
23.2 AaTh 500ff.+ Supernatural Helpers; 530ff.+ Animals as Helpers; 750ff.+ Religious Tales.

23.3.1 BUL-E0225, BUL-E0259, BUL-E0292, BUL-E0489, BUL-E0572, BUL-E0593, BUL-E0920, BUL-E1267, BUL-E1435, BUL-E1803, 1853, BUL-E1854, BUL-E1857
23.3.2 Gurma: Zwernemann 1985: 32f.: 'O Tyen setzt das Tieropfer ein'.
23.4 LH 1.2
23.5.1 *sunsueli* 23.5.2 mythological fairy tale

24.1 INITIAL SITUATION, DETERIORATION/ TRICKERY/ EXPOSURE/ REACTION/ DANGER/ PROVISION OF A MAGICAL AGENT, ADVICE, RESCUE

26. (1) Chief orders all newborn girls to be killed; his junior wife gives birth to a girl.
INITIAL SITUATION, DETERIORATION

(2-3) The chief and his wife say that she had a miscarriage, but in fact they hide their daughter in a room; there she grows up in secret.
TRICKERY

(5-15) A boy discovers the grown-up girl and exposes the chief's violation of his own rule.
EXPOSURE

(16-18) All people who killed their daughters according to the chief's order assemble and demand that the chief's daughter should also be killed.
REACTION

(19-55) The boy who betrayed her is sent to fetch her; when the girl comes out, she sings her own funeral song lamenting her death.
DANGER

(56-60) A woman comes from the sky, telling them to let that girl and all other girls live because if they are killed, no man would have a family. The girl is left alive.
PROVISION OF A MAGICAL AGENT, ADVICE, RESCUE

27.1 A woman from the sky (God) said: '(58) If they [people in a village] had born them all [both boys and girls], they should keep [them], if, however, they continued to [kill all newborn girls] in [a very short] time, a man would no longer have a family. (59) Even they themselves[447] who live in God's house, they are mixed [men and women]; therefore they should exempt her [the girl, from being killed].'

27.2 A chief who gives orders to his people is also bound to follow them; he is not exempt. - God is Lord over life and death.

447) The celestial woman and her consorts.

04. **BUL-E0182**

05. Three supernatural women come down from the sky and marry three brothers.

06. Buli 07. Gur 08. English
09. Ms: MS-SfV
10.
11. Sandema-Kalijiisa, Akpe-yeri 12. 23. 01. 89
13. Rüdiger Schott
14. C-BUL-Lit 118/1

15. From the journal of R. Schott: 'At 7:30 p.m. I went with James Agalic to a compound in the north of Kalijiisa, at the 'road' to Chiana [Kassena village to the north of Sandema, at the Navrongo - Tumu road] [...] About 20-30 people had assembled in the compound Akpe-yeri. They told their stories with much enthusiam until after 10 p.m.'

16.1 Amoak Bili (Amoabil)
16.2
16.3 in Kumasi as a worker, forestry department
16.4
17. c. 32 18. male
19.1 Sandema-Kalijiisa, Ayegaamba-yeri
19.2
20. Bulsa 21. Buli 22. Gur

23.1.1 MM, SW, AM 23.1.2 Brothers marry women from the sky.
23.2 AaTh 100ff.+ Wild Animals and Domestic Animals; 150ff.+ Man and Wild Animals; 219* Miscellaneous Tales of Domestic Animals; 400ff.+ Supernatural or Enchanted Husband (Wife) or Other Relatives; 545+ The Cat as Helper; 645+ The Three Brothers.
23.3.1 BUL-E0426, BUL-E1445
23.3.2 Kasena: Zwernemann 1985: 24-27, 39.
23.4 LH 4
23.5.1 *sunsueli* 23.5.2 mythological fairy tale

24.1 INITIAL SITUATION, LACK / LACK LIQUIDATED / RECONNAISSANCE, RECOGNITION, PROVISION OF SUPERNATURAL AGENTS / DEPARTURE / FAILURE / SOLUTION I / DEPARTURE / DANGER, FAILURE, RETURN / ADVICE, DANGER, COUNTERACTION / HOSPITALITY, DANGER / HELP, SOLUTION II / RETURN, LACK LIQUIDATED / ETIOLOGICAL MOTIF / MORAL

26. (1-2) Three men (brothers) live in a house and farm without having wives.
INITIAL SITUATION, LACK

(3-4) Whenever they return home from their field in the bush, they find food that has been prepared for them in secret.
LACK LIQUIDATED

(5-11) They want to find out who has done this. The eldest brother hides in a chicken coop and discovers that three women from the sky come to prepare the food for the three brothers.
RECONNAISSANCE, RECOGNITION, PROVISION OF SUPERNATURAL AGENTS

(12) After having prepared the food, the women go up to the sky again.
DEPARTURE

(13-21)	When the other two brothers return, they accuse the senior brother that he has not held back the women. The same happens to the middle brother. FAILURE
(22-38)	The youngest brother succeeds in holding back the women from the sky by means of magic; they all live together. SOLUTION I
(39-42)	The women from the sky want to visit their parents; they are accompanied by their husbands. DEPARTURE
(43-50)	When a leopard in front of the womens' parents' house threatens them, the two elder brothers flee, leaving their wives behind. DANGER, FAILURE, RETURN
(51-66)	The wife tells the junior brother what the true identity of the ferocious animals is which they meet in her parents' house; he greets her relatives kindly. ADVICE, DANGER, COUNTERACTION
(67-73)	In return, the junior brother is welcomed by various people in his wife's house. They prepare food for him - human meat and the meat of bush animals. HOSPITALITY, DANGER
(74-111)	A cat offers its help if the man feeds it with meat to its satisfaction: it helps him to avoid the human meat and to identify his wife and his brothers' wives among many women all looking alike. HELP, SOLUTION II
(112-114)	The junior brother arrives home with his wife and his brothers' wives. RETURN, LACK LIQUIDATED
(115-118)	Origin of women in the sky, they came to prepare food for men. ETIOLOGICAL MOTIF
(119)	Junior persons have a 'stronger heart' than senior ones. MORAL

27.1 1. '(115) [...] how women came to live on earth. (116) In the past there existed only men. (117) Formerly the women used to come from the sky and prepare food for mankind. (118) That is how women live on earth at present.

2. (119) [...] a younger person may be anything, but certainly he has a stronger heart than any other thing [on earth].'

27.2 1. Women are a gift of the sky (God). The sky (God) will not tolerate that men live as bachelors. The origin of the sexual division of labour.

2. The youngest are often more clever and braver than their seniors.

04. **BUL-E0225**

05. A chief orders his people to kill all girls, but he lets his own daughter live. His people want to kill her as well by sacrificing her to a *tanggbain*[448]. A ram, sent by God, is killed (sacrificed) in the girl's stead.

06. Buli 07. Gur 08. English
09. Ms: MS-SfV
10.
11. Yuesi (Wiasi), Section: Atong-yeri, House: Anoangko[?]-yeri
12. 01. 11. 88
13. Rüdiger Schott
14. C-BUL-Lit 104/2

15. From the journal of R. Schott: 'Mr. James Agalic had arranged a session of storytelling with the Chief of Yuesi. When we arrived there around 18 hrs., the Chief had gone to Navrongo and none of his elders were present. Instead, we went to a big house nearby, called Atong-yeri. There we met the Headteacher of the local primary school, Mr. J. B. Agriba. An old man sitting in the *kusung* declared himself prepared to tell stories. He was later joined by a woman who sat beside him in the *kusung*. Repeater was, in most cases, a young man. About two dozen children and several adults assembled around the storytellers. The children joined in most of the songs vociferously. The general spirit was lively. The telling lasted from approximately 18 h to 20 h.'

16.1 Awenpok
16.2
16.3 housewife
16.4
17. c. 35 18. female
19.1 Fumbisi-Bachiesa
19.2 married to a man in Yuesi-Atong-yeri
20. Bulsa 21. Buli 22. Gur

23.1.1 MCda, MP, SA, SB, SD, SU
23.1.2 All girls must be killed (sacrificed).
23.2 AaTh 500ff.+ Supernatural Helpers; 530ff.+ Animals as Helpers; 750ff.+ Religious Tales.
23.3.1 BUL-E0008, BUL-E0259, BUL-E0292, BUL-E0489, BUL-E0572, BUL-E0593, BUL-E0920, BUL-E1267, BUL-E1435, BUL-E1803, BUL-E1853, BUL-E1854, BUL-E1857

23.3.2 Gurma: Zwernemann 1985: 32f.: 'O Tyen setzt das Tieropfer ein'.
23.4 LH 1.2
23.5.1 *sunsueli* 23.5.2 mythological fairy tale

24.1 INITIAL SITUATION/ TRICKERY, VIOLATION/ EXPOSURE, REACTION, DANGER/ DETERIORATION/ DANGER/ DETERIORATION/ PROVISION OF A MAGICAL AGENT, RESCUE/ ETIOLOGICAL MOTIF

---

448) An earth-shrine, or 'spirit of an earth-shrine, sacred place of the earth-divinity, inhabited by an earth-spirit, who receives regular sacrifices from the (human) owner of the *tanggbain*; it may be a sacred grove, tree, rock, hill, river, lake etc....' (Kröger BED). See also glossary.

26. (1-2) Chief orders all newborn girls to be killed; he himself begets a daughter.
INITIAL SITUATION

(2-3) The chief hides her in a room; thus, he himself does not abide by his order.
TRICKERY, VIOLATION

(4-9) When the chief's people discover this, they want to kill his daughter.
EXPOSURE, REACTION, DANGER

(9-78) She is to prepare the millet-beer to be used at her sacrifice. In the course of her work, a bird comes six times and sings a song announcing her death.
DETERIORATION

(79-81) At daybreak the people come, take the millet-beer and the girl to the *tanggbain* in order to sacrifice her there.
DANGER

(82-92) When they offer the girl to the *tanggbain*, the bird comes again and announces her death in a song.
DETERIORATION

(93) When they want to kill the girl on the *tanggbain*, a ram, sent by God, appears and tells them not to kill the girl; they should kill the ram in her stead.
PROVISION OF A MAGICAL AGENT, RESCUE

(94) This is the reason why girls are no longer sacrificed to earth-shrines (*tanggbana*).
ETIOLOGICAL MOTIF

27.1 '(94) [...] nowadays, when they bring forth a girl, they let her [live], saying that a girl is not something to be carried [to a shrine] [...]'. Human sacrifices are substituted by animals as victims.

27.2 A chief who gives orders to his people is also bound to follow them; he is not exempt. - God is Lord over life and death.

04. **BUL-E0259**

05. A man wants to have a child from his barren wife. They are given children by a *tanggbain*; the oldest child, a girl, must be sacrificed to it. God sends a ram to be sacrificed in her stead.

06. Buli 07. Gur 08. English
09. Ms: MS-SfV
10.
11. Yuesi (Wiasi), Atong-yeri, Naa-yeri 12. 06. 11. 88
13. Rüdiger Schott
14. C-BUL-Lit 106/2

15. From the journal of R.Schott: 'A considerable crowd of people, men, women and children, had assembled under and by the Yuesi Chief's *kusung*. With the exception of the first five stories, all the other stories of this session were told by women. The teller Ayabalie Awulei, a woman full of temperament and vitality, was prominent among the tellers due to her vivid performance, her marked gestures and, most of all, by her enthusiastic singing, which fired the whole crowd to join in with the refrains. The mood was extremely spirited and animated.'

16.1 Ayabalie Awulei
16.2
16.3 housewife, farmer
16.4
17. c. 40 18. female
19.1 Yuesi, Atong-yeri, Naa-yeri
19.2
20. Bulsa 21. Buli 22. Gur

23.1.1 SU, SB, MP
23.1.2 Girl to be sacrificed to a shrine.
23.2 AaTh 500ff.+ Supernatural Helpers; 750ff.+ Religious Tales; 930ff.+ Tales of Fate; 1440ff.+ Stories about a Woman (Girl).
23.3.1 BUL-E0008, BUL-E0225, BUL-E0292, BUL-E0489, BUL-E0572, BUL-E0593, BUL-E0920, BUL-E1267, BUL-E1435, BUL-E1803, BUL-E1853, BUL-E1854, BUL-E1857
23.3.2 Gurma: Zwernemann 1985: 32f.: 'O Tyen setzt das Tieropfer ein'.
23.4 LH 1.2
23.5.1 *sunsueli* 23.5.2 mythological fairy tale

24.1 INITIAL SITUATION, LACK/ HELPER, CONTRACT/ LACK LIQUIDATED/ WARNING/ DANGER, REFUSAL, REPETITION/ PROMISE KEPT/ HELPER, RESCUE/ ETIOLOGICAL MOTIF

26. (1) A man's wife is barren and he marries another woman.
INITIAL SITUATION, LACK

(2-3) The man still wants his first wife to have children and he asks a *tanggbain* (earth-shrine) for help. The *tanggbain* agrees. [And the man promises to sacrifice his firstborn to the *tanggbain*.]
HELPER, CONTRACT

(4) Soon they have six children; the firstborn is a beautiful girl.
LACK LIQUIDATED

(5-19) The man orders his wives to prepare millet beer and guinea corn malt for a sacrifice for the *tanggbain*. When the daughter is grinding corn malt, a bird warns her in a song talking about her death.
WARNING

(20-127) The girl asks her mother several times about the meaning of the bird's song, but the mother refuses to explain and always tells her to continue her work. The bird repeats its song several times.
DANGER, REFUSAL, REPETITION

(128-133) When they assemble for the sacrifice, the father tells the *tanggbain* that he had rejected his daughter's suitors and saved her to fulfill his promise of sacrificing his firstborn to the *tanggbain.*
PROMISE KEPT

(134-141) They are ready to kill the girl, when suddenly something from the sky appears and tells them to wait. The 'thing' turns into a ram and one of the men takes the ram and they sacrifice it to the *tanggbain* in the girl's stead.
HELPER, RESCUE

(142-147) In former times, Bulsa people used to sacrifice their firstborn to a *tanggbain.* Since God has sent the ram, they use animals as sacrifices.
ETIOLOGICAL MOTIF

27.1 (142) ' [...] in former times, [...] if you begot your first child, you had to give it to a *tanggbain.* (143) It is God who sent a ram to use for sacrifice to a shrine. [...] (145) Otherwise, if you had given birth to a first child, you would have to give it to a *tanggbain.* (146) God saw that this wasn't good and he gave a ram [to the people] in order that they should sacrifice [this] to the shrine.'

27.2 Human lives should be saved, (domestic) animals should be sacrificed instead.

04. **BUL-E0292**

05. All girls are to be killed. A woman nurses her daughter secretly. When she is discovered and they are about to kill her, she is saved by a ram coming down from the sky (God).

06. Buli 07. Gur 08. English
09. Ms: MS-SfV
10.
11. Yuesi-Yipaala, Akpe-yeri 12. 07. 12. 88
13. Rüdiger Schott
14. C-BUL-Lit 111/1

15. From the journal of R. Schott: 'With James Agalic and Karolina Becker I went to Yuesi. Our visit was not announced beforehand. The Chief of Yuesi directed us to the section Yipaala. In the house Akpe-yeri many women and children had gathered in a spacious *dabiak* of a big compound. Only women told stories this evening. The meeting was improvised, but the storytelling was directed to the microphone of the White Man. The general mood was not very enthusiastic. The telling took place in almost total darkness. The telling began around 19.30 h and ended at 21.15 h after some of the women said that they were tired. The children began to get restless. Some young men carried on their conversation in the background. Many of the stories told this evening consisted, for the greater part, of songs.'

16.1 Anamsidek
16.2
16.3 housewife
16.4
17. c. 22 18. female
19.1 Fumbisi-Nyaandem
19.2 Yuesi-Yipaala, Akpe-yeri
20. Bulsa 21. Buli 22. Gur

23.1.1 MP, SD, Y 23.1.2 All girls must be killed.
23.2 AaTh 530ff.+ Animals as Helpers; 750ff.+ Religious Tales; 930ff.+ Tales of Fate; 1440ff.+ Stories about a Woman (Girl).
23.3.1 BUL-E0008, BUL-E0225, BUL-E0259, BUL-E0489, BUL-E0572, BUL-E0593, BUL-E0920, BUL-E1267, BUL-E1435, BUL-E1803, BUL-E1853, BUL-E1854, BUL-E1857
23.3.2 Gurma: Zwernemann 1985: 32f.: 'O Tyen setzt das Tieropfer ein'.
23.4 LH 1.2, 4.1
23.5.1 *sunsueli* 23.5.2 mythological fairy tale

24.1 INITIAL SITUATION/ INTERDICTION/ VIOLATION/ VIOLATION/ EXPOSURE/ DETERIORATION/ DANGER, PROVISION OF A SUPERNATURAL AGENT, RESCUE/ ETIOLOGICAL MOTIF

26.
(1) A woman gives birth to several boys, but only to one girl.
INTITIAL SITUATION
(2) It is forbidden to bring forth girls; they have to be killed.
INTERDICTION
(3) The mother hides her daughter in a room and brings her up secretly.
VIOLATION
(4-6) The girl grows up, is discovered by people who demand that she be killed.
EXPOSURE
(9-29) The girl's brothers cry and take her out of the house to be killed.
DETERIORATION

(30-31) When the girl is about to be killed by having her throat cut, a ram comes down from the sky (God) and asks to be slaughtered in her stead.
DANGER, PROVISION OF A SUPERNATURAL AGENT, RESCUE

(32-34) Since then, sheep have been killed (sacrificed) instead of girls.
ETIOLOGICAL MOTIF

27.1 When a girl was to be killed, a ram came down from the sky (God) to be slaughtered in her stead. '(32) [...] from thenceforth they have killed sheep. [...] (34) Formerly, when they gave birth to us girls, they killed [us] indeed.'

27.2 Animal sacrifices are to be substituted for human sacrifices. - Girls (women) are human beings and have the same right to live as men.

04. **BUL-E0402**

05. Man's message to God that he wants to die and return, whereas Moon shall stay dead, not delivered by a dog, but confounded by a goat.

06. Buli 07. Gur 08. English
09. Ms: MS-SfV
10.
11. Sandema-Kobdem, Presbyterian Mission 12. 13. 07. 78
13. Franz Kröger
14. C-BUL-006/1

15. The teller is a specialist in astronomy (oral information of F. Kröger).

16.1 Gilbert Angmaanina
16.2 *Yeri-nyono* (Head of a compound), at the same time Christian, related to the Presbyterian Mission at Sandema; at the time of recording, cook to a group of American missionaries.
16.3
16.4
17. c. 35 18. male
19.1 Sandema-Bilinsa
19.2 Sandema-Bilinsa
20. Bulsa 21. Buli 22. Gur

23.1.1 AM, SB, SD, Y
23.1.2 Origin of Man's and Moon's death through confounded message to God.
23.2 AaTh 335+ Death's Messengers.
23.3.1
23.3.2 Baumann 1936: 268-279; Mwaba (North Togo): Surgy, A. de 1984: 129.
23.4 LH 2.1
23.5.1 *sunsueli* 23.5.2 mythological fairy tale

24.1 INITIAL SITUATION/ TASK, FAILURE/ DETERIORATION/ FINAL LACK/ ETIOLOGICAL MOTIF 1/ ETIOLOGICAL MOTIF 2

26.
(1) In primeval times, God lets Man die and return to life, whereas Moon died and remained dead.
INITIAL SITUATION
(2-4) Dog, waiting for food, fails to deliver the message from Man to God that Man wants to continue living in this way.
TASK, FAILURE
(5-7) A he-goat confounds the message and tells God that Man wants to die and remain dead, whereas Moon shall die and return (to life).
DETERIORATION
(8-12) When dog at last comes with the right message, God is not willing to correct himself. Consequently, from then on, when Man dies, he remains dead.
FINAL LACK, ETIOLOGICAL MOTIF 1
(13-15) Ever since, Man eats dog's meat in revenge.
ETIOLOGICAL MOTIF 2

27.1 (1) Because a dog was late and a he-goat confounded Man's message to God, Moon dies and returns to life, whereas Man dies and remains dead.
(2) Because of dog's fault, man remains dead forever. In revenge, Man takes dog's meat and eats it.

27.2 Man's final death is attributed to a mistake (confounded message of dog and goat).

04. **BUL-E0426**

05. Supernatural women come down from the sky and marry three bachelors. (The origin of witches on earth.)

06. Buli 07. Gur 08. English
09. Ms: MS-SfV
10.
11. Sandema-Kobdem 12. 15. 04. 79
13. James Agalic
14. C-BUL-Lit 051/1-2

15. James Agalic: 'A group composed of Rev. Johnson Akobrika, his family (his wife, five children and a niece) and Miss Imke Swart (a student from Frankfurt, West Germany, a former student of Prof. R. Schott, Münster) had gathered. The time was 8 p.m. and the Pastor's family had just had their evening meal and were relaxing. The children were lying on their mats, the Pastor was sitting in a 'lazy' chair. James Agalic and Imke Swart were sitting on a bench facing the storytellers who had come at the special invitation of James Agalic. The storytellers were Ayuk, Ambabiik, Amoosa and Gilbert Abrunya, all from Sandema-Tankunsa. Amoosa and Ambabiik (blind) are from Akatuk-yeri. Ambabiik is popularly known as 'M and B' (i.e. a nickname and signifies a type of drug of the sulphate group which is common among the people for healing various sicknesses of bacterial origin. The sale and distribution of this drug is forbidden by law except if it is done by the appropriate authorities). Ambabiik, a man of about 25, attended school up to the form of Primary Four. Then he became a 'truant'; he went down to the South and became blind. He returned to Sandema two years ago (i.e. in 1977). He is very popular in Tankunsa and in other parts of Sandema because of his ability to sing, joke and tell stories. Abrunya is merely a 'follower' (*ngaang-viiro*) of the storytellers. Before the storytelling started, the tellers asked the *dok-nyono* (lit. 'room-owner', a woman 'owning' or heading the compartment of a compound), the wife of the Pastor, for permission.'

The story was transcribed by James Agalic from the tape recording. He sent the written version together with his English translation to Prof. R. Schott in Münster. Mr. Agalic commented on this and further stories of this series: 'There are a number of proverbs in this story which need explanations... Much is lost in the translation'.

16.1 Ambabiik
16.2 blind man, storyteller: 'He is very popular in [Sandema-]Tankunsa and in other parts of Sandema because of his ability to sing, joke and tell stories.' (James Agalic)
16.3
16.5 school up to Primary Four
17. c. 25 18. male
19.1 Sandema-Tankunsa, Akatuk-yeri
19.2 Sandema-Tankunsa, Akatuk-yeri
20. Bulsa 21. Buli 22. Gur

23.1.1 MM, MS, SW 23.1.2 Brothers marry women from the sky (God).
23.2 AaTh 209*+ Miscellaneous Tales of Domestic Animals; 334+ Household of the Witch; 400ff.+ Supernatural or Enchanted Husband (Wife) or Other Relatives; 545+ The Cat as Helper; 654+ The Three Brothers.
23.3.1 BUL-E0182, BUL-E1445.
23.4 LH 4.
23.5.1 *sunsueli* 23.5.2 mythological fairy tale

24.1 INITIAL SITUATION, LACK/ (MATERIAL) LACK LIQUIDATED/ PROVISION OF A MAGICAL AGENT, RECOGNITION/ [REPETITION]/ TRICKERY, (SOCIAL) LACK LIQUIDATED/ DEPARTURE/ DANGER, FAILURE, ABSENTATION, [REPETITION]/ SUCCESS OF HERO/ DANGER, DIFFICULT TASK/ HELP, TASK FULFILLED, RETURN/ FINAL LACK, ETIOLOGICAL MOTIF/ TERMINAL MARKER

26.

(1)	Three brothers live alone as bachelors in their house and farm their bush field, in spite of their having no wives. INITIAL SITUATION, LACK
(2-5)	Although they close their house before leaving for the bush, they find food prepared whenever they return home. (MATERIAL) LACK LIQUIDATED
(6-25)	In order to find out how the food comes to be prepared, the senior brother hides in a hen house and sees three women coming down from the sky and doing all the work necessary for preparing the food. PROVISION OF A MAGICAL AGENT, RECOGNITION
(26-41)	When the two younger brothers return from the field, the senior brother refuses to tell them what he has seen. The same happens with the middle brother. [REPETITION]
(42-62)	The junior brother strews ashes and succeeds in retaining the celestial women who marry the men. TRICKERY, (SOCIAL) LACK LIQUIDATED
(63-69)	After some time, the women want to go and see their parents in the sky; they are accompanied by their husbands. DEPARTURE
(70-91)	The senior and the middle brother flee from the wild animals guarding the womens' father's house. DANGER, FAILURE, ABSENTATION, [REPETITION]
(92-106)	The junior brother stands the test of intrepidity. SUCCESS OF HERO
(107-110)	Before the junior brother returns home, a cow is slaughtered for him, but a cat warns him that he is going to die if he does not identify his wife and his brothers' wives among many women, God's wives and daughters, who all look alike. DANGER, DIFFICULT TASK
(111-148)	The cat promises to help the hero in identifying the women if he lets the cat have the meat of the slaughtered cow. The cat helps by brushing against the women to be identified, thus pointing them out to the hero. He, having solved the task, returns home with the women. HELP, TASK FULFILLED, RETURN
(149-151)	On returning home, the wives of the senior and middle brother pass by the Sun's house where they are given human flesh to eat by their maternal uncle. This is the origin of witchcraft. FINAL LACK, ETIOLOGICAL MOTIF
(153-162)	Nonsensical final formula TERMINAL MARKER

27.1 '(150) [...] why there are witches as well as innocent persons on earth. (151) Had they [God's daughters] not deviated [and eaten human flesh with their maternal relatives in Sun's house] there would not be a [any] witch on earth.'

27.2 Man needs the help of women. Women came down to earth from the sky (God), but some of them are dangerous as they are witches.

04. **BUL-E0438**

05. Common-Son-Of-Ten-Women wrestles with God's bull; origin of the thunderstorm.

06. Buli 07. Gur 08. English
09. Ms: MS-SfV
10.
11. Sandema-Tankunsa, Anaankum Primary School 12. 20. 04. 79
13. James Agalic
14. C-BUL-Lit 052/2

15. Remarks by James Agalic: 'By the time this story was told, the tellers were very tired and sleepy - it was past midnight. It is, therefore, not complete and not properly told.'

16.1 Ambabiik
16.2
16.3
16.4
17. c. 25 18. male
19.1 Sandema-Tankunsa, Akatuk-yeri
19.2
20. Bulsa 21. Buli 22. Gur

23.1.1 MCwi, SA, SB, SM, SO, Y 23.1.2 'Strong Boy'.
23.2 AaTh 300ff.+ Supernatural Adversaries; 513+ The Extraordinary Companions; 650A Strong John; 650B The Quest for a Strong Companion; 700ff.+ Other Tales of the Supernatural; 1070+ Wrestling Contest
23.3.1 BUL-E0522, BUL-E0587, BUL-E0654, BUL-E0806, BUL-E0828.
23.3.2
23.4 LH 1.8
23.5.1 *sunsueli* 23.5.2 mythological fairy tale

24.1 INITIAL SITUATION, UNUSUAL CONCEPTION/ CHALLENGE 1/ DEPARTURE, CHALLENGE 2/ STRUGGLE, VICTORY, FRIENDSHIP/ VILLAINY, CHALLENGE 3/ INTERDICTION, VIOLATION, STRUGGLE/ PROVISION OF A SUPERNATURAL AGENT/ SUSPENSE/ ETIOLOGICAL MOTIF

26. (1-2) Ten women, wives of a chief, are pregnant together and give birth to a son together.
INITIAL SITUATION, UNUSUAL CONCEPTION

(3-6) The boy grows quickly. The chief asks for the name of the boy; he names himself 'Common-Son-Of-Ten-Women'.
CHALLENGE 1

(7-12) 'Common-Son-Of-Ten-Women' goes into the bush to hunt; he dries his meat on a rock, disturbing an ogre in a river, named 'Beard-Covers-River'.
DEPARTURE, CHALLENGE 2

(13-16) In a wrestling match, 'Common-Son-Of-Ten-Women' conquers 'Beard-Covers-River'; they go hunting together and dry their meat on the rock.
STRUGGLE, VICTORY, FRIENDSHIP

(17-39) God sends his bull from the sky; it secretly takes and swallows the meat from the rock. 'Common-Son-Of-Ten-Women' tells 'Beard-Covers-River' to watch the meat, but he is helpless against God's bull.
VILLAINY, CHALLENGE 3

(40-47) When God's bull comes again, 'Common-Son-Of-Ten-Women' forbids him to take the meat, hits him with his iron stick and wrestles with him for three (four) days.
INTERDICTION, VIOLATION, STRUGGLE

(48-49) When God sees that both are equally strong, he pulls them up into the sky.
PROVISION OF A SUPERNATURAL AGENT

(50) God does not judge their case, but suspends it.
SUSPENSE

(51) Wrestling of 'Common-Son-Of-Ten-Women' and God's bull continues; cause of thunderstorms.
ETIOLOGICAL MOTIF

27.1 Origin of thunderstorms: '(51) Whenever Common-Son-Of-Ten-Women and God's bull come across each other, [...] the sky always cries [...] because they [God's bull and Common-Son-Of-Ten-Women] wrestle [with one another].'

27.2 God is powerful, but not almighty: If he releases supernatural beings (*kikita*), their fighting one another may launch cosmic forces. God may suspend judgment, but he cannot decide and settle their 'quarrel' in favour of the one or the other once and for all.

30. Comments by James Agalic: 'This story has many versions. It tells of the *kikiruk* who is invincible, having been born in a peculiar way. He, the *kikiruk*, is now wrestling with another one up in the sky, causing the rain and thunder.' Cf.the similar story BUL-E0522; it has a very different message.

04. **BUL-E0489**

05. Man promises his daughter, a young girl, to the Earth. A relative kills one of his ugly sons in her stead.

06. Buli 07. Gur 08. English
09. Ms: MS-SfV
10.
11. Kadema-Kpipaluk, Akpiak-yeri 12. 15. 02. 89
13. Martin Striewisch and Barbara Meier
14. C-BUL-Lit 126/2

15. Comments by Martin Striewisch: 'Organized storytelling evening. Market-day in Kadema; most men were drunk. Strong smell of Akpeteshi [schnapps]; Mr. Philip, a schoolteacher directed the storytelling, chose tellers and kept the other people quiet. About 100 people gathered; not traditional circumstances, people had to give a hand signal if they wanted to tell a story. The compound was a very modern one, without cattle in the yard. Ulrike Schott, Martin Striewisch and Barbara Meier came instead of Prof. Schott. Three armchairs had been brought out for the purpose.' [Faults in recording - weak batteries?]

16.1 Abalie
16.2
16.3 housewife
16.4
17. c. 35 18. female
19.1 Kadema-Changsa, Ayirikadi-yeri
19.2 Kadema-Kpipaluk, Apientichaab-yeri
20. Bulsa 21. Buli 22. Gur

23.1.1 SU, SB, MP
23.1.2 Girl to be sacrificed to a shrine.
23.2 AaTh 450+ Little Brother and Little Sister; 500ff. Supernatural Helper; 750ff.+ God Repays and Punishes; 750A+ The Wishes; 1440ff. Stories about a Woman (Girl).
23.3.1 BUL-E0008, BUL-E0225, BUL-E0259, BUL-E0292, BUL-E0572, BUL-E0593, BUL-E0920, BUL-E1267, BUL-E1435, BUL-E1853, BUL-E1854, BUL-E1857.
23.3.2
23.4 LH 1.5, 4.1
23.5.1 *sunsueli* 23.5.2 mythological fairy tale

24.1 LACK, CONTRACT, PROMISE/ LACK LIQUIDATED/ DANGER/ INTERLUDE/ RESCUE

26. (2) A man promises to sacrifice his daughter to the Earth (earth-shrine, *teng*) if his wife gives birth to many children.
LACK, CONTRACT, PROMISE
(3) The man's wife gives birth to nine ugly boys and one fair-skinned (beautiful) girl.
LACK LIQUIDATED
(5) The Earth reminds the man of his promise and demands his daughter.
DANGER
(6-27) Some of the girl's brothers ask her to come out of the house to be killed (sacrificed); others prophesy that God will help her.
INTERLUDE

(82-30) **One of the girl's paternal relatives kills her youngest brother in her stead and placates the Earth. The girl is left alive.**
RESCUE

27.1 -
27.2 **Promises (vows) to the Earth must be fulfilled unconditionally; God, however, may help in finding a substitute for the victim promised to the Earth.**

04. **BUL-E0503**

05. Man marries half-woman who is God's daughter.

06. Buli 07. Gur 08. English
09. Ms: MS-SfV
10.
11. Sandema 12. 11. 01. 67
13. Godfrey Achaw
14. handwritten (no tape recording)

15. The story was written down by Mr. Godfrey Achaw in his own room.

16.1 Godfrey Achaw
16.2 male nurse, at that time assistant and interpreter of R. Schott
16.3
16.4 literate, has absolved Middle School
17. c. 20 18. male
19.1 Sandema-Kalijiisa-Yongsa
19.2 Sandema-Kalijiisa-Yongsa and Sandema town
20. Bulsa 21. Buli 22. Gur

23.1.1 MC, MM, MP, SB, SW 23.1.2 Man marries half-woman.
23.2 AaTh 400ff.+ Supernatural or Enchanted Wife.
23.3.1 BUL-E0049, BUL-E0196, BUL-E0258, BUL-E0272, BUL-E0514, BUL-E0831, BUL-E1272, BUL-E1443.
23.3.2 LYE-E0100.
23.4 LH 1.5, 4
23.5.1 *sunsueli* 23.5.2 mythological fairy tale

24.1 INITIAL SITUATION, LACK, REFUSAL/ ABSENTATION, PROVISION OF A MAGICAL AGENT, LACK FALSELY LIQUDATED/ REFUSAL, STRUGGLE, FAILURE/ REACTION, DEPARTURE, REFUSAL, STRUGGLE/ UNRECOGNIZED ARRIVAL, DISGUISE, RETRANSFORMATION/ IMPROVEMENT, LACK LIQUIDATED, DEPARTURE/ RETURN, CHALLENGE/ COUNTERACTION, VILLAINY, DANGER, DETERIORATION/ RESCUE, SOLUTION, FINAL STABILITY/ MORAL/ ETIOLOGICAL MOTIF

26. (1-5) A boy [man], living together with his parents, refuses to marry.
INITIAL SITUATION, LACK, REFUSAL

(6-8) In the bush, he cuts wood for his mother. Out of a dead tree comes a 'half-woman' (woman with half a body). She insists that he take her home and that he marry her.
ABSENTATION, PROVISION OF A MAGICAL AGENT, LACK FALSELY LIQUDATED

(9-12) When the boy refuses, the half-woman makes him drop dead and revives him again. In the end, he gives in to her demand and takes her home.
REFUSAL, STRUGGLE, FAILURE

(13-28) As his parents want to get rid of her, he takes her back to the bush. Against his will, she forces him to follow her into a hole underneath a termite-hill.
REACTION, DEPARTURE, REFUSAL, STRUGGLE

(29-45) Her subterranean house belongs to God, her father. The boy does not recognize his wife, God's daughter, because in the underworld she changes from a half-woman into a beautiful woman.
UNRECOGNIZED ARRIVAL, DISGUISE, RETRANSFORMATION

(46-58) God sends them back to earth with many followers and horses and gifts of magic objects.
IMPROVEMENT, LACK LIQUIDATED, DEPARTURE

(59-71) On return, the hero uses God's magic gifts to establish his own house and to separate from his parents. He is made chief and replaces the former one.
RETURN, CHALLENGE

(72-84) The return of the hero causes misgivings among his parents and elders. The chief of the village revenges himself: He and his men all want to sleep with the boy's beautiful wife. The chief incites his men to throw the boy [man] into a fire, kills him and tries to get hold of the boy's wife.
COUNTERACTION, VILLAINY, DANGER, DETERIORATION

(85-90) His wife asks his mother and his father to follow him into the flames, but they shrink back from the fire. Thereupon his wife, God's daughter, takes a new calabash, throws herself into the flames and from the ashes of the boy's body she resuscitates him. Both of them go home.
RESCUE, SOLUTION, FINAL STABILITY

(91) A wife loves her husband more than his parents do.
MORAL

(92) Origin of the custom of using new calabashes for ritual purposes.
ETIOLOGICAL MOTIF

27.1 (1) A wife loves her husband more than his parents do.
(2) Why one uses new calabashes in performing rituals.

27.2 God will not tolerate a man who remains unmarried. He has the power to force him to marry a woman; he has the power to make him rich and to bring him back to life after he has been killed by envious fellow beings.

04. **BUL-E0514**

05. God, transformed into a leper, marries chief's daughter.

06. Buli 07. Gur 08. English
09. Ms: MS-SfV
10. Agalic 1978: 267-269; Schott 1980e: 195-197.
11. Sandema 12. 05. 01. 67
13. Godfrey Achaw
14. handwritten (no tape recording)

15. The story was dictated to and written down by Godfrey Achaw from Sandema-Kalijiisa, assistant and interpreter to R. Schott.

16.1 Awunyok
16.2 mechanic, cook in the service of R. Schott
16.3
16.4 illiterate
17. c. 30 18. male
19.1 Sandema-Punsa
19.2 Sandema-Punsa
20. Bulsa 21. Buli 22. Gur

23.1.1 SB, MCda, MH, MM, SD, SF, SJ, Y
23.1.2 Girl marries leper.
23.2 AaTh 751A*+ A Man invites God to his house... [he] orders that a beggar, who has come to his door, be driven away... The beggar, it turns out, was God himself; 753A+ Unsuccessful Resuscitation; 779+ Miscellaneous Divine Rewards and Punishments; 853+ The Hero Catches the Princess with her Own Words; 900+ King Thrushbeard.
23.3.1 BUL-E0049, BUL-E0196, BUL-E0258, BUL-E0272, BUL-E0503, BUL-E0831, BUL-E1272, BUL-E1443.
23.3.2 LYE-E0100.
23.4 LH 3.1
23.5.1 *sunsueli* 23.5.2 mythological fairy tale

24.1 INITIAL SITUATION, DISEQUILIBRIUM/ INTERDICTION/ TRANSFORMATION, DISGUISE, PROVOCATION, VIOLATION/ PUNISHMENT, DEPARTURE/PROVOCATION, FAILURE/ EXPOSURE/ RE-TRANSFORMATION, PROVISION OF MAGICAL AGENT, INTERDICTION/ VIOLATION, PUNISHMENT, DETERIORATION/ ETIOLOGICAL MOTIF, MORAL

26. (1-2) A chief has a beautiful daughter who refuses to marry any suitor.
INITIAL SITUATION, DISEQUILIBRIUM

(3-5) The chief says that his daughter must no longer speak to any man; the first man she does speak to will become her husband.
INTERDICTION

(6-14) God turns into a leper, comes to the chief's daughter and makes her speak by committing an abominable act: he pretends to feed puppies through their anuses.
TRANSFORMATION, DISGUISE, PROVOCATION, VIOLATION

(15-23) The chief orders his daughter to follow her husband, the leper, home.
PUNISHMENT, DEPARTURE

(24-29) The chief's daughter maltreats her husband in various ways and in vain tries to provoke him into breaking up the marriage.
PROVOCATION, FAILURE

(30-37) When the chief dies, the leper, when going to the funeral, denounces the chief's daughter's misdeeds in a funeral dirge.
EXPOSURE

(38-47) At the funeral house, the leper resuscitates the chief by striking his dead body with a magic tail. The leper retransforms himself into God, giving the chief his tail under the provision that it is not to be taken into any room.
RETRANSFORMATION, PROVISION OF A MAGICAL AGENT, INTERDICTION

(48-53) A chief's wife misappropiates God's magic tail to resuscitate her dead father. He takes the tail into a room where immediately it looses its powers.
VIOLATION, PUNISHMENT, DETERIORATION

(54-55) In consequence, people can no longer be resuscitated and women must not be shown the use of 'medicines'.
ETIOLOGICAL MOTIF, MORAL

27.1 '(54) [...] because of him [a man] who took the tail [God's magic tail] and put it on the ceiling [in a room], that if someone dies, one cannot again strike [him] and make him rise [from the dead] as in former times, when they struck people and made them truly rise [from the dead] after they had died. (55) Because of this, they [also] don't take (lit. eat) medicine in the presence of women.'

27.2 Girls must not refuse to get married; otherwise God himself will enforce this rule.

30. Comments by James Agalic (cf. from his publication: 'Storytelling among the Bulsa of Northern Ghana', 1978: 267): 'Prominent among the ethics of the Bulsa people is the demand that one should take a positive attitude towards people like orphans, strangers and the handicapped. The ancestors are believed to visit their people, appearing as beggars, lepers and strangers. It is therefore imperative that such unfortunate ones be treated with respect and kindness. A man should not maltreat such people as he cannot be sure whether he is not in fact facing an ancestor or some other supernatural being who is appearing in that form to test him. Either blessings or curses may fall upon the one who treats those unfortunate ones with either respect or contempt. Other social vices like theft, adultery, disobedience, pride and arrogance are condemned and may be punished by the ancestors who intervene in human affairs as custodians of the ethics. The ancestors (*kpilima*, lit. 'the dead') or even *Naawen* (or *wen-naab*, God, lit. 'Lord of the Sky') may appear in the form of *kikita* (sing. *kikiruk*, 'monster') to inflict punishment on people who disobey the social norms of the society. This belief is expressed in another story from the unpublished collection of Professor Schott. It was recorded by his interpreter and assistant, Mr. Godfrey Achaw, from a dictation of Mr. Awunyok of Sandema-Punsa in January 1967 (at that time he was about 30 years old).' Here follows the story rendered above.

04. **BUL-E0572**

05. Childless couple receives children from an earth-shrine (*tanggbain*) which demands one child as a sacrifice. God sends a ram to be killed instead.

06. Buli 07. Gur 08. English
09. Ms: MS-SfV
10.
11. Kadema-Gaadem 12. 24. 01. 89
13. Rüdiger Schott
14. C-BUL-Lit 121/1

15. From the journal of R. Schott: 24. January, 1989: At my home in Sandema-Kobdem, Stephen Azantinlow, a chief's son, introduces himself. 'At 18.30 hrs he accompanied me to Kadema where I recorded another series of stories in front of a compound in the section of Gaadem .' In spite of interferences by the chief's son - he wanted the tellers to tell stories with a moral and not only for entertainment - ' ... the evening passed in a good mood. Shortly before 23 hours I stopped the session because I felt very tired. The people, if left to themselves, would have continued in other circumstances for a long time.'

16.1 Akansalinkum
16.2
16.3 farmer
16.4
17. c. 26 18. male
19.1 Kadema-Gaadem
19.2 Kadema-Gaadem
20. Bulsa 21. Buli 22. Gur

23.1.1 SU, SB, MP, Y
23.1.2 Girl to be sacrificed to a shrine.
23.2 AaTh 500ff.+ Supernatural Helpers; 750ff.+ Religious Tales; 930ff.+ Tales of Fate; 1440ff.+ Stories about a Woman (Girl).
23.3.1 BUL-E0008, BUL-E0225, BUL-E0259, BUL-E0292, BUL-E0489, BUL-E0593, BUL-E0920, BUL-E1267, BUL-E1435, BUL-E1803, BUL-E1853, BUL-E1854, BUL-E1857.
23.3.2 Gurma: Zwernemann 1985: 32f.: 'O Tyen setzt das Tieropfer ein'.
23.4 LH 1.2
23.5.1 *sunsueli* 23.5.2 mythological fairy tale

24.1 LACK/ PROVISION OF A MAGICAL AGENT, HELP, EXTORTION/ LACK LIQUIDATED/ DETERIORATION/ DEPARTURE/ DANGER, RESCUE/ ETIOLOGICAL MOTIF

26. (1) A man and his wife do not get children.
LACK

(2-7) The man consults an earth-shrine (*tanggbain*) who promises to help them, but demands the firstborn child as a sacrifice.
PROVISION OF A MAGICAL AGENT, HELP, EXTORTION

(7) The man and his wife bring forth children.
LACK LIQUIDATED

(8-56) A girl born to the couple grows up and is to be sacrificed to the *tanggbain*. Together with her mother, she prepares millet-beer and shea nut oil as sacrificial gifts. The mother announces the girl's death in a mourning song.
DETERIORATION

(57-70) When everything is prepared, the father takes his daughter to the *tanggbain*.
DEPARTURE

(71-99) When her father wants to slaughter his daughter by cutting her throat with a knife, God sends a ram from the sky to be slaughtered instead.
DANGER, RESCUE

(100-103) Since that event, animals instead of human beings are promised and sacrificed to shrines.
ETIOLOGICAL MOTIF

27.1 '(100) [...] how it happened that we take an animal and sacrifice it to an earth-shrine. (101) Concerning a human being, when [someone] has consulted an earth-shrine and has [received] riches, is healthy and has a lot of people [relatives], it is not forbidden that he should name anything and promise it [to the earth-shrine] by mentioning [it]. (102) However, God said that if you make a vow to an earth-shrine, do promise [it] an animal, but do not take a human being as something promised with a vow.'

27.2 Even girls (women) are human beings; God ordained that they are not fit for bloody sacrifices, instead one has to use domestic animals.

04. **BUL-E0674**

05. God created man and woman, hen and cock. The fowls show the human couple how to perform sexual intercourse and how to procreate.

06. Buli 07. Gur 08. English
09. Ms: MS-SfV
10.
11. Sandema-Balansa 12. 26. 11. 74
13. Godfrey Achaw
14. C-BUL-Lit 021/1 (Copy on: T-BUL 17)

15. No notes on the conditions of recording available. (There is no entry in the journal of R. Schott on recording stories on November 26 and 27, 1974.) The stories no. BUL-E0671 - BUL-E0680 seem to have been recorded by Godfrey Achaw in his own private room. Godfrey Achaw himself acts as repeater, i.e. he repeats sentence by sentence what the teller says, as is the custom of storytelling among the Bulsa. Most of the stories recorded on November 26 and 27, 1974 were told by a man named Adaaye or Adoayie from Sandema-Balansa. (At the storytelling session on November 17, 1974 he also told the stories no. BUL-E0650, BUL-E0654, BUL-E0658 and BUL-E0660.)

16.1 Adaaye, Adoayie [?]
16.2
16.3 farmer
16.4 illiterate
17. c. 52 18. male
19.1 Sandema-Balansa
19.2 Sandema-Balansa
20. Bulsa 21. Buli 22. Gur

23.1.1 SB, AM, BS, Y 23.1.2 Chickens teach humans sexual intercourse.
23.2 AaTh 219+ Miscellaneous Tales of Domestic Animals; 530ff.+ Animals as Helpers; 670+ The Animal Languages [...] The Advice of the Cock; 1430ff.+ The Foolish Couple; 1550ff.+ Stories about Married Couples.
23.3.1 23.3.2
23.4 LH 1.8
23.5.1 *sunsueli* 23.5.2 mythological fairy tale

24.1 INTRODUCTION/ INTITIAL SITUATION, EQUILIBRIUM/ LACK/ HELP, CONTRACT/ ADVICE/ LACK LIQUIDATED/ INTERDICTION/ COUNTERACTION BY SUPERNATURAL AGENT/ ETIOLOGICAL MOTIF

26. (1) Introductory statement of the teller.
INTRODUCTION

(2-6) God creates man and woman and gives them hen and cock. God gives them enough millet to eat and both the human couple and chickens are young enough to produce children.
INTITIAL SITUATION, EQUILIBRIUM

(7-24) The hen lays eggs and produces chicks because the fowls know how to copulate, whereas the human beings are ignorant of it. The woman complains that she has no children whereas the hen has many.
LACK

(25-38) The hen tells the cock of the woman's complaints; the cock asks the woman to provide him with millet, and then he would show her how to get children.
HELP, CONTRACT

(39-40) The cock, after having received his millet, shows the woman how to copulate.
ADVICE

(41-44) The woman imitates the fowl's acts and puts the man's penis into her vagina. The man copulates with the woman, who becomes pregnant and gives birth to a child.
LACK LIQUIDATED

(45-48) The man curses the fowl and tells his child to beware of it.
INTERDICTION

(49-56) God interferes by coming down from the sky and scolding the man for cursing the fowl. God ordains that man and fowl will no longer understand each others' language.
COUNTERACTION BY SUPERNATURAL AGENT

(57-61) The primeval man's grandchild ordains that henceforth a fowl must be slaughtered first of all in every ritual with animal sacrifices. Origin of this custom.
ETIOLOGICAL MOTIF

27.1 '(59) [...] when someone dies nowadays and they do not ask for a fowl [to be sacrificed][449)], then they will [also] not ask for a cow. (60) It was the fowl which taught mankind to live [to procreate]. (61) That is the reason why a fowl takes the first place[450)].'

27.2 Human beings are removed from nature; in primeval times they did not even know how to procreate, they had to learn it from the fowls. The man, being humiliated (?), curses the cock; ever since there has existed a fundamental cleavage between human beings and (domestic) animals.

---

449) I. e. if there is no sacrifice of an animal at all.

450) In all sacrificial rites, when animals are being slaughtered.

04. **BUL-E0761**

05. A barren woman promises her (first) child to the Earth (earth-shrine, *teng*). When her daughter is about to be sacrificed to the Earth, God sends animals to be slaughtered in her stead.

06. Buli 07. Gur 08. English
09. Ms: MS-SfV
10.
11. Gbedema-Gbinaansa, Anjia-Yeri 12. 06. 02. 89
13. Margaret L. Arnheim
14. C-BUL-Lit 313/2

15. Note by Mrs. Arnheim: 'The story was told inside the house at night. There were a lot of children around, all very good in singing '*sunsuelima*'-songs, but some were poor in narrating the stories.'

16.1 Akumweni Amoak
16.2
16.3
16.4
17. c. 15 18. male
19.1 Gbedema-Gbinaansa, Anjia-Yeri
19.2 Gbedema-Gbinaansa, Anjia-Yeri
20. Bulsa 21. Buli 22. Gur

23.1.1 MP, SU, SB 23.1.2 Girl to be sacrificed to a shrine.
23.2 AaTh 500ff.+ Supernatural Helpers; 750ff.+ Religious Tales; 930ff.+ Tales of Fate; 1440ff.+ Stories about a Woman (Girl).
23.3.1 BUL-E0008, BUL-E0225, BUL-E0259, BUL-E0292, BUL-E0489, BUL-E0572, BUL-E0593, BUL-E0920, BUL-E1267, BUL-E1435, BUL-E1803, BUL-E1853, BUL-E1854, BUL-E1857.
23.3.2 Gurma: Zwernemann 1985: 32f.: 'O Tyen setzt das Tieropfer ein'.
23.4 LH 1.2, 4.1
23.5.1 *sunsueli* 23.5.2 mythological fairy tale

24.1 LACK/ PROVISION OF A MAGICAL AGENT/ PROMISE/ HELP, LACK LIQUIDATED/ TASK/ TASK ACCOMPLISHED, ANNOUNCEMENT OF DEATH/ INTERLUDE/ SPATIAL TRANSFERENCE BETWEEN TWO PLACES/ DANGER, PROVISION OF A SUPERNATURAL AGENT/ RESCUE/ ETIOLOGICAL MOTIF

26. (1) A woman cannot give birth to children.
LACK
(2) She goes to the Earth (earth-shrine, *teng*) and makes a vow.
PROVISION OF A MAGICAL AGENT
(3) She promises the Earth(-shrine) her firstborn child.
PROMISE
(4) In less than three days she gives birth to a child (a girl).
HELP, LACK LIQUIDATED
(5-10) The mother asks the girl to prepare millet beer (to be offered as a libation to the earth-shrine (*teng*) on the occasion of her sacrifice).
TASK
(11-56) The girl sings a song announcing her death while going through the different stages of brewing millet beer.
TASK ACCOMPLISHED, ANNOUNCEMENT OF DEATH

(57-60) After having brewed the beer, the girl sleeps.
INTERLUDE

(61-79) The mother takes her daughter to the earth-shrine (*teng*).
SPATIAL TRANSFERENCE BETWEEN TWO PLACES

(80) When they are about to slaughter the girl, God sends down animals and birds to be sacrificed in the girl's stead.
DANGER, PROVISION OF SUPERNATURAL AGENT

(81) God asks them to slaughter the animals instead of human beings and to let the girl live.
RESCUE

(82) Since then people have killed animals instead of human beings and man continues to live on earth.
ETIOLOGICAL MOTIF

27.1 '(82) Since then they have killed the 'things' [animals and birds] and left the children and the children [have continued] to live. (83) This is the reason why man lives and exists on earth. (84) [Otherwise] they would by now get hold of human beings and kill them indeed.'

27.2 Human beings must not be promised as sacrifices to the Earth (earth-shrines). God (*Naawen*) is opposed to human sacrifices.

04. **BUL-E0920**

05. Parents dislike their daughter; her father tries to burn her. She is saved by a being from the sky (God).

06. Bùli 07. Gur 08. English
09. Ms: MS-SfV
10.
11. Sandema-Longsa, Adoabisa-yeri 12. 11. 01. 89
13. Akamara Atogtemi
14. C-BUL-Lit 511/1

15. Comments by Mr. Akamara Atogtemi: 'It was a big gathering consisting of six households with many adults and children. It took place at Adoabisa-yeri during the night, in the courtyard (*dabiak*) of Awienate, mother of the children in the house.'

16.1 Awienate
16.2
16.3 housewife
16.4
17. c. 41 18. female
19.1 Sandema-Kalibiisa
19.2 Sandema-Longsa, Adoabisa-yeri
20. Bulsa 21. Buli 22. Gur

23.1.1 MP, MS, SB
23.1.2 Girl to be killed.
23.2 AaTh 500ff.+ Supernatural Helpers; 750ff.+ Religious Tales; 1440ff.+ Stories about a Woman (Girl).
23.3.1 BUL-E0008, BUL-E0225, BUL-E0259, BUL-E0292, BUL-E0489, BUL-E0572, BUL-E0593, BUL-E1267, BUL-E1435, BUL-E1853, BUL-E1854, BUL-E1857
23.3.2
23.4 LH 1.2
23.5.1 *sunsueli* 23.5.2 mythological fairy tale

24.1 DISEQUILIBRIUM/ HELPER/ DANGER/ DANGER, SUSPENSE/ DANGER, DETERIORATION/ HELPER, RESCUE/ EQUILIBRIUM/ MORAL

26.
(1) A man begets three children with his wife, one of them is a daughter.
INTITIAL SITUATION
(2-3,6) Father and mother say that they do not like the girl.
DISEQUILIBRIUM
(4-5) Her brother disagrees and stresses the value of sisters for men.
HELPER
(7-8) The father tells his sons to fetch firewood. The girl is to be burnt on a pile of firewood set on fire.
DANGER
(9-28) The girl's brothers, by singing a song, call her to come out of her house and room, but she does not move.
DANGER, SUSPENSE
(29) At last, after her favourite brother called her, she gets up and runs into the fire.
DANGER, DETERIORATION

(29-30) A supernatural being comes down from the sky (God) and puts her out of danger. Water from the sky quenches the fire.
HELPER, RESCUE

(31) The girl's favourite brother is blessed with women, children and riches.
EQUILIBRIUM

(32-34) The importance of having sisters.
MORAL

27.1 If you do not give birth to girls, boys and girls would be unhappy because they would not have a sister.
Daughters perpetuate the roots of their mother's clan.

27.2 One should not reject daughters. Daughters perpetuate the maternal lineage.

04. **BUL-E1267**

05. Father promises a child to a *tanggbain*, if his wife gives birth to many children. Fair-skinned daughter, claimed by the *tanggbain*, is saved by an old woman from the sky.

06. Buli 07. Gur 08. English
09. Ms: MS-SfV
10.
11. Navrongo 12. 29. 01. 89
13. Sabine Dinslage/ Francis Adocta
14. handwritten

15. Noted by Sabine Dinslage: 'Peter Atiniak wrote down the story during his holidays.'

16.1 Peter Atiniak
16.2
16.3 student
16.4 literate
17. 20 18. male
19.1 Sandema-Kori
19.2 Sandema-Kori
20. Bulsa 21. Buli 22. Gur

23.1.1 SU, SB, MP
23.1.2 Girl to be sacrificed to a shrine.
23.2 AaTh 500ff.+ Supernatural Helpers; 750ff.+ Religious Tales; 930ff.+ Tales of Fate; 1440ff.+ Stories about a Woman (Girl).
23.3 BUL-E0225, BUL-E0259, BUL-EO292, BUL-E0572, BUL-E0593, BUL-E0920, BUL-E1853, BUL-E1854, BUL-E1857
23.4 LH 1.3, 4.1
23.5.1 *sunsueli* 23.5.2 mythological fairy tale

24.1 LACK/ PROMISE/ LACK LIQUIDATED/ DEMAND/ INTERLUDE/ DANGER/ PROVISION OF A MAGICAL AGENT, RESCUE/ MORAL

26. (1) A man and his wife remain childless.
LACK
(2-3) The man promises a child to an earth-shrine (*tanggbain*), if it makes him able to beget children.
PROMISE
(4-5) The man and his wife bring forth many children, among them a beautiful fair-skinned girl.
LACK LIQUIDATED
(6) The earth-shrine claims the daughter as sacrifice to it.
DEMAND
(7-18) Preparation of the girl's sacrifice to the earth-shrine.
INTERLUDE
(19-21) Father is ready to slaughter his daughter with a knife. She is made to lie down before the altar.
DANGER
(22-25) An old woman descends from the sky; she tells the people to refrain from killing the girl and disappears again to the sky.
PROVISION OF A MAGICAL AGENT, RESCUE

(26) Human beings should not be sacrificed to a shrine.
MORAL

27.1 (26) '[...] one does not take human beings and sacrifice them to a shrine.'
27.2 Human beings may not be sacrificed.

04. **BUL-E1328**

05. Hare marries chief's daughter after he promised to be buried when his mother-in-law dies. When she pretends to die, he threatens to take agricultural tools and products as well as a domestic animal into his grave.

06. Buli 07. Gur 08. English
09. Ms: MS-SfV
10.
11. Sandema-Kalijiisa-Yongsa, Agbedem-yeri 12. 13. 02. 89
13. Sabine Dinslage
14. C-BUL-Lit 212/2

15. Sabine Dinslage: 'Just one hour before we reached the compound, a child was born and everyone felt happy. Eight women and about ten children sat together, later one man joined the storytelling session. The cassette was defective, side one did not record all the stories.'

16.1 Ayomalie Awoke
16.2
16.3
16.4 literate
17. c. 20 18. female
19.1 Sandema-Kalijiisa-Yongsa, Agbedem-yeri
19.2 Sandema-Kalijiisa-Yongsa, Agbedem-yeri
20. Bulsa 21. Buli 22. Gur

23.1.1 AM, ML, SB, SF, Y 23.1.2 [Hare and his mother-in-law.]
23.2 AaTh 150ff.+ Man and Wild Animals; 160B*+ The Hare's Last Will; 500ff.+ Supernatural Helpers.
23.3.1
23.3.2
23.4 LH 1.5
23.5.1 *sunsueli* 23.5.2 mythological fairy tale

24.1 INITIAL SITUATION, LACK/ LACK LIQUIDATED, CONDITION IMPOSED/ DETERIORATION/ PROVISION OF MAGICAL AGENT, ADVICE/ DEPARTURE/ HELP, TRICKERY, EXTORTION/ IMPROVEMENT, SOLUTION/ ETIOLOGICAL MOTIF

26. (1-3) Hare woos chief's daughter.
INITIAL SITUATION, LACK

(4-6) The girl's mother gives her consent to the marriage on the condition that when she dies, Hare will also be buried. Hare agrees.
LACK LIQUIDATED, CONDITION IMPOSED

(7-20) Shortly afterwards, Hare's mother-in-law is said to be dead. Hare is desperate and goes lamenting into the bush.
DETERIORATION

(21-32) A supernatural being from the sky advises Hare on what to do.
PROVISION OF MAGICAL AGENT, ADVICE

(34-45) Mourning, Hare goes to the chief's house.
DEPARTURE

(46-51) He asks God to give him a hoe, farm products and a [domestic] animal and threatens to take them with him into the realm of the dead. God gives him the requested things.
HELP, TRICKERY, EXTORTION

(52-53) Hare's mother-in-law gets up from her feigned death and tells him not to take the things away. She only wanted to test his faithfulness.
IMPROVEMENT, SOLUTION

(55-57) Owing to Hare's mother-in-law, the Bulsa can produce their food with a hoe and today they have farm products and animals.
ETIOLOGICAL MOTIF

27.1 Food exists because Hare's mother-in-law prevented him from taking a hoe, farm products and [domestic] animals into the realm of the dead.

27.2 God is the giver of a hoe, farm products and domestic animals to mankind; otherwise the Bulsa could not produce their food.

04. **BUL-E1435**

05. Parents want to kill their daughter, because she does not belong to their clan. God saves her by sending a being, half-human, half-animal, from the sky.

06. Buli 07. Gur 08. English
09. Ms: MS-SfV
10.
11. Sandema-Kobdema, Abeliwan-yeri 12. 26. 02. 89
13. John Anankpieng
14. C-BUL-Lit 219/1

15. No information on the conditions of telling available.

16.1 Azaagoam, Abeliwan
16.2
16.3 farmer
16.4 illiterate
17. c. 40 18. male
19.1 Sandema-Kobdema, Abeliwan-yeri
19.2 Sandema-Kobdema, Abeliwan-yeri
20. Bulsa 21. Buli 22. Gur

23.1.1 MP, SA, SB 23.1.2 Girl to be killed.
23.2 AaTh 500ff.+ Supernatural Helpers; 750ff.+ Religious Tales; 930ff.+ Tales of Fate; 1440ff.+ Stories about a Woman (Girl).
23.3.1 BUL-E0008, BUL-E0225, BUL-E0259, BUL-E0292, BUL-E0489, BUL-E0572, BUL-E0593, BUL-E0920, BUL-E1267, BUL-E1853, BUL-E1854, BUL-E1857.
23.3.2 Gurma: Zwernemann 1985: 32f.: 'O Tyen setzt das Tieropfer ein'.
23.4 LH 1.2
23.5.1 *sunsueli* 23.5.2 mythological fairy tale

24.1 INITIAL SITUATION/ LACK/ DETERIORATION/ PURSUIT/ INTERLUDE, TRAVESTY OF RITUAL/ DANGER/ PROVISION OF A SUPERNATURAL AGENT, RESCUE/ ETIOLOGICAL MOTIF

26. (1-3) A man and his wife brought forth first a boy, then a girl.
INITIAL SITUATION
(4-5) The parents declare that the girl is not of their lineage (clan or family).
LACK
(6-9) They decide to kill the girl on the ninth day after her birth.
DETERIORATION
(10-13) On the ninth day, they send the girl's senior brother to take her out of her mother's rooms and out of the house to be killed.
PURSUIT
(14-30) The outdoor ceremony for the girl has not yet been performed. The boy, singing a song, goes from one station to the next whilst his sister is brought finally to the *kusung* where her father is waiting for her.
INTERLUDE, TRAVESTY OF RITUAL
(31-32) The girl is laid down, ready to be slaughtered, and a knife is put to her throat.
DANGER

(33-39) A supernatural being, half-human, half-animal, comes from the sky (God) and tells the people not to kill the girl. When threatened with the extinction of their clan, the people desist from what they are doing.
PROVISION OF A SUPERNATURAL AGENT, RESCUE

(40-41) God sent his servant in order to stop the killing of women; ever since then they have lived on earth, as well as men.
ETIOLOGICAL MOTIF

27.1 Women live on earth because God sent a supernatural being which forbade the killing (slaughtering) of women (girls).

27.2 God's will made men respect women; they have an equal right to be treated as human beings and not as animals which are slaughtered as sacrifices.

30. Comment by R. Schott: The text is incoherent in that the teller seems to have remembered the tale type 'All girls are to be killed' and 'God sends a ram (or any other animal or being) to be killed in the girl's stead', but he does not come out with either of these themes. Instead, he attributes the girl's fate to the individual decision of her parents to kill her because they think that she is not of their type or kind, i.e. that she does not belong to their lineages (clans or families). This may be an allusion to the fact that the parents regard the girl as being a *kikiruk*, a kind of ogre. It is interesting that her senior brother is charged with calling her outside. This again is vaguely reminiscent of a motif in other stories where the adult brother calls his adult sister out of her room. This does not make sense in the present story because the girl cannot possibly answer him nine days after her birth. Instead, the boy performs the different steps of the outdoor ceremony - this is probably a travesty of the proper ceremony with its deep religious and social symbolic meanings of taking a newborn human being into the social group where he or she belongs. The story poses the problem whether women are in fact fit to become members of the essential social groups, namely lineages such as clans or families. In a patrilineal and patriarchal society such as that of the Bulsa, the standing of women is a matter of debate. The story expresses the idea that God's decision was needed to allow women to live on earth as safely as men.

04. **BUL-E1445**

05. Hunter marries women who come down from the sky to cook his food. (Origin of marriage and the division of labour.)

06. Buli 07. Gur 08. English
09. Ms: MS-SfV
10.
11. Sandema-Kobdema, courtyard of Abeliwan-yeri 12. 26. 02. 89
13. John Anankpieng
14. C-BUL-Lit 219/2

15. No information on the conditions of telling available.

16.1 Ama Ayaaji
16.2
16.3 housewife
16.4 illiterate
17. c. 33 18. female
19.1 Sandema-Balansa, Ayaaji-yeri
19.2 Sandema-Kobdem, Abeliwan-yeri
20. Bulsa 21. Buli 22. Gur

23.1.1 SB, MW, Y
23.1.2 Man marries women from the sky (God).
23.2 AaTh 500+ Supernatural Helpers.
23.3.1 BUL-E0182, BUL-E0426. 23.3.2
23.4 LH 1.2
23.5.1 *sunsueli* 23.5.2 mythological fairy tale

24.1 INITIAL SITUATION, LACK/ PROVISION OF A MAGICAL AGENT, HELP/ INTERLUDE/ DEPARTURE/ RETURN, TRICKERY/ LACK LIQUIDATED/ ETIOLOGICAL MOTIF

26.

(1) A hunter lives alone in his house (without a wife).
INITIAL SITUATION, LACK

(3-4) Whenever he goes to the bush, women come down from the sky (God) and secretly prepare food for him and take off to the sky before the hunter returns.
PROVISION OF A MAGICAL AGENT, HELP

(6-50) When descending and doing their work, the women sing a song, accompanying the different stages of preparing the millet porridge.
INTERLUDE

(51-59) After having prepared the millet porridge, the women return to the sky again, leaving the food for the hunter.
DEPARTURE

(60-62) One day the hunter hides himself and sees the women descend from the sky and prepare food for him.
RETURN, TRICKERY

(63-68) When the women are about to leave again, the hunter steps forward and begs them to stay with him in his house.
LACK LIQUIDATED

(69-70) **Men and women have lived together since the hunter had brought a woman from the sky (God) to earth. - Origin of marriage and the division of labour.**
ETIOLOGICAL MOTIF

27.1 **Why men and women live together; formerly women lived in the sky (with God). A hunter brought a woman down to earth.**

27.2 **Gen. 2, 18: 'And the Lord God said: It is not good that the man should be alone; I will make him a help mate for him.' - Man cannot live by himself; he needs a helper in his house. - The woman is a gift of Heaven.**

04. **BUL-E1698**

05. God (*Naawen*) offers himself as food; he retires from mankind after a woman breaks a taboo.

06. Buli 07. Gur 08. Engl.,Germ.
09. Ms: MS-SfV
10. Schott 1982b: 131f.
11. Sandema-Abilyeri, Chief's house 12. 20. 03. 67
13. Rüdiger Schott
14. C-BUL-Lit 006/1 (copied from T-BUL 6a/1)

15. From the journal of R.Schott: 'Ayieta Azantinlow, the Paramount Chief of the Bulsa, told the stories BUL-E1686-1699 (formerly BUL-E0094) in his reception room in the presence of R. Schott and Mr. Abu Gariba, at that time Head Teacher of the Local Authority Middle School in Sandema. Also present was Prof. Schott's assistant and interpreter, Mr. Godfrey Achaw. It was shortly before R. Schott left Bulsa country at the end of March, 1967. The atmosphere was friendly, but formal; there was no Bulsa audience present and the stories were not told in the traditional fashion, i.e. by having each sentence repeated by someone from the audience.' - The stories in the series BUL-E1686-E1699 were corrected by a son of the Paramount Chief, Mr. Clement Azaksuk Azantinlow, on the occasion of his visit to Germany in August 1968 and by Mrs. Margaret Lariba-Arnheim in November 1979.

16.1 Ayieta Azantinlow
16.2 Sandem-naab and Paramount Chief of the Bulsa
16.3 Paramount Chief
16.4 illiterate
17. c. 65 18. male
19.1 Sandema-Abilyeri
19.2 Sandema-Abilyeri
20. Bulsa 21. Buli 22. Gur

23.1.1 SB, Y 23.1.2 God gives himself as food.
23.2 AaTh 750 ff.+ God Repays and Punishes.
23.3.1
23.3.2 Kassena: Zwernemann 1985: 36.
Mossi: Baumann 1936: 149, 328, 363.
Lyela: unpubl. collection of Sabine Steinbrich (LYE-E779).
23.4 LH 2.2
23.5.1 *wa-magsini* 23.5.2 mythological tale, myth

24.1 EQUILIBRIUM/ INTERDICTION/ VIOLATION/ DETERIORATION/ PUNISHMENT, LACK, DISEQUILIBRIUM

26. (1) When God leaves mankind, he tells the humans that they should not do any work; he would be near the Earth and they should cut off pieces of him to eat him as food (meat).
EQUILIBRIUM
(2-4) No one should grind millet; no one should work (farm) in order to obtain food. God makes it taboo to add a certain spice (*kaam*[451)]) to the meat.
INTERDICTION

---

451) See glossary.

(5) A very old woman refuses to obey God's command; she breaks the taboo by adding *kaam* to the meat.
VIOLATION

(6) God becomes angry because his taboo on not using *kaam* together with meat cut from his body was broken; he ascends.
DETERIORATION

(7-10) God declares that every man shall suffer and henceforth work in order to obtain food.
PUNISHMENT, LACK, DISEQUILIBRIUM

27.1 (10) '...why every man has to work in order to get food.'

27.2 It is the fault of an old woman that God, who offered himself as food, retired and thence man has to toil for his food.

04. **BUL-E1856**

05. Sky (God) and a river argue with one another; river boasts that he is not dependent on the sky (God) for his water (rain).

06. Buli 07. Gur 08. English
09. Ms: MS-SfV
10.
11. Sandema-Longsa, Agalisui-yeri[452)] 12. 22. 05. 89
13. Barbara Meier
14. C-BUL-Lit 804/2 (B17)

15. From Barbara Meier's notes: 'The storytelling took place at the *kusung* of Agalisui-yeri. Young people and children from the neighbouring compounds came to tell stories. They quarrelled about who may hold the recorder. The main tellers were two girls of about 15.'

16.1 Avika Azaayam
16.2 school-girl (Sandema Secondary School)
16.3
16.4 speaks hardly any English, understands a little
17. c. 14 18. female
19.1 Sandema-Kobdema
19.2 Sandema-Kobdema, Adaasing-yeri
20. Bulsa 21. Buli 22. Gur

23.1.1 SB, SR, WF
23.1.2 [Sky (God) and a river argue with one another.]
23.2 AaTh 750ff. God Repays and Punishes; 934D Nothing Happens without God.
23.3.1 23.3.2
23.4 LH 1.1
23.5.1 *sunsueli* 23.5.2 mythological fairy tale

24.1 CONFLICT/ CHALLENGE/ PUNISHMENT, LACK/ REQUEST, REFUSAL/ REACTION/ RECOGNITION/ LACK LIQUIDATED/ MORAL

26.
(1-6) A river and the sky (God) quarrel; the river boasts that he is not dependent on the sky (God) for his water.
CONFLICT
(7-9) The river and God challenge one another; each of them saying that the other will beg for the other one's help first.
CHALLENGE
(10-12) The sky (God) withholds the rain; the River dries up and his children die.
PUNISHMENT, LACK
(13-31) The river despairs and sends his children to God's house to ask for rain, but in vain; finally he goes himself.
REQUEST, REFUSAL
(32-35) God states that no one can argue with him; he is most powerful.
REACTION
(36) River recognizes his fault and begs God to forgive him.
RECOGNITION

452) This was the house (compound) in which Ms. Barbara Meier lived.

(37-40)	God sends rain which fills the river.
	LACK LIQUIDATED
(41)	No one can argue with God.
	MORAL

27.1 (41) '[...] one cannot argue with God.'

27.2 God is more powerful than anyone and anything else in the world. He rules over natural phenomena like rain and rivers.

IV. INDEX OF KEYWORDS

BUL-E0503 **Arrival** of son, returning with his wife from God's house, the son is announced to his parents and elders.

BUL-E1445 **Ascend,** supernatural women a. to the sky after having prepared food for a lone hunter absent in the bush.

BUL-E0426 **Ascend,** three women having come from the sky, a. again after having cooked food for three bachelors.

BUL-E1445 **Ashes,** 'A chief's son never refuses a.' (proverb).

BUL-E0426 **Ashes,** 'A chief may not walk over a.' (proverb).

BUL-E0503 **Ashes,** boy revived by his wife, God's daughter, from the a. to which he was burnt.

BUL-E0572 **Ashes,** God says that a ram represents the a. placed before a father who is about to sacrifice his daughter to an earth-shrine (*tanggbain*).

BUL-E0426 **Ashes,** junior brother blows a. and stops women from returning to the sky.

BUL-E0182 **Ashes,** junior brother takes a. into his hiding place and spreads them to prevent women from the sky from returning to the sky.

BUL-E0489 **Ashes** placed before earth-shrine (*tanggbain*) after brother has been killed by relative in a girl's stead;

BUL-E1435 **Ashes,** supernatural being throws a. to save girl from being killed by her parents;

BUL-E0259 **Assemble,** people a. to sacrifice a girl at an earth-shrine (*tanggbain*).

BUL-E0426 **Bachelors,** at noon, three fair-skinned women come from the sky to cook millet porridge for three b.

BUL-E0426 **Bachelors,** three b. live alone in a house and go to make a bush farm without the help of wives.

BUL-E0182 **Bachelors,** three b. live together in one house and go farming in the bush.

BUL-E1445 **Barn,** women from the sky (God) take millet from a hunter's b. in order to prepare food for him during his absence.

BUL-E0572 **Barren** woman gives birth to children after her husband consulted an earth-shrine (*tang-gbain*).

BUL-E0761 **Barren** woman gives birth to a girl after having consulted an earth-shrine (*teng*).

BUL-E1267 **Barren** woman gives birth to a girl after having consulted an earth-shrine (*teng*).

BUL-E0259 **Barren** woman is loved by her husband who wants a child from her; she gives birth to a girl after having consulted an earth-shrine (*teng*).

BUL-E0438 **Beard** of a *kikiruk* covers a whole river.

BUL-E0438 **Beard-Covers-River** follows Common-Son-Of-Ten-Women when the latter goes hunting.

BUL-E0503 **Cap,** chief's c. taken away from him and given to boy after the boy returned from God with many men, women and riches.

BUL-E0674 **Care,** God created human beings and fowls in pairs so that they should take c. of each other.

BUL-E0225 **Carry,** girl has to c. the millet beer she brewed to the earth-shrine (*tanggbain*) to which she will be sacrificed.

BUL-E0259 **Carry,** mother orders her daughter to c. the millet beer to be used at the girl's sacrifice.

BUL-E0761 **Carry,** mother orders her daughter to c. the millet beer to be used at the girl's sacrifice.

BUL-E0438 **Case,** God is to judge c. between Common-Son-Of-Ten-Women and God's bull.

BUL-E0182 **Cat** brushes against food and women to show the husband of a woman from the sky the ones he should choose.

BUL-E0182 **Cat** comes to see the husband of a woman from the sky who sleeps on a platform roof.

BUL-E0182 **Cat** helps husband of a woman from the sky to identify his own wife and the wives of his brothers.

BUL-E0426 **Cat** helps man to identify his wife and his brothers' wives in the sky.

BUL-E0426 **Cat** receives cow's meat for showing a man his and his brothers' wives in the sky.

BUL-E0182 **Cat,** the husband of a woman from the sky gives c. meat so that it can eat to its satisfaction.

BUL-E0426 **Cat** warns man of his imminent death in the sky.

BUL-E0182 **Cattle yard,** bush cow standing in the c. y. of God's house is junior brother of woman from the sky.

BUL-E0292 **Cattle yard,** girl is brought into a c. y. in order to be killed.

BUL-E0008 **Cattle yard**, girl comes out of her room where she had been hidden since infancy, and stands in the c.y. singing her own mourning song.

BUL-E1435 **Cattle yard,** girl, to be killed by her parents, is taken from her mother's room into the c.y. before being taken out of the house.

BUL-E0674 **Ceremony,** a fowl is used (sacrificed) first in every religious c.

Change, see Transform, Retransform.

BUL-E0426 **Chicken coop,** one of three bachelors hides in a c. c. to see who prepares millet porridge for them.

BUL-E0182 **Chicken coop,** three brothers hide in a c.c. to watch women from the sky.

BUL-E0674 **Chickens,** hen breeds with c., whereas primeval woman does not know how to have sexual intercourse or how to give birth.

BUL-E0761	**God** does not approve of the killing of human beings; he asks men to kill animals in their stead.
BUL-E1435	**God** ensures that women are not killed (slaughtered), but that they may live on earth as well as men;
BUL-E0503	**God,** father of half-woman, has his house in the underworld.
BUL-E0674	**God** gives a hen and a cock to primeval human couple.
BUL-E0503	**God** gives his daughter and her husband many riches on their way home: ninety girls, one hundred men and their wives, twenty horses etc.
BUL-E1328	**God,** Hare begs G. to send him a hoe, farm products and an animal to take with him into the realm of the dead.
BUL-E0438	**God** has to judge the case between Common-Son-Of-Ten-Women and God's bull.
BUL-E0182	**God** in the shape of a male dog with eyes wide open greets his son-in-law in the courtyard.
BUL-E1698	**God** leaves man and retires to sky.
BUL-E0402	**God** lets Moon die and return, Man die and remain dead.
BUL-E1698	**God,** man should cut G. as meat (food).
BUL-E1856	**God,** no one can challenge G.
BUL-E1698	**God** offers himself as food (meat) to man.
BUL-E1267	**God,** old woman comes down from the sky (from G.) to prevent people from sacrificing a girl to an earth-shrine (*tanggbain*).
BUL-E0572	**God** orders men to vow and sacrifice animals, not human beings, to earth-shrines (*tanggba-na*).
BUL-E0674	**God** provides human beings and fowls with food.
BUL-E0438	**God** pulls Common-Son-Of-Ten-Women and his bull up to the sky.
BUL-E0402	**God** receives wrong message about Man's death.
BUL-E0514	**God** revives dead chief with magic tail.
BUL-E0438	**God** sees that Common-Son-Of-Ten-Women is so strong that God's bull cannot overcome him.
BUL-E0761	**God** sends animals from the sky to be sacrificed in a girl's stead.
BUL-E0438	**God** sends his bull from the sky down to earth to take away Common-Son-Of-Ten-Women's meat.
BUL-E0503	**God** sends his daughter, disguised as a half-woman, to earth in order to force a man to marry her.

BUL-E0259 **Malt,** girl dries m. to prepare millet beer to be offered to an earth-shrine (*tanggbain*) before she herself is sacrificed to it.

BUL-E0572 **Malt,** mother measures and grinds m. used for millet beer when her daughter is to be sacrificed to an earth-shrine (*tanggbain*).

BUL-E0761 **Malt,** mother orders her daughter to grind the m. for the millet beer to be used at the girl's sacrifice.

BUL-E0514 **Maltreat,** chief's daughter m.s her husband, a leper (God), by shitting and pissing into his food.

BUL-E0402 **Man** and Moon return from death.

BUL-E0674 **Man** and woman receive a cock and a hen from God.

BUL-E0920 **Man,** brother says that you need a sister to become a m.

BUL-E0514 **Man,** chief's daughter must not speak to any m., otherwise she must marry him.

BUL-E0402 **Man** dies and returns from death at the beginning of the Earth.

BUL-E1698 **Man** had to work in order to get food after an old woman violated God's command not to add a certain spice (*kaam*) to the meat cut off from (Fall of m.).

BUL-E1267 **Man** promises a child to an earth-shrine (*tanggbain*), if he begets children.

BUL-E0489 **Man** promises the Earth his daughter, if his wife gives birth to many children.

BUL-E0674 **Mankind,** in former times, m. and fowl understood each other's language (had been on good terms).

BUL-E0514 **Market,** chief's daughter and leper (God) on m.

BUL-E1445 **Marriage,** origin of m.: hunter begs women from the sky (God) to stay in his house and cook for him.

BUL-E0514 **Marry,** chief's daughter has to m. leper (God) because she broke a taboo against speaking.

BUL-E0514 **Marry,** chief's daughter refuses to m.

BUL-E1445 **Marry,** man m.ies women from the sky (God).

BUL-E1328 **Marry,** Hare marries chief's daughter on the condition of his being buried when his mother-in-law dies.

BUL-E0503 **Marry,** man marries half-woman after she has demonstrated her power to kill him if he refuses.

BUL-E0503 **Marry,** man refuses to m.

BUL-E0182 **Marry,** three brothers m. women from the sky.

BUL-E0426 **Maternal relatives** of women from the sky, God's daughters, live in Sun's house.

BUL-E0572 **Pity,** mother feels p. for her daughter who is to be sacrificed to an earth-shrine (*tanggbain*).

BUL-E0182 **Platform roof,** the husband of a woman from the sky sleeps on a p. r.

BUL-E1445 **Polygamy,** hunter marries several women from the sky (God).

BUL-E0572 **Pound,** girl helps her mother p. shea-nuts to prepare oil that is to be used in her sacrifice to an earth-shrine (*tanggbain*).

BUL-E0674 **Pound,** primeval woman p.s millet in a mortar.

BUL-E0225 **Pour,** girl p.s the millet beer of her death [in a song].

BUL-E0259 **Pour,** girl p.s the millet beer of her death [in a song].

BUL-E0259 **Pour,** girl p.s the millet beer into another vessel.

BUL-E0225 **Pour,** people p. libation to an earth-shrine (*tanggbain*) with millet beer brewed by the girl to be sacrificed.

BUL-E0920 **Pour,** water p.s down from the sky and quenches fire in which a girl was about to burn herself.

BUL-E0674 **Pregnancy** occurs three days after having had sexual intercourse.

BUL-E0438 **Pregnant**, ten women are p. with one and the same son: Common-Son-Of-Ten-Women.

BUL-E0674 **Pregnant,** woman does not know how to become p.

BUL-E1445 **Prepare,** women come down from the sky (God) and p. millet-porridge and other kinds of food for hunter.

BUL-E1328 **Pretend,** Hare's mother-in-law p.s to be dead.

BUL-E0514 **Pretend,** leper (God) p.s to feed puppies through their anuses in order to make chief's daughter talk.

BUL-E0674 **Primeval** human couple does not know how to perform sexual intercourse.

BUL-E0674 **Procreate,** fowl teaches human beings how to p.

BUL-E0761 **Promise,** barren woman p.s to sacrifice her first-born child to an earth-shrine (*teng*) if it makes her fecund.

BUL-E0572 **Promise,** God orders that any animal may be p.ed as sacrifice to an earth-shrine (*tanggbain*), but not human beings.

BUL-E1328 **Promise,** Hare p.s to be buried when his mother-in-law dies.

BUL-E1267 **Promise,** man p.s a child to an earth-shrine (*tanggbain*), if he begets children.

BUL-E0489 **Promise,** man p.s to sacrifice his daughter to the Earth, if his wife gives birth to many children;

BUL-E1435 **Room,** senior brother has to take his sister out of her room (house?) nine days after she has been born so that she may be killed.

BUL-E0292 **Room,** woman hides and nurses her only daughter in a r.

BUL-E0674 **Room,** woman performs first sexual intercourse with a man in a r.

BUL-E0438 **Ropes,** God pulls Common-Son-Of-Ten-Women and his bull up into the sky with r.

BUL-E0008 **Rubbish heap,** girl is to be killed on the r. h.

BUL-E1328 **Rubbish heap,** Hare begs God for a hoe, farm products and an animal while standing on top of a r. h.;

BUL-E0182 **Rubbish heap,** leopard jumps out from behind a r. h. and threatens husbands of women in the sky.

BUL-E0426 **Run away,** senior and middle brothers r.a. when they meet wild animals in their wives' house in the sky.

BUL-E0514 ***Saab*** (millet porridge), chief's daughter shits and pisses into the *s.* she prepares for her husband, a leper.

BUL-E0426 ***Saab*** (millet porridge) cooked by women coming down from the sky.

BUL-E0503 ***Saab*** (millet porridge) given to half-woman to eat.

BUL-E0514 ***Saab*** (millet porridge), leper pretends to feed puppies with *s.* through their anuses in order to make chief's daughter talk.

BUL-E1267 **Sacrifice,** an earth-shrine (*tanggbain*) demands beautiful (fair-skinned) girl as a s.

BUL-E0225 **Sacrifice,** animals are to be s.d instead of human beings (girls).

BUL-E0225 **Sacrifice,** chief's daughter is to be s.d to an earth-shrine (*tanggbain*).

BUL-E0572 **Sacrifice,** childless husband and his wife promise to s. a child to an earth-shrine (*tanggbain*) if it gives them children.

BUL-E0259 **Sacrifice,** earth-shrine (*tanggbain*) claims s. of firstborn child for making barren wife fecund.

BUL-E0761 **Sacrifice,** God sends down animals to be sacrificed in a girl's stead.

BUL-E0259 **Sacrifice,** God sends ram from the sky to be used as a s. in a girl's stead.

BUL-E0572 **Sacrifice,** God sends ram from the sky to be used as a s. in a girl's stead.

BUL-E1267 **Sacrifice,** human beings are not to be used as s.s to a shrine.

BUL-E0572 **Sacrifice,** human s. substituted by animal s.

BUL-E1435 **Sacrifice,** in former times women (girls) were killed and s.d.

BUL-E0514 **Speak,** leper (God) makes chief's daughter s. again by pretending to feed puppies through their anuses.

BUL-E0426 **Speechless,** bachelor is s. after having watched three women from the sky who prepared food for him and his brothers.

BUL-E0438 **Splash,** Common-Son-Of-Ten-Women s.es water in a river, thereby provoking Beard-Covers-River.

BUL-E0514 **Spoil,** father of chief's wife, after having been resuscitated by God's magic tail, s.s it by taking it into a room.

BUL-E0438 **Steal,** God's bull s.s Common-Son-Of-Ten-Women's meat.

BUL-E0259 **Stir,** girl s.s millet beer to be offered to an earth-shrine (*tanggbain*) before she herself is sacrificed to it.

BUL-E0225 **Stir,** girl s.s the millet beer of her death [in a song].

BUL-E0426 **Stop,** junior brother blows ashes and s.s women from returning to the sky.

BUL-E0438 **Strength,** Common-Son-Of-Ten-Women has remarkable s.

BUL-E0514 **Strike,** leper (God) s.s the body of his dead father-in-law and revives him with a tail.

BUL-E1698 **Suffer,** man has to s. after God withdrew from Earth because an old woman violated a taboo.

BUL-E0920 **Suicide,** girl is about to commit s. by throwing herself into a fire when a being coming from the sky saves her.

BUL-E0514 **Suitors,** chief's daughter refuses all her s.; in the end she has to marry a leper.

BUL-E0259 **Suitors** refused because girl is promised to be sacrificed to an earth-shrine (*tanggbain*).

BUL-E0426 **Sun,** maternal relatives of women from the sky, God's daughters, live in the s.'s house and eat human flesh.

BUL-E1328 **Supernatural being** comes down from the sky and helps Hare by giving him advice.

BUL-E0920 **Supernatural being** comes from the sky (God) and saves girl from throwing herself into a fire.

BUL-E1435 **Supernatural being** comes from the sky and asks people not to kill (slaughter) the girl.

BUL-E1435 **Supernatural being,** half-animal, half-human, saves girl from being killed by her parents;

BUL-E1445 **Supernatural women** come down from the sky and prepare food for a hunter.

BUL-E0426 **Supernatural women,** three s.w. come down from the sky.

BUL-E0438 **Suspend,** God s.s judgment of the case between Common-Son-Of-Ten-Women and God's bull.

V. INDEX OF MOTIFS

0000uncl.	BUL-E0225:005-008	Chief orders all girls to be killed.
0000uncl.	BUL-E0761:006-	Millet beer is prepared for ceremony performed on a girl (daughter) who is to be sacrificed to an earth-shrine (*teng*).
0000uncl.	BUL-E1328:029-051	Hare begs God to send him a hoe, farm products and an animal's young to take with him into the realm of the dead.
0000uncl.	BUL-E1435:014-	Outdoor ceremony performed on a girl (daughter) who is to be killed.
A0000ff.+	BUL-E0674:001-002	Creator; here: God creates husband and wife and gives them fowls, a hen and a cock.
A0021.1+	BUL-E0182:007-	Woman who falls from the sky; here: Three women, God's daughters, descend from the sky to cook food for three brothers (bachelors).
A0021.1+	BUL-E0426:012-	Woman who falls from the sky; here: Three women, God's daughters, descend from the sky to cook food for three bachelors.
A0081.0	BUL-E1698:006	Creator goes to sky.
A0101.0+	BUL-E0402:002-	Supreme God; here: God lets Man die and return and Moon die and remain dead.
A0101.1+	BUL-E0674:001-002	Supreme God as creator; here: God creates husband and wife and gives them fowls, a hen and a cock.
A0102.4+	BUL-E1856:002-	Omnipotent god; here: God rules over the waters (rain).
A0103.0+	BUL-E0503:034-	Father God; here: God, who is half-woman's father, has his house in the underworld.
A0125.0+	BUL-E0514:006-	Deity in human form; here: God turns into a leper and marries chief's daughter.
A0125.4+	BUL-E0503:041-044	Beautiful goddess; here: God's daughter, a half-woman, turns into a beautiful woman in her father's house.
A0153.8+	BUL-E0182:073-080	Cannibal gods; here: The Sky-god's daughters visit their relatives in the sky, who prepare human flesh for their youngest husband.
A0153.8+	BUL-E0426:149	Cannibal gods; here: The Sky-god's daughters visit their maternal relatives in Sun's house, where they receive human flesh.

A0164.0+	BUL-E0008:059	Marriage or liason of gods; here: People living in God's house are men and women (married).
A0165.2+	BUL-E0008:056	Messengers of the gods; here: God (sky-god) sends a woman to prevent the slaughtering of a girl.
A0165.2+	BUL-E0292:030	Messengers of the gods; here: God (sky-god) sends a ram to prevent the slaughtering of a girl.
A0171.0.3+	BUL-E1445:004-	God descends from heaven; here: Women from the sky (God) descend and prepare food for lone hunter while he is absent in the bush.
A0179.6+	BUL-E0674:001-002	God has power to create men; here: God creates husband and wife.
A0180.0+	BUL-E0503:007-	God in relation to mortals; here: God sends his daughter, disguised as a half-woman, to earth in order to force a man to marry her.
A0180.0+	BUL-E0514:006-	God in relation to mortals; here: God turns into a leper and marries chief's daughter;
A0189.0+	BUL-E1328:029-051	Gods in relation to mortals - miscellaneous; here: God, begged by Hare, sends him a hoe, farm products and an animal's young;
A0196.2+	BUL-E0420:011-012	Decree of Gods irrevocable; here: God's decree that Man will die and not return, Moon will die and return, is irrevocable.
A0205.0+	BUL-E0426:149-150	Witch-woman of the upper world; here: In sun's house live maternal relatives of God's daughters, who become witches by eating human flesh.
A0210.0+	BUL-E0008:059	Sky-god; here: People in God's house are of both sexes (men and women).
A0210.0+	BUL-E0182:007-	Sky-god; here: Three women, God's daughters, descend from the sky to cook food for three bachelors.
A0210.0+	BUL-E0225:096	Sky-God; here: Sky-God sends a ram to save girl from being sacrificed.
A0210.0+	BUL-E0259:141-	Sky-God; here: Sky-God sends a ram and orders it to be sacrificed instead of a human being.
A0210.0+	BUL-E0292:030-031	Sky-God; here: Ram, sent down from the sky, is to be killed in a girl's stead.
A0210.0+	BUL-E0402:002-	Sky-god; here: At the beginning, God lets Man die and return, and Moon die and remain dead.

A0210.0+	BUL-E0438:017-	Sky-god; here: God sends his bull from the sky to take away Common-Son-Of-Ten-Women's meat.
A0210.0+	BUL-E0438:049	Sky-god; here: God pulls wrestling pair of Common-Son-Of-Ten-Women and his bull up into the sky.
A0210.0+	BUL-E0438:050	Sky-god; here: God has to judge the case between his bull and Common-Son-Of-Ten-Women.
A0210.0+	BUL-E0462:012-	Sky-god; here: Three women, God's daughters, descend from the sky to cook food for three bachelors.
A0210.0+	BUL-E0489:017-027	Sky-God; here: Brothers prophesy that God will help in a wonderful way to save their sister from being sacrificed.
A0210.0+	BUL-E0572:097-099	Sky-God; here: Sky-God sends a ram to be sacrificed instead of a human being (girl).
A0210.0+	BUL-E0761:080-082	Sky-God; here: God sends down animals and birds to be sacrificed in a girl's stead.
A0210.0+	BUL-E0920:029	Sky-god; here: Supernatural being from the sky (God) saves girl from being sacrificed;
A0210.0+	BUL-E1267:022-025	Sky-god; here: Old woman comes down from the sky (sky-god) to prevent people from sacrificing a girl to an earth-shrine (*tanggbain*);
A0210.0+	BUL-E1328:029-051	Sky-god; here: God, begged by Hare, sends him a hoe, farm products and a domestic animal.
A0210.0+	BUL-E1435:035	Sky-God; here: God sends down a being from the sky who saves girl from being killed.
A0210.0+	BUL-E1445:004-	Sky-god; here: Women from the sky (God) descend to earth and prepare food for lone hunter.
A0210.0+	BUL-E1698:001,006	Sky-god; here: God (Naawen), identified with the sky, ascends after an old woman broke a taboo.
A0210.0+	BUL-E1856:001-	Sky-god; here: Sky-god and a river argue with one another over who is dependent on whom.
A0210.0+	BUL-E1856:003-	Sky-god; here: Sky-god controls the water (rain).
A0210.0+	BUL-E1856:033	Sky-god; here: No one can argue with the sky (God).
A0220.2+	BUL-E0462:149	The sun-god and his family; here: God's daughters visit their maternal relatives in Sun's house, where they receive human flesh. (Origin of witchcraft)
A0287.0+	BUL-E1856:011-	Rain-god; here: Sky-god controls the water (rain).

A0300.0+	BUL-E0503:023-	God of the underworld; here: Hole under termite hill leads to God's house.
A0400.0+	BUL-E0489:002	God of earth; here: Man promises the Earth to give it his daughter, if his wife gives birth to many children.
A0400.0+	BUL-E0489:005	God of earth; here: Earth reminds man to 'pay his debt', i.e. to sacrifice his daughter to it.
A0521.0+	BUL-E1328:029-051	Culture hero as trickster; here: Hare asks God to send him a hoe, farm products and a domestic animal. He threatens to take them away into the realm of the dead.
A0522.1.2+	BUL-E1328:029-051	Rabbit as Culture Hero; here: Hare asks God to send him a hoe, farm products and a domestic animal.
A0625.2	BUL-E1698:006	Raising of the sky. Originally the sky is near the Earth [...]. It is raised to its present place.
A0670.0+	BUL-E0503:023-	Nature of the lower world; here: Hole under termite hill leads to God's house.
A0702.0+	BUL-E1698:006	Nature of the sky; here: God, identical with the sky, retreats from the Earth after an old woman broke a taboo.
A0711.2+	BUL-E0426:149	Sun as a cannibal; here: Two daughters of God, married to bachelors, branch off to visit their maternal parents, who serve them human flesh in a soup.
A0736.0+	BUL-E0426:149	Sun as a human being; here: Sun is living in a house where maternal relatives of God's daughters live. They eat human flesh; in this way witchcraft originates.
A0755.0+	BUL-E0402:001	Causes of moon's phases; here: Moon's phases related to death of Man (confounded message).
A0930.1+	BUL-E1856:003-	Creator of rivers; sky (God) claims that he is the ruler of a river which says it is not dependent on the sky (God).
A1131.0+	BUL-E1856:010-	Origin of rain; here: God is the origin of rain.
A1142.1+	BUL-E0259:138	Creator's (deity's) voice makes thunder; here: Thunder comes from the sky (God) when a ram is sent down to be sacrificed to an earth-shrine in a girl's stead.
A1142.9+	BUL-E0438:051	Thunder made by giants in the sky; here: God's bull and Common-Son-Of-Ten-Women wrestle in the sky and thereby cause thunder.
A1210ff.+	BUL-E0674:001-002	Creation of man by creator; here: God creates husband and wife.
A1270.1	BUL-E0674:001-008	Primeval human pair live in innocence.

A1277.0+	BUL-E0674:001-038	Offspring of first parents; here: Primeval human couple beget a child (son) after learning from fowl how to perform sexual intercourse.
A1300.0+	BUL-E0182:038,115-	Ordering human life; here: How women coming from the sky came to live on earth.
A1330.0+	BUL-E0426:149-151	Beginning of trouble for man; here: Origin of witchcraft: Cannibals on the sun give God's daughters human flesh to eat.
A1331.1.1+	BUL-E1698:008-	Paradise lost because of forbidden food; here: Paradise lost because of forbidden spice added to pieces of meat which man cut off from God.
A1335.0+	BUL-E0402:001-	Origin of death; here: Moon and Man exchange fates of dying and returning from death.
A1335.1	BUL-E0402:001-	Origin of death from falsified message.
A1335.1.1	BUL-E0402:005	Origin of death: wrong messenger goes to God.
A1346.0	BUL-E1698:008,010	Man to earn bread by sweat of his brow.
A1346.2.2	BUL-E1698:001-	First people have everything they wish (life without work).
A1352.0+	BUL-E0674:034	Origin of sexual intercourse; here: Fowls (hen and cock) demonstrate to human couple how to have sexual intercourse.
A1372.0+	BUL-E0225:097	Origin of other special characteristics of women; here: The reason why nowadays women are not used as sacrifices.
A1372.0+	BUL-E1435:040-041	Origin of other special characteristics of women; here: The reason why there are women on earth.
A1420.0+	BUL-E1328:029-051	Acquisition of food supply for human race; here: Hare asks God to send him a hoe and 'things a hoe produces' (farm products).
A1420.4+	BUL-E1698:001-	Food originally obtained without effort; here: God offers himself as food.
A1441.0+	BUL-E1328:029-051	Acquisition of agriculture; here: Hare asks God to send him a hoe and 'the things a hoe produces' (farm products).
A1443.0+	BUL-E1328:029-051	Origin of domestication of animals; here: Hare asks God to send him a [domestic] animal.
A1455.0+	BUL-E1445:003-	Origin of cooking; here: Women from the sky (God) descend to earth and cook food for lone hunter.
A1470.0+	BUL-E0182:038,115-	Beginning of social relationships; here: Women coming from the sky married men and came to live on earth.

A1472.0+	BUL-E1445:067-	Beginning of division of labour; here: Women from the sky come to prepare food for lone hunter who suggests that they stay together in his house.
A1516.0+	BUL-E0426:149-151	Origin of cannibalism; here: Cannibals on the sun cook human flesh and give it to God's daughters to eat.
A1541.0+	BUL-E0674:001-	Origin of religious ceremonials; here: Why a fowl is used in every religious ritual.
A1545.2+	BUL-E0259:136-146	Animal substituted for human sacrifice; here: Ram is sent by God to be sacrificed in a girl's stead.
A1545.2+	BUL-E0292:030-031	Animal substituted for human sacrifice; here: Ram, coming down from the sky, is to be killed in a girl's stead.
A1545.2+	BUL-E0572:097-099	Animal substituted for human sacrifice; here: Ram is sent by God to be sacrificed instead of a human being (girl).
A1545.2+	BUL-E0761:081-082	Animal substituted for human sacrifice; here: Animals are sent by God to be sacrificed in a girl's stead.
A1545.3.0+	BUL-E0225:096	Origin of animal sacrifices; here: Ram, sent by God, to be sacrificed instead of human being (girl).
A1545.3.0+	BUL-E0259:138-146	Origin of animal sacrifices; here: Ram, sent by God, to be sacrificed instead of human being (girl).
A1545.3.0+	BUL-E0292:030-031	Origin of animal sacrifices; here: Ram, coming down from the sky, is to be killed instead of a human being (a girl).
A1545.3.0+	BUL-E0572:097-099	Origin of animal sacrifices; here: Ram is sent by God to be sacrificed instead of a human being (girl).
A1545.3.0+	BUL-E0761:080-082	Origin of animal sacrifices; here: God sends down animals and tells people that they should use them as sacrifices instead of human beings.
A1545.3.3	BUL-E0674:001-	Origin of cock sacrifice.
A1547.1+	BUL-E0674:058-	Origin of funeral sacrifices; here: Origin of funeral sacrifices: custom to first sacrifice a fowl.
A1549.0+	BUL-E0503:092	Origin of religious ceremonials - miscellaneous; here: Origin of the custom to use new calabashes in performing rituals.
A1555.0+	BUL-E1445:067-	Origin of marriage; here: Hunter asks women from the sky (God) to stay in his house and to prepare his food.
A2435.3.2+	BUL-E0182:074-	Food of cat; here: Cat in the sky eats meat to its satisfaction.

A2496.0+	BUL-E0674:034	Sexual intercourse of animals; here: Cock and hen demonstrate to human couple how to have sexual intercourse.
A2525.1	BUL-E1328:056	Why hare is deceptive.
B0007.0+	BUL-E0438:051	Animals in the heavens; here: God's bull in the sky causes thunderstorms by wrestling with Common-Son-Of-Ten-Women.
B0015.4+	BUL-E0438:017	Animals with unusual eyes; here: God's bull is one-eyed.
B0015.7+	BUL-E0438:017	Other animals with unusual limbs or members; here: God's bull is one-eyed, has one hind leg and one foreleg.
B0020.0+	BUL-E1435:036	Beast-men; here: Supernatural being, coming from the sky, half-human, half-animal (with hairs on its hindquarters).
B0122.1+	BUL-E0674:034	Bird as adviser; here: Fowls demonstrate to human couple how to have sexual intercourse.
B0143.1+	BUL-E0225:012-094	Bird gives warning; here: Bird announces girl's death.
B0143.1+	BUL-E0259:009-	Bird gives warning; here: Bird warns girl that the beer she brews will be her 'death beer'.
B0172.2+	BUL-E0225:012-094	Magic bird's song; here: Bird announces girl's death by singing a song.
B0172.2+	BUL-E0259:009-	Magic bird's song; here: Bird warns girl in a song that the beer she brews will be her 'death beer'.
B0181.1+	BUL-E0182:073-	Magic cat; here: Cat helps junior brother to avoid eating human flesh and to identify his wife and his brothers' wives in the sky.
B0181.1+	BUL-E0426:109-	Magic cat; here: Cat helps junior brother to identify his wife and his brothers' wives in the sky.
B0211.1.2+	BUL-E0402:005-006	Speaking goat; here: Speaking goat takes false message of Man's and Moon's death to God.
B0211.1.7+	BUL-E0402:009-010	Speaking dog; here: Speaking dog fails to take message about Man's and Moon's death to God in time.
B0211.1.8+	BUL-E0182:074-	Speaking cat; here: Cat speaks to man, telling him how to avoid eating human flesh and how to identify his wife and his brothers' wives.
B0211.1.8+	BUL-E0426:109-	Speaking cat; here: Cat speaks to man, telling him how to behave at his imminent death.
B0211.2.6	BUL-E1328:005-	Speaking hare (rabbit).

B0211.3.0+	BUL-E0225:012-094	Speaking bird; here: Bird announces girl's death by singing a song.
B0211.3.0+	BUL-E0259:013-	Speaking bird; here: Bird announces death of girl in a song.
B0211.3.2	BUL-E0674:022-028	Speaking cock.
B0214.1+	BUL-E0225:012-094	Singing animal; here: Bird announces girl's death by singing a song.
B0214.1+	BUL-E0259:009-	Singing animal; here: Bird announces death of a girl in a song.
B0214.1+	BUL-E1328:008-	Singing animal; here: Singing hare.
B0214.4+	BUL-E1328:008-	Weeping animal; here: Weeping hare.
B0250.0+	BUL-E0674:001-	Religious animals; here: A fowl is used in every religious ritual (sacrifice).
B0291.2.0+	BUL-E0402:005-006	Domestic beast as messenger; here: Goat as messenger.
B0291.2.2+	BUL-E0402:003-010	Dog as messenger; here: Dog fails to bring message when it sees food.
B0322.0+	BUL-E0182:074	Helpful animal demands food; here: Helpful cat demands meat and promises to help human being in return.
B0322.0+	BUL-E0426:111	Helpful animal demands food; here: Helpful cat demands cow's meat from man in the sky.
B0322.0+	BUL-E0674:028-034	Helpful animal demands food; here: Cock demands millet for demonstrating to human couple how to have sexual intercourse.
B0391.0+	BUL-E0182:074-	Animal grateful for food; here: Cat helps junior brother after he has given it meat.
B0391.0+	BUL-E0426:111	Animal grateful for food; here: Cat offers man its help for letting it eat his cow's meat until it is satisfied.
B0391.0+	BUL-E0674:028-034	Animal grateful for food; here: Cock demonstrates to human couple how to have sexual intercourse after receiving millet from man.
B0422.0+	BUL-E0182:077-110	Helpful cat; here: Cat helps junior brother to avoid eating human flesh and to identify his wife and his brothers' wives in the sky.
B0422.0+	BUL-E0426:110-145	Helpful cat; here: Cat helps man to identify his wife and his brothers' wives in the sky.

B0469.5+	BUL-E0674:034	Helpful cock; here: Cock demonstrates to human couple how to have sexual intercourse.
B0529.0+	BUL-E0426:109-	Animal saves person's life - miscellaneous; here: Cat saves man's life by helping him to identify his wife and his brother's wives in the sky.
B0569.0+	BUL-E0674:034	Animals advise men; here: Fowls demonstrate to human couple how to have sexual intercourse.
B0599.0+	BUL-E0182:074-110	Other services of helpful animals; here: Cat helps man to avoid eating human flesh and to identify his wife and his brothers' wives in the sky.
B0599.0+	BUL-E0426:109-	Other services of helpful animals; here: Cat helps man to identify his wife and his brothers' wives in the sky.
B0601.13+	BUL-E1328:004-006	Marriage to hare; here: Hare marries chief's daughter;
B0800.0+	BUL-E0182:043-066	Miscellaneous animal motifs; here: Wild animals (leopard, bush cow, python) in the sky are transformed domestic animals and human relatives of the Sky-god's daughters.
B0800.0+	BUL-E0426:071-105	Miscellaneous animal motifs; here: Domestic animals in father-in-law's compound (dog, goat, flies) are in reality transformed ferocious beasts (leopard, lion, bees).
C0031.3+	BUL-E0503:010-	Taboo: disobeying supernatural wife; here: God's daughter makes man die and revive when he disobeys her order.
C0060.0+	BUL-E1698:004-	Taboo: offending the gods; here: Taboo on offending God by adding a certain spice to meat cut off from him.
C0210.0+	BUL-E0514:055	Tabu: eating in certain place; here: Medicine (magic substance) must not be taken (eaten) in the presence of women.
C0221.0+	BUL-E1698:004	Taboo: eating meat; here: Taboo on eating meat cut off from God together with a certain spice.
C0400.0+	BUL-E0514:005-	Speaking tabu; here: Chief's daughter not allowed to speak to any man after she refused to marry.
C0600.0+	BUL-E0514:047	Unique prohibition; here: Taboo on taking magic tail, used to resuscitate people, into a room.
C0600.0+	BUL-E1698:004-	Unique prohibition; here: Man is not allowed to eat meat together with a particular spice.
C0900.0+	BUL-E0514:021-023	Punishment for breaking taboo; here: Father forces his daughter to marry leper who succeeded in making her speak to him (breach of taboo).

C0900.0+	BUL-E0514:053	Punishment for breaking taboo; here: Magic tail loses its power to resuscitate dead persons when taken into a room.
C0901.1+	BUL-E0514:005-	Taboo imposed by certain person; here: Chief imposes taboo on daughter not to talk to any man because she refused to marry.
C0901.1+	BUL-E0514:047	Taboo imposed by certain person; here: Taboo imposed by God: magic tail, used to resuscitate people, must not be taken into a room.
C0937.0+	BUL-E1698:006-	God's favour lost for breaking taboo; here: Taboo of using a particular spice together with pieces of meat cut off from God.
C0987.0+	BUL-E1698:006-010	Curse as punishment for breaking taboo; here: God curses man after an old woman broke a taboo when using a certain spice together with meat cut off from God;
D0027.0+	BUL-E0514:006	Transformation into leper; here: God turns into leper and marries chief's daughter.
D0042.0+	BUL-E0503:007-	God in guise of mortal; here: God's daughter comes in guise of half-woman to a man who refuses to marry any woman;
D0042.0+	BUL-E0514:006-	God in guise of mortal; here: God turns into leper and marries chief's daughter.
D0112.1+	BUL-E0182:053,061	Transformation: man to lion; here: Senior brother of Sky-god's daughter transformed into lion.
D0114.1+	BUL-E0182:054,62	Transformation: man to bovine animal (wild); here: Junior brother of Sky-god's daughter transformed into bush cow.
D0141.0+	BUL-E0182:055,063	Transformation: man to dog; here: Sky-god transformed into dog.
D0191.0+	BUL-E0182:056,065	Transformation: man to serpent (snake); here: Mother of Sky-god's daughter transformed into python.
D0411.0+	BUL-E0182:052,058	Transformation: mammal (wild) to another animal; here: Leopard transformed into dog in the sky (God's house).
D0411.0+	BUL-E0426:071-	Transformation: mammal (wild) to another animal; here: Leopard transformed to dog in the sky (God's house).
D0411.0+	BUL-E0426:072-	Transformation: mammal (wild) to another animal; here: Lion transformed to billy-goat in the sky (God's house).
D0415.0+	BUL-E0426:073-	Transformation: insect into another animal; here: Bees transformed to flies in the sky (God's house).

D0431.2+	BUL-E0503:007	Transformation: tree to person; here: Half-woman comes out of the wood of a dead tree.
D0522.0+	BUL-E0503:089	Transformation through magic word; here: God's daughter resuscitates her burnt husband by speaking certain words.
D0659.0+	BUL-E0503:045	Miscellaneous reasons for voluntary transformation; here: As a man does not want to marry a woman, God sends his daughter in the form of a half-woman, who forces him to marry her.
D0681.0+	BUL-E0514:030-044	Mourning customs; here: Leper (God) goes to mourn at the funeral of his father-in-law.
D0811.0+	BUL-E0503:057	Magic object received from God; here: God gives magic egg and magic clod of earth to his daughter and her husband.
D0811.0+	BUL-E0514:047	Magic object received from God; here: Chief receives magic tail, used to resuscitate people, from God.
D0902.0+	BUL-E0920:030	Magic rain; here: Suddenly water pours down from the sky and quenches fire on which daughter is to be burnt.
D0931.1.2+	BUL-E0182:027-029	Magic ashes; here: Junior brother strews ashes in order to prevent women from returning to the sky.
D0931.1.2+	BUL-E0426:048-055	Magic ashes; here: Magic ashes prevent supernatural women from returning into the sky.
D0931.1.2+	BUL-E1435:037,041	Magic ashes; here: Supernatural being throws ashes to prevent people from killing a girl.
D0935.2+	BUL-E0503:057,067	Magic clay; here: Magic clod of clay dropped down turns into a big house.
D0965.2+	BUL-E0503:088	Magic calabash; here: New calabash used to gather ashes of burnt man in order to resuscitate him.
D1024.0+	BUL-E0503:057,067	Magic egg; here: Magic egg dropped down turns into river.
D1029.2+	BUL-E0514:045	Magic tail of animal; here: Magic tail used by leper (God) to resuscitate chief.
D1045.0+	BUL-E0259:006-	Magic beer; here: Girl is to brew beer to be offered to an earth-shrine along with herself.
D1241.0+	BUL-E0514:045-	Magic medicine; here: Magic substance in a tail, used to resuscitate people, must not be taken into a room.
D1242.0+	BUL-E0920:030	Magic water; here: Water pours down from the sky and quenches fire on which daughter is to be burnt.

D1273.1.1+	BUL-E0182:001-	Three as magic number; here: Three women from the sky cook food for three unmarried brothers.
D1273.1.1+	BUL-E0426:001-	Three as magic number; here: Three brothers, bachelors, marry three women who came down from the sky.
D1274.0+	BUL-E0514:045-	Magic fetish; here: Tail used as magic fetish to revive the dead.
D1347.0+	BUL-E0259:002-004	Magic object produces fecundity; here: Earth-shrine produces fecundity for barren wife.
D1347.0+	BUL-E0572:001-007	Magic object produces fecundity; here: Earth-shrine produces fecundity for barren wife.
D1347.0+	BUL-E0761:002-004	Magic object produces fecundity; here: Earth-shrine (*teng*) makes barren woman fecund.
D1347.0+	BUL-E1267:004	Magic object produces fecundity; here: Earth-shrine produces fecundity for barren couple.
D1380.8+	BUL-E1435:037,041	Magic ashes protect; here: Supernatural being throws ashes to protect girl from being killed.
D1391.1+	BUL-E0920:030	Miraculous rain extinguishes fire used at stake; here: Suddenly water pours down from the sky and quenches fire on which daughter is to be burnt.
D1566.0+	BUL-E0920:030	Magic object controls fire; here: Magic water pours down from the sky and quenches fire on which daughter is to be burnt.
D1610.35+	BUL-E1856:004-	Speaking river; here: River and God argue with one another over who is dependent on whom.
D1610.35+	BUL-E1856:016-021	Speaking river; here: River's children beg the sky (God) for rain.
D1710.0+	BUL-E0503:010-	Possession of magic powers; here: God's daughter makes her human husband die and revive.
D1726.0+	BUL-E0514:047	Magic power from deity; here: God gives chief magic tail by which people can be resuscitated.
D1753.0+	BUL-E0503:088-090	Magic power by jumping into the fire; here: God's daughter jumps into the fire in order to resuscitate her burnt husband from the ashes.
D1766.2+	BUL-E0259:003-	Magic results produced by sacrifices; here: Barren wife made fecund by promising sacrifice of firstborn child (girl) to earth-shrine.

D1766.2+	BUL-E0572:001-007	Magic results produced by sacrifices; here: Barren wife made fecund by promising the sacrifice of her firstborn child to an earth-shrine.
D1766.2+	BUL-E0761:002-004	Magic results produced by sacrifices; here: Barren wife made fecund by promising the sacrifice of her firstborn child to an earth-shrine (*teng*).
D1766.2+	BUL-E1267:002-004	Magic results produced by sacrifices; here: Childless couple begets children when man promises to sacrifice his daughter to an earth-shrine.
D1810.9+	BUL-E0514:047	Magic knowledge from God; here: Resuscitation by God's magic knowledge.
D1840.0+	BUL-E0503:088-090	Magic invulnerability; here: God's daughter jumps into the fire in order to resuscitate her burnt husband.
D1841.3+	BUL-E0920:029	Burning magically evaded; here: here: Supernatural thing, coming down from the sky (God), saves girl from being burnt.
D1853.0+	BUL-E0402:002	Immortality exchanged; here: Man and Moon exchange immortality because of false message.
D1925.0+	BUL-E0259:002-004	Fecundity magically induced; here: Earth-shrine agrees to make barren wife fecund in exchange for the sacrifice of her firstborn child.
D1925.0+	BUL-E0572:001-007	Fecundity magically induced; here: Earth-shrine agrees to make barren wife fecund in exchange for the sacrifice of her firstborn child.
D1925.0+	BUL-E0761:002-004	Fecundity magically induced; here: Earth-shrine (*teng*) makes barren wife fecund in exchange for the sacrifice of her firstborn child.
D1925.0+	BUL-E1267:002-004	Fecundity magically induced; here: Earth-shrine gives fecundity to childless couple when man promises to sacrifice his daughter.
D2020.0+	BUL-E0426:025,037	Magic dumbness; here: Two men are speechless (dumbfounded) when they have seen woman from the sky.
D2143.1+	BUL-E0920:030	Rain produced by magic; here: Suddenly water pours down from the sky and quenches fire on which daughter is to be burnt.
D2161.3.11+	BUL-E0259:002-	Barrenness magically cured; here: Barrenness of wife cured by powers of earth-shrine.
D2161.3.11+	BUL-E0572:001-007	Barrenness magically cured; here: Barrenness of wife cured by powers of earth-shrine.

D2161.3.11+	BUL-E0761:002-004	**Barrenness magically cured; here: Barren woman becomes fecund due to an earth-shrine (*teng*).**
D2161.3.11+	BUL-E1267:002-004	**Barrenness magically cured; here: Powers of an earth-shrine enable childless couple to beget children;**
E0001.0+	BUL-E0514:045	**Person comes to life; here: Leper (God) resuscitates chief by striking his dead body with a magic tail.**
E0011.0+	BUL-E0514:045	**Resuscitation by beating; here: Leper (God) resuscitates chief by striking his dead body with a magic tail.**
E0026.1+	BUL-E0503:010-	**Resuscitation by command to arise; here: God's daughter orders her human husband to die and to revive.**
E0050.0+	BUL-E0503:010-	**Resuscitation by magic; here: God's daughter makes her human husband die and revive several times.**
E0050.0+	BUL-E0514:045	**Resuscitation by magic; here: Leper (God) resuscitates chief by striking his dead body with a magic tail.**
E0064.0+	BUL-E0503:088-090	**Resuscitation by magic object; here: God's daughter uses new calabash when resuscitating her burnt husband from the ashes.**
E0064.16+	BUL-E0514:045	**Resuscitation by animal's tail; here: Leper (God) resuscitates chief by striking his dead body with a magic tail.**
E0121.1+	BUL-E0503:088-090	**Resuscitation by a god; here: Man, after being burnt to ashes, is resuscitated by the help of his wife, God's daughter.**
E0121.1+	BUL-E0514:045	**Resuscitation by a god; here: Leper (God) resuscitates chief by striking his dead body with a magic tail.**
E0151.0+	BUL-E0503:010-	**Repeated resuscitation; here: God's daughter makes her human husband die and revive several times.**
E0600.1+	BUL-E0402:002	**Origin of reincarnation: miscarried message of immortality; here: Moon reincarnated, whereas Man has to die because of false message.**
F0010.0+	BUL-E0182:039-	**Journey to upper world; here: Women from the sky return to their parents' home together with their husbands.**
F0010.0+	BUL-E0426:065-	**Journey to upper world; here: Women from the sky return to their parents' home together with their husbands.**
F0010.1+	BUL-E0182:044-	**Return from upper world; here: Two elder brothers flee from the sky; junior brother returns with their three wives.**
F0011.0+	BUL-E0182:039-	**Journey to heaven (upper-world paradise); here: Three brothers follow their wives home into the sky.**

F0012.1+	BUL-E1856:013-028	Journey to Sky-god; here: River sends his children and goes himself to Sky-god to beg him for rain.
F0017.0+	BUL-E0426:149	Visit to land of the sun; here: Visit to sun's house where the maternal relatives of God's daughters live.
F0030.0+	BUL-E0182:007-	Inhabitant of upper world visits earth; here: Three women from the sky (God) come down to earth in order to visit three bachelors.
F0030.0+	BUL-E1445:004-	Inhabitant of upper world visits earth; here: Women from the sky (God) visit lone hunter and prepare food for him while he is in the bush.
F0031.0+	BUL-E0182:007-	Child of deity visits earth; here: God's daughters visit three unmarried brothers and cook food for them.
F0031.0+	BUL-E0426:003-	Child of deity visits earth; here: God's daughters visit three bachelors and cook food for them.
F0032.0+	BUL-E0514:006-	God visits earth; here: God transforms into leper and marries chief's daughter.
F0080.0+	BUL-E0503:024-028	Journey to lower world; here: Man travels with half-woman, God's daughter, to lower world, God's house.
F0092.1+	BUL-E0503:028-	Visit to lower world through hole made by lifting clumps of grass; here: Visit to lower world through hole made by lifting termite hill.
F0101.0+	BUL-E0503:046-062	Return from the lower world; here: Man and his wife (God's daughter) return from God's house in the lower world to the man's father's house.
F0166.11+	BUL-E0182:080-	Abundant food in otherworld; here: People in the sky cook abundant food from human flesh and from wild bush animals.
F0167.1.0+	BUL-E0182:043-066	Animals in otherworld; here: Leopard, lion, python, bush cow and dogs as wives' relatives in otherworld.
F0183.0+	BUL-E0182:080-	Food in otherworld; here: People in the sky cook food from human flesh and from wild bush animals.
F0239.2.0+	BUL-E0182:032,101-	Fairy women identical in form and feature; here: Women from the sky resemble each other.
F0420.4.9+	BUL-E0438:008-012	Water spirit controls water supply; here: Ogre 'Beard-Covers-Water', who lives in the water, challenges Common-Son-Of-Ten-Women to splash the water.
F0424.0+	BUL-E0438:008-012	River spirit; here: Ogre 'Beard-Covers-River', living in the water, challenges Common-Son-Of-Ten-Women.

F0500.0+	BUL-E1445:004-	Remarkable persons; here: Women from the sky (God) descend to earth and prepare food for lone hunter.
F0521.1+	BUL-E1435:036	Man covered with hair like animal; here: Supernatural being, coming from the sky, half-human, half-animal (with hairs on its hindquarters).
F0525.0+	BUL-E0503:007-024	Person with half a body; here: God's daughter appears as woman with half a body.
F0525.0+	BUL-E0503:013-017	Person with half a body; here: Man marries half a woman and puts food into half of her mouth.
F0545.1+	BUL-E0438:008-039	Remarkable beard; here: Ogre called Beard-Covers-River.
F0569.3.1+	BUL-E0514:005	Silent princess; here: Chief's daughter forbidden to speak to any man. The one who makes her speak will be her husband.
F0575.1+	BUL-E0514:001-	Remarkably beautiful woman; here: Chief's daughter is so beautiful that she surpasses all other women.
F0575.1+	BUL-E1267:005,009	Remarkably beautiful woman; here: Fair-skinned daughter admired by her father.
F0576.0+	BUL-E0489:003-	Extraordinary ugliness; here: Woman gives birth to nine ugly sons.
F0577.0+	BUL-E0182:032,101-	Persons identical in appearance; here: God's daughters and wives all look alike.
F0577.0+	BUL-E0426:121-	Persons identical in appearance; here: God's daughters and wives all look alike.
F0601.2+	BUL-E1328:021-032	Extraordinary companions help hero in suitor test; here: Supernatural being helps Hare to avoid fulfilment of his promise to be buried when his mother-in-law dies.
F0696.5+	BUL-E0438:006-007	Skillful hunter; here: Common-Son-Of-Ten-Women goes into the bush to hunt.
F0715.0+	BUL-E1856:001-	Extraordinary river; here: River and the sky (God) argue with one another over who is dependent on whom.
F0721.0+	BUL-E0503:028-	Subterranean world; here: God's house in subterranean world under a termite hill.
F0851.0+	BUL-E0182:003-038	Extraordinary food; here: Three brothers find cooked food every day when they return home.
F0851.0+	BUL-E0182:073-089	Extraordinary food; here: People in the sky cook meat of human beings and of bush animals.

F0851.0+	BUL-E0426:003-	Extraordinary food; here: Three bachelors find cooked food every day when they return home from field work.
F0900.0+	BUL-E1445:004-	Extraordinary occurrences; here: Women from the sky (God) descend to earth and prepare food for lone hunter.
F0962.0+	BUL-E0920:030	Extraordinary precipitation (rain, etc.); here: Suddenly water pours down from the sky and quenches fire on which daughter is to be burnt.
F0968.0+	BUL-E0259:138	Extraordinary thunder; here: Thunder comes from the sky (God) when a ram is sent down to be sacrificed to an earth- shrine in a girl's stead.
F0968.0+	BUL-E0438:051	Extraordinary thunder; here: Thunder caused by wrestling of Common-Son-Of-Ten-Women and God's bull in the sky.
G0010.0+	BUL-E0182:073-089	Cannibalism; here: People in the sky, in-laws of junior brother, offer him human meat.
G0011.3+	BUL-E0426:149	Cannibal witch; here: God's daughters' mother's brother, living on the Sun, cooks human flesh. (Origin of witches)
G0036.0+	BUL-E0426:149-150	Taste of human flesh leads to habitual cannibalism; here: God's daughters taste human flesh and become cannibal witches.
G0121.0+	BUL-E0438:008-	Physical characteristics of giant ogres; here: Ogre called Beard-Covers-River has a huge beard.
G0121.1.1+	BUL-E0438:017	One-eyed giant (ogre); here: God's bull has one eye, one hind leg and one foreleg.
G0203.0+	BUL-E0426:149-150	Origin of witches; here: God's daughters visit their mother's brother on the sun, eat human flesh and become witches.
G0249.0+	BUL-E0426:149-150	Habits of witches - miscellaneous; here: Witches eat human flesh.
G0262.0+	BUL-E0426:149-150	Murderous witch; here: Witches eat human flesh.
G0317.0+	BUL-E0438:013	Wrestling ogre; here: Ogre 'Beard-Covers-River' wrestles with Common-Son-Of-Ten-Women.
G0317.0+	BUL-E0438:045-051	Wrestling ogre; here: God's bull wrestles with Common-Son-Of-Ten-Women.
G0351.0+	BUL-E0438:017	Domestic beast as ogre; here: God's bull has one eye, one hind leg and one foreleg.
G0360.0+	BUL-E0438:008-	Ogres with monstrous features; here: Ogre 'Beard-Covers-River' has huge beard.

G0360.0+	BUL-E0438:017	Ogres with monstrous features; here: God's bull has one eye, one hind leg and one foreleg.
H0045.1+	BUL-E1856:036	God recognized by his supernatural powers; here: River recognizes that he is dependent on God who supplies him with water.
H0161.0.1+	BUL-E0182:101-	Recognition of person among identical companions; here: Man has to identify his own wife and those of his brothers in a row of identical women in the sky.
H0161.0.1+	BUL-E0426:121-	Recognition of person among identical companions; here: Man has to identify his own wife and those of his brothers in a row of identical women in the sky.
H0324.0+	BUL-E0182:094-111	Suitor test: Choosing princess from others identically clad; here: Junior brother has to choose his wife and his brothers' wives among women in the sky who all look alike.
H0338.0+	BUL-E1328:004-	Suitor tests: faithfulness; here: Hare may marry chief's daughter if he promises to be buried when his mother-in-law dies.
H0343.0+	BUL-E0514:005-0013	Suitor test: bringing dump princess to speak; here: Suitor who succeeds in making chief's daughter speak may marry her.
H0359.0+	BUL-E1328:004-	Other suitor tests; here: Hare may marry chief's daughter if he is ready to let himself be buried when his mother-in-law dies.
H0901.0+	BUL-E0426:110-	Task imposed on pain of death; here: Man has to identify his wife and his brothers' wives on pain of death.
H0974.0+	BUL-E0182:052-066	Task performed with help of supernatural wife; here: Junior brother performs task of greeting his in-laws by following his wife's advice.
H0974.0+	BUL-E0426:094-106	Task performed with help of supernatural wife; here: Junior brother is able to enter the compound of his in-laws in God's house by following the advice of his wife, God's daughter.
H0982.0+	BUL-E0182:105-	Animals help man perform task; here: Cat helps man to identify his wife and his brother's wives in the sky.
H0982.0+	BUL-E0426:111-	Animals help man perform task; here: Cat helps man to identify his wife and his brother's wives in the sky.
H1194.0.1+	BUL-E0514:005-013	Task: causing silent person to speak; here: Suitor who suceeds in making chief's daughter speak may marry her.
H1199.0+	BUL-E0182:102-	Other tasks; here: Man has to identify his wife and his brother's wives from God's identical daughters and wives.

H1199.0+	BUL-E0426:121-	Other tasks; here: Man has to identify his wife and his brother's wives from God's identical daughters and wives.
H1406.0+	BUL-E1328:004-	Suitor tested by apparent threats to his person; here: Hare is tested as a suitor by his mother-in-law with the threat to be buried when she dies.
H1557.0+	BUL-E0259:002-	Tests of obedience; here: Parents tested to see if they keep their promise to sacrifice their daughter.
H1569.0+	BUL-E1328:004-	Tests of character - miscellaneous; here: Test of faithfulness, Hare's faithfulness tested by his mother-in-law.
J0702.0+	BUL-E1698:007-010	Necessity of work; here: God declares that every man has to work after an old woman broke a taboo.
J1050.0+	BUL-E1698:005	Attention to warnings; here: Old woman does not pay attention to God's warnings not to mix meat cut off from him with a certain spice.
J1112.0+	BUL-E0674:034-038	Clever wife; here: Wife shows husband how to perform sexual intercourse; she learnt it from the fowl.
J1745.0+	BUL-E0674:001-008	Absurd ignorance of sex; here: Primeval husband and wife do not know how to perform sexual intercourse.
J1749.0+	BUL-E1856:005-	Absurd ignorance - miscellaneous; here: River is ignorant of the fact that he depends on the sky for water.
J2671.4+	BUL-E0402:005-006	Foolish messenger muddles message; here: Goat, as messenger of Man, muddles message of Man's death and Moon's revival.
K0300.0ff.+	BUL-E0438:019-044	Thefts and cheats; here: God's bull secretely takes away and swallows Common-Son-Of-Ten-Women's meat.
K0515.1+	BUL-E0008:001-018	Children hidden in order to avoid their execution (death); here: Chief hides his own daughter in a room even though he had ordered to kill all girls.
K0515.1+	BUL-E0225:002-	Children hidden to avoid their execution (death); here: Chief hides his daughter, although he ordered all newborn girls to be killed.
K0515.1+	BUL-E0292:003	Children hidden in order to avoid their execution (death); here: Woman hides her daughter in a room to avoid her being killed.
K0925.0+	BUL-E0503:082	Victim pushed into fire; here: Man thrown into the fire because everyone wants to sleep with his wife.
K0955.0+	BUL-E0503:082-083	Murder by burning; here: Chief orders to throw man into the fire after he returned from God with a beautiful wife, many men, women and riches.

K0955.0+	BUL-E0920:007-008	Murder by burning; here: Father plans to burn disliked daughter.
K0978.1+	BUL-E0402:0005-013	Message of death; here: Message of death concerning Man and Moon delayed by Dog, confounded by Goat.
K1302.0+	BUL-E0514:010-015	Woman won and lost by a ruse; here; here: Leper (God) succeeds to marry chief's daughter by pretending to feed puppies through their anuses in order to make her talk (breach of taboo).
K1700.0+	BUL-E0514:012-015	Deception through bluffing; here: Leper (God) pretends to feed puppies through their anuses in order to make chief's daughter talk (breach of taboo).
K1771.0+	BUL-E1328:028-	Bluffing threat; here: Hare threatens to take a hoe, farm products and domestic animals with him into the realm of the dead leaving mankind without food.
K1811.0+	BUL-E0514:006-047	Gods (saints) in disguise visit mortals; here: God transforms into a leper and marries chief's daughter.
K1818.1+	BUL-E0514:006-047	Disguise as leper; here: God transforms into leper and marries chief's daughter.
K1860.0+	BUL-E1328:007-	Deception by feigned death; here: Hare's mother-in-law feigns death in order to test his faithfulness.
K2210.0+	BUL-E1435:006-	Treacherous relatives; here: Parents decide to kill their daughter because she does not belong to their clan.
K2211.0.1+	BUL-E1435:015-030	Treacherous elder brother(s); here: Senior brother has to take out his sister in order for her to be killed by her parents.
K2213.0+	BUL-E0514:024	Treacherous wife; here: Wife maltreats her husband, a leper (God), by shitting and pissing into his food.
K2213.0+	BUL-E0514:026-030	Treacherous wife; here: Wife smears slimy soup on the compound wall so that her husband, a leper (God), may slip and fall.
K2320.0+	BUL-E1328:028-	Deception by frightening; here: Hare frightens people by threatening to take away all means of gaining food.
L0010.0+	BUL-E0182:029-114	Victorious youngest son; here: Youngest brother wins wives from the sky for himself and his elder brothers. He also makes their wives return from the sky.
M0002.0+	BUL-E0008:001-	Inhuman decisions of king; here: Chief orders all newborn girls to be killed.
M0002.0+	BUL-E0225:005-	Inhuman decision of king; here: Chief orders all newborn girls to be killed.

M0114.0+	BUL-E0489:002	Oath taken on sacred object; here: Man takes oath on the Earth to give (sacrifice) his daughter, if his wife gives birth to many children;
M0114.0+	BUL-E1267:002	Oath taken on sacred object; here: Man takes vow on earth-shrine to sacrifice one of his children;
M0150.0+	BUL-E0259:002-	Other vows and oaths; here: Father vows to sacrifice his firstborn child to an earth- shrine.
M0150.0+	BUL-E0572:001-007	Other vows and oaths; here: Father vows to sacrifice first-born child to earth-shrine.
M0150.0+	BUL-E0572:102	Other vows and oaths; here: God orders people never to vow to bring a human sacrifice, but to sacrifice an animal instead.
M0150.0+	BUL-E0761:002-003	Other vows and oaths; here: Woman vows to sacrifice her firstborn child to an earth-shrine (*teng*).
M0150.0+	BUL-E1267:002-003	Other vows and oaths; here: Father promises to sacrifice one of his children to an earth-shrine, if he begets children.
M0183.0+	BUL-E0489:002	Religious vows; here: Man vows to the Earth to sacrifice his daughter, if his wife gives birth to many children;
M0202.0+	BUL-E0489:006-	Fulfilling of bargain or promise; here: Father is ready to kill his daughter which he promised to sacrifice to the Earth (earth-shrine).
M0202.0+	BUL-E1328:004-	Fulfilling of bargain and promise; here: Hare promises to be buried when his mother-in-law dies.
M0242.0+	BUL-E1267:002-003	Bargains and promises between mortals and supernatural beings; here: Father promises one of his children to an earth-shrine if he begets children.
M0250.0+	BUL-E1328:004-	Promises connected with death; here: Hare promises to be buried when his mother-in-law dies.
M0310.0+	BUL-E0489:017-027	Favourable prophecies; here: Brother prophesies that God will help in a wonderful way to save his sister from being sacrificed.
M0341.0+	BUL-E0225:012-094	Death prophesied; here: Bird announces girl's death by singing a song.
M0341.0+	BUL-E0259:009-	Death prophesied; here: Bird prophesies death to girl in a song.
M0341.0+	BUL-E0489:008-027	Death prophesied; here: Brother announces that his sister will be killed (sacrificed).

M0411.1+	BUL-E0674:045-	Curse by parent; here: Father curses fowl, who taught him how to perform sexual intercourse.
M0411.4.1+	BUL-E1698:007-	Curse by a god; here: After breaking a taboo, God ordains that every man shall suffer by having to work for his food.
M0414.8+	BUL-E0674:045-	Animals cursed; here: Man curses cock because it taught him to perform sexual intercourse.
N0130.0+	BUL-E0225:096	Changing of luck or fate; here: Girl, condemned to be sacrificed, is finally saved by God, who sends a ram to be killed in her stead.
N0130.0+	BUL-E0489:028-030	Changing of luck and fate; here: Girl, condemned to be sacrificed, is finally saved when her youngest brother is killed.
N0130.0+	BUL-E0761:080-081	Changing of luck or fate; here: Girl condemned to be sacrificed is suddenly saved by God, who sent animals to be killed instead of her.
N0130.0+	BUL-E1435:033-039	Changing of luck or fate; here: Girl, condemned to be killed, is suddenly saved by supernatural being from the sky.
N0343.3+	BUL-E1328:007-	Woman feigns death ...; here: Woman (Hare's mother-in-law) feigns death in order to test Hare's faithfulness.
N0380.0+	BUL-E0008:005-	Other unlucky accidents; here: Chief's daughter, hidden in a room, is discovered by accident and ordained to be killed like all other girls.
N0380.0+	BUL-E0292:004-006	Other unlucky accidents; here: Girl, hidden in a room, is discovered by accident and ordained to be killed like all other girls.
N0610.0+	BUL-E0008:005-007	Accidental discovery of crime; here: Boy finds out accidentally that chief's daughter is hidden and allowed to live while all other daughters were killed according to the chief's orders.
N0610.0+	BUL-E0292:004	Accidental discovery of crime; here: People find out accidentally that a woman has hidden her daughter while all other girls were killed.
N0788.0+	BUL-E0426:003-	Incidents when wife takes food to husband in field or forest; here: On returning home, bachelors find food, prepared by women from the sky.
N0810.0+	BUL-E0008:056-061	Supernatural helpers; here: Woman from sky saves girl's life and advises people not to kill their newborn daughters any more.

N0810.0+	BUL-E0225:096	Supernatural helpers; here: God sends down a ram to save girl from being sacrificed.
N0810.0+	BUL-E0761:080-081	Supernatural helpers; here: God saves girl from being sacrificed by sending down animals to be killed instead of her.
N0810.0+	BUL-E1435:033-039	Supernatural helpers; here: Supernatural being saves girl from being killed.
N0810.4.+	BUL-E0182:007-	Supernatural helper comes from the sky; here: Three women come down from the sky and secretly cook food for three unmarried brothers.
N0810.4+	BUL-E0292:030	Supernatural helper comes from sky; here: Ram, coming down from the sky, saves girl from being killed.
N0810.4+	BUL-E0426:012-	Supernatural helper(s) come from the sky; here: Three women from the sky come down to prepare food for three bachelors.
N0810.4+	BUL-E0920:029	Supernatural helper comes from sky; here: Supernatural thing, coming down from the sky (God), saves girl from being burnt.
N0810.4+	BUL-E1267:022-023	Supernatural helper comes down from sky; here: Old woman comes down from the sky and rescues girl from being sacrificed.
N0810.4+	BUL-E1328:013-019	Supernatural helper comes down from the sky; here: Supernatural being from the sky helps Hare to avoid keeping his promise to be buried when his mother-in-law dies.
N0817.0.0+	BUL-E0182:052-	Deity as helper; here: God's daughter helps her husband, the junior brother by telling him what to do when entering God's house.
N0817.0.0+	BUL-E0426:070-	Deity as helper; here: God's daughters try to help their mortal husbands by telling them what to do when entering God's house.
N0817.0.1+	BUL-E0489:017-027	God as helper; here: God helps in a wonderful way to save girl from being sacrificed to the Earth.
N0817.0.1+	BUL-E0503:054-057	God as helper; here: Man receives many gifts from God when returning to his family with God's daughter.
N0817.0.1+	BUL-E1328:032	God as helper; here: God sends Hare a hoe, farm products and an animal's young for which he was begging.
N0817.0.1+	BUL-E1445:004-	God as helper; here: Women from the sky (God) help lone hunter by preparing his food while he is away in the bush.

N0817.0.1+	BUL-E1856:039-040	God as helper; here: God sends rain for a river which has dried up.
N0818.0+	BUL-E1698:001	Sky as helper; here: God, identical with the sky, is near man who may cut off pieces of him to eat as food (meat).
N0825.3+	BUL-E1267:022-023	Old woman helper; here: Old woman comes down from the sky and rescues girl from being sacrificed.
N0831.0+	BUL-E0920:031	Girl as helper; here: Girl helps brother to marry women.
N0832.0+	BUL-E0920:004-005	Boy as helper; here: Brother defends sister against parents who dislike their daughter.
P0010.0+	BUL-E0008:001	Kings; here: Chief orders all newborn girls to be killed, whereas boys should be kept alive.
P0011.0+	BUL-E0503:069-071	Choice of kings; here: People want boy to become their chief after he returned from God with a beautiful wife, many men, women and riches.
P0013.0+	BUL-E0008:001-018	Customs connected with kings; here: A chief who gives orders to his people is also bound to follow them himself.
P0016.0+	BUL-E0503:069-071	End of king's reign; here: Chief is deposed and young rich man becomes chief in his stead.
P0019.0+	BUL-E0503:073-	Other motifs connected with kings; here: Former chief wants to marry (sleep with) new chief's wife.
P0019.0+	BUL-E0503:077-080	Other motifs connected with kings; here: Deposed chief incites his people against a boy after he returned from God with a beautiful wife, many men, women and riches.
P0019.0+	BUL-E0503:082-083	Other motifs connected with kings; here: Jealous former chief orders to throw new chief into the fire.
P0040.0+	BUL-E0008:001-	Princesses; here: Chief orders that all girls must be killed, but hides gis won daughter.
P0040.0+	BUL-E0225:002-006	Princesses; here: Chief orders that all girls must be killed, but hides gis won daughter.
P0040.0+	BUL-E1328:004-006	Princesses; here: Chief's daughter married to Hare.
P0040.0+	BUL-E0514:002-015	Princesses; here: Chief's daughter refuses to marry any of her suitors; in the end, she has to marry a leper.
P0162.0+	BUL-E0514:006	Leper; here: God transforms himself into a leper.
P0200.0+	BUL-E0008:058	The family; here: Within a short time, there would be no longer any family (lineage) if all girls were killed.

P0200.0+	BUL-E0182:001-	The family; here: Three bachelors living together without women.
P0200.0+	BUL-E0426:001-	The family; here: Three bachelors living together without women.
P0200.0+	BUL-E0514:025	The family; here: Leper sends gifts of money to his wife's paternal relatives through his wife.
P0210.0+	BUL-E0182:011-038	Husband and wife; here: Three brothers marry three women from the sky who have secretly cooked food for them.
P0210.0+	BUL-E0259:001-002	Husband and wife; here: Barren wife goes with husband to earth-shrine who makes wife fecund in exchange for her firstborn child.
P0210.0+	BUL-E0259:002	Husband and wife; here: Husband loves barren wife, although he has another wife (wives?) who has (have) born him children.
P0210.0+	BUL-E0426:012-	Husband and wife; here: Three bachelors are visited by three women, their wives, from the sky; they cook food for them.
P0210.0+	BUL-E0503:008-	Husband and wife; here: Man marries half-woman, God's daughter.
P0210.0+	BUL-E0514:006-025	Husband and wife; here: Wife maltreats her husband, a leper (God), by shitting and pissing into his food and by smearing slimy soup on the compound wall.
P0210.0+	BUL-E0572:001-007	Husband and wife; here: Barren wife becomes fecund after her husband consulted an earth-shrine.
P0210.0+	BUL-E1435:004-006	Husband and wife; here: Husband and wife decide to kill their daughter because she does not belong to their clan.
P0230.0+	BUL-E0008:016-018	Parents and children; here: All newborn girls are to be killed, all newborn boys are to be kept alive.
P0230.0+	BUL-E0225:001-	Parents and children; here: Parents are to kill all newborn girls.
P0230.0+	BUL-E0225:002-	Parents and children; here: Chief hides his daughter so as not to kill her, as all other girls were, according to his orders.
P0230.0+	BUL-E0259:004	Parents and children; here: Man begets six children with his barren wife after having visited an earth-shrine.
P0230.0+	BUL-E0503:003-	Parents and children; here: Parents try in vain to marry their son to an ordinary woman; he marries a half-woman instead.

P0230.0+	BUL-E0572:005	Parents and children; here: Parents promise to sacrifice their firstborn child to an earth-shrine.
P0230.0+	BUL-E0920:002-006	Parents and children; here: Parents dislike their daughter; they plan to kill her.
P0230.0+	BUL-E1435:006-	Parents and children; here: Parents decide to kill their daughter because she does not belong to their clan.
P0230.0+	BUL-EO503:014-020	Parents and children; here: Parents complain that their son has married a half-woman and tell him to leave their house with her.
P0231.0+	BUL-E0438:001-002	Mother and son; here: Ten mothers give birth to one son.
P0231.0+	BUL-E0503:004	Mother and son; here: Son helps his mother in collecting firewood.
P0231.3+	BUL-E0503:085-086	Mother-love; here: Mother does not love her son as much as her own life.
P0232.0+	BUL-E0259:011-	Mother and daughter; here: Daughter, who is to be sacrificed to an earth-shrine, asks her mother for the meaning of a bird's song announcing her death. Mother rebukes her daughter.
P0232.0+	BUL-E0292:001-003	Mother and daughter; here: Mother gives birth to a girl and although all girls are to be killed, she hides her in a room and nurses her secretly.
P0232.0+	BUL-E0572:018-056	Mother and daughter; here: Daughter helps mother in grinding and pounding in order to prepare millet beer and shea-nut oil for her own sacrifice.
P0232.0+	BUL-E0572:019-055	Mother and daughter; here: Mother announces in a song that her daughter is grinding her 'death flour' and her 'death oil' before being sacrificed to an earth-shrine.
P0232.0+	BUL-E0761:003	Mother and child; here: Mother promises to sacrifice her firstborn child to an earth-shrine (*teng*).
P0232.0+	BUL-E0761:006-	Mother and daughter; here: Mother orders her daughter to prepare millet beer for her own sacrifice.
P0232.0+	BUL-E0920:003	Mother and daughter; here: Mother dislikes her daughter.
P0232.0+	BUL-E1328:004-006	Mother and daughter; here: Mother marries daughter to Hare under the condition that Hare agrees to be buried when she dies.
P0233.0+	BUL-E0503:087	Father and son; here: Father does not love his son as much as his own life.

P0234.0+	BUL-E0225:002-	Father and daughter; here: Chief hides his daughter, although he ordered all newborn girls to be killed.
P0234.0+	BUL-E0489:002	Father and daughter; here: Father promises to sacrifice his daughter to the Earth (earth-shrine), if his wife gives birth to many children.
P0234.0+	BUL-E0514:021-023	Father and daughter; here: Father forces his daughter to marry leper who succeeded in making her speak to him (breach of taboo).
P0234.0+	BUL-E0572:071-097	Father and daughter; here: Father keeps his promise to sacrifice one of his children to an earth-shrine.
P0234.0+	BUL-E0572:088	Father and daughter; here: Father feels dizzy when he is about to cut daughter's throat for a sacrifice to earth-shrine.
P0234.0+	BUL-E0920:002	Father and daughter; here: Father does not like his daughter; he plans to kill her.
P0234.0+	BUL-E1267:002	Father and daughter; here: Father promises his daughter as a sacrifice to an earth-shrine.
P0234.0+	BUL-E1267:005	Father and daughter; here: Beautiful, fair-skinned daughter admired by her father.
P0251.0+	BUL-E0489:028	Brothers; here: Paternal relative kills youngest brother with a club in girl's stead.
P0251.6.1	BUL-E0182:011-038	Three brothers; here: Three brothers marry three women from the sky.
P0251.6.1+	BUL-E0426:001-	Three brothers; here: Three brothers, bachelors, are working on a farm together. Women from the sky cook their food for them.
P0251.6.5+	BUL-E0489:003-027	Nine brothers; here: Girl has nine ugly brothers; some of them prophesy that she will be killed, some of them that God will help her in a wonderful way.
P0253.0.0+	BUL-E0292:009-	Sister and brother; here: Brothers sing song, calling their sister out of the room to be killed.
P0253.0.0+	BUL-E0920:004-005	Sister and brother; here: Brother says that one cannot be a man without a sister.
P0253.0.0+	BUL-E0920:004-005	Sister and brother; here: Brother defends sister who is disliked by her parents.
P0253.0.0+	BUL-E0920:009-025	Sister and brother; here: Brothers call out disliked sister who is to be killed by parents.

P0253.0.0+	BUL-E0920:031	Sister and brother; here: Sister helps brother to marry women.
P0253.0.0+	BUL-E1435:012-029	Sister and brother; here: Senior brother is to take his new-born sister out of the house to be killed.
P0253.0.5+	BUL-E0489:003-028	Sister and (nine) brothers; here: Brothers prophesy that their sister will be killed.
P0253.0.5+	BUL-E0489:028-030	Sister and (nine) brothers; here: Youngest of nine brothers is killed in his sister's stead as a sacrifice to the Earth.
P0260.0+	BUL-E0182:041-	Relations by law; here: Husbands accompany their wives to their family of origin and are scared by wild animals in their compound.
P0260.0+	BUL-E0426:064-	Relations by law; here: Husbands accompany their wives to their family of origin and are scared by wild animals in their compound.
P0261.0+	BUL-E0514:038-045	Father-in-law; here: Leper (God) goes to the funeral of his father-in-law and resuscitates him by striking his dead body with a magic tail.
P0262.0+	BUL-E1328:004-	Mother-in-law; here: Mother marries daughter to Hare under the condition that he agress to be buried when she dies.
P0262.0+	BUL-E1328:033-034	Mother-in-law; here: Mother-in-law feigns death to find out whether Hare keeps his promise to be buried when she dies.
P0265.0+	BUL-E0514:038-045	Son-in-law; here: Son-in-law, a leper (God) goes to the funeral of his father-in-law and resuscitates him by striking his dead body with a magic tail.
P0290.0+	BUL-E0489:006,0028	Other relatives; here: Man calls together his paternal relatives before sacrificing his daughter to the Earth; one of the paternal relatives kills her youngest brother in her stead.
P0414.0+	BUL-E1445:001-	Hunter; here: Women from the sky prepare food for hunter while he is absent in the bush.
P0681.0+	BUL-E0514:030-044	Mourning customs; here: Leper comes to mourn at his wife's father's funeral.
P0682.0+	BUL-E0182:058-071	Greeting customs; here: Man greets kindly wild animals in the sky and is welcomed by them in return after they have transformed into their human shape.
P0682.0+	BUL-E1856:015-029	Greeting customs; here: River's children observe greeting customs when coming to God's house.

Q0221.5+	BUL-E0514:053-054	Disobedience to God punished; here: Magic tail loses its force to resuscitate people when it is taken into a room against God's instructions.
Q0221.5+	BUL-E1698:008-	Disobedience to God punished; here: After an old woman refused to obey God's command, all humans were punished by having to work for their food;
Q0306.0+	BUL-E1856:001-	Quarrelsomeness punished; here: River quarrels with sky (God) and is punished by being dried up.
Q0330.0+	BUL-E1856:004-	Overweening punished; here: River boasts to be independent of the sky (God) and is punished by being dried up.
Q0556.0+	BUL-E1698:007-010	Curse as punishment; here: God ordains humans to work for their food as punishment for having broken a taboo.
R0152.0+	BUL-E0503:088-090	Wife rescues husband; here: Wife goes into the fire and revives her burnt husband by collecting the ashes of his body.
R0169ff.+	BUL-E0292:030-031	Other rescuers; here: Ram, coming down from the sky, saves girl from being killed.
R0169ff.+	BUL-E0920:029	Other rescuers; here: Supernatural thing, coming down from the sky (God), saves girl from being burnt by fire.
R0215.0+	BUL-E0008:001-061	Escape from execution; here: Girl hidden in chief's house and discovered by boy is to be killed on rubbish heap. Woman from the sky saves her life.
R0215.0+	BUL-E0292:031	Escape from execution; here: Girl, hidden in her mother's room and discovered by the people, is to be killed. Ram from the sky saves her life.
S0010.0+	BUL-E0225:001-	Cruel parents; here: Parents killed their newborn girls.
S0010.0+	BUL-E1435:006-	Cruel parents; here: Parents decide to kill their daughter because she does not resemble their family.
S0011.0+	BUL-E0489:002	Cruel father; here: Father promises to sacrifice his daughter to the Earth (earth-shrine).
S0011.3+	BUL-E1267:019-023	Father kills child; here: Father intends to kill daughter as a sacrifice to an earth-shrine.
S0011.4	BUL-E1435:006-	Father plans child's death.
S0011.4.0+	BUL-E0920:007-008	Father plans child's death; here: Father plans disliked daughter's death.
S0011.4.3+	BUL-E0920:002-009	Cruel fathers threaten to kill their children if they are of undesirable sex; here: Father dislikes his daughter; he plans to kill her.

S0012.0+	BUL-E0920:003	Cruel mother; here: Mother dislikes her daughter.
S0012.3+	BUL-E1435:006-	Mother orders son's death; here: Mother decides on daughter's death.
S0070.0+	BUL-E0489:028	Other cruel relatives; here: Paternal relative kills youngest brother in a daughter's stead.
S0110.0+	BUL-E0489:028	Murders; here: Paternal relative murders youngest son by slaying him with a club.
S0112.0+	BUL-E0503:082-083	Burning to death; here: Chief has boy who usurped his position thrown into fire and burnt to death.
S0112.0+	BUL-E0920:007-008	Burning to death; here: Parents plan to burn disliked daughter to death.
S0118.2+	BUL-E0259:136	Murder by cutting throat; here: Girl (daughter) is to be slaughtered by cutting her throat.
S0118.2+	BUL-E0292:030	Murder by cutting throat; here: Girl (daughter) is to be slaughtered by cutting her throat.
S0118.2+	BUL-E0572:097	Murder by cutting throat; here: Girl (daughter) is to be slaughtered by cutting her throat.
S0118.2+	BUL-E1435:032,037	Murder by cutting throat; here: Girl (daughter) is to be slaughtered by cutting her throat.
S0210.0+	BUL-E0259:005-	Children sold or promised; here: Firstborn child (daughter) promised as an offering to an earth-shrine which has made barren wife fecund.
S0210.0+	BUL-E0489:002	Children sold or promised; here: Father promises to sacrifice his daughter to the Earth (earth-shrine).
S0210.0+	BUL-E0572:005	Children sold or promised; here: Firstborn child promised as an offering to an earth-shrine, which has made barren wife fecund.
S0210.0+	BUL-E0761:003	Children sold or promised; here: Firstborn child promised as an offering to an earth-shrine (*teng*) which made barren woman fecund.
S0210.0+	BUL-E1267:003	Children sold or promised; here: Child promised to be sacrificed to earth-shrine by its father.
S0223.0+	BUL-E0259:005-	Childless couple promise child to the devil if they may only have one; here: Man promises firstborn child (girl) to an earth-shrine if his barren wife bears children.
S0223.0+	BUL-E0572:005	Childless couple promise child to the devil if they may only have one; here: Man promises firstborn child to an earth-shrine if his barren wife bears children.

S0223.0+	BUL-E0761:003	Childless couple promise child to the devil if they may only have one; here: Barren woman promises her firstborn child to an earth-shrine (*teng*) if it makes her fecund.
S0255.0+	BUL-E0008:057-059	Deity saves person about to be sacrificed; here: Woman from the sky saves girl about to be sacrificed.
S0255.0+	BUL-E0225:096	Deity saves person about to be sacrificed; here: God sends ram in order to save girl about to be sacrificed.
S0255.0+	BUL-E0259:136-146	Deity saves person about to be sacrificed; here: Sky-God saves girl about to be sacrificed to earth-shrine by sending down a ram to be sacrificed in her stead.
S0255.0+	BUL-E0292:030-031	Deity saves person about to be sacrificed; here: Ram, sent down from the sky, saves girl about to be killed.
S0255.0+	BUL-E0489:017-027	Deity saves person about to be sacrificed; here: God saves girl about to be sacrificed.
S0255.0+	BUL-E0572:097-099	Deity saves person about to be sacrificed; here: Sky-God saves girl about to be sacrificed to earth-shrine by sending down a ram to be sacrificed in her stead.
S0255.0+	BUL-E0761:080-082	Deity saves person about to be sacrificed; here: God saves girl about to be sacrificed to an earth-shrine (*teng*) by sending down animals to be sacrificed in her stead.
S0255.0+	BUL-E1267:023	Deity saves person about to be sacrificed; here: Old woman from the sky saves girl about to be sacrificed.
S0255.0+	BUL-E1435:033-039	Deity saves person about to be sacrificed; here: God sends supernatural being to save girl from being killed.
S0260.1.1+	BUL-E0008:001-	Child sacrifice as religious rite; here: All newborn girls are to be sacrificed.
S0260.1.1+	BUL-E0225:079-096	Child sacrifice as religious rite; here: Girl is to be sacrificed to an earth-shrine.
S0260.1.1+	BUL-E0259:005-	Child sacrifice as religious rite; here: Firstborn child (girl) to be sacrificed to an earth-shrine which has made barren wife fecund.
S0260.1.1+	BUL-E0489:002-	Child sacrifice as religious rite; here: Father promises to sacrifice his daughter to the Earth (earth-shrine), if his wife gives birth to many children.
S0260.1.1+	BUL-E0572:005	Child sacrifice as religious rite; here: Firstborn child to be sacrificed to an earth-shrine which has made barren wife fecund.

S0260.1.1+	BUL-E0761:002-	Child sacrifice as religious rite; here: Firstborn child to be sacrificed to an earth-shrine (*teng*) which made barren woman fecund.
S0260.1.1+	BUL-E1267:003-	Child sacrifice as religious rite; here: Daughter to be sacrificed to earth-shrine which made childless couple fecund.
S0263.2.1+	BUL-E0225:096	Gods furnish substitute for child sacrifice; here God sends a ram from the sky to be sacrificed in a girl's stead.
S0263.2.1+	BUL-E0259:136-146	Gods furnish substitute for child sacrifice; here: Sky-God sends down a ram to be sacrificed to an earth-shrine instead of a daughter.
S0263.2.1+	BUL-E0292:030-031	Gods furnish substitute for child sacrifice; here: Ram, sent down from the sky, is to be killed in a girl's stead.
S0263.2.1+	BUL-E0572:097-099	Gods furnish substitute for child sacrifice; here: Sky-God sends down ram to be sacrificed to earth-shrine in a daughter's stead.
S0263.2.1+	BUL-E0761:080-082	Gods furnish substitute for child sacrifice; here: Sky-God sends down animals to be sacrificed to an earth-shrine (*teng*) in a girl's stead.
S0271.0+	BUL-E0259:002-	Sacrifice of child to remove barrenness; here: Firstborn child (girl) promised to earth-shrine if it cures wife of her barrenness.
S0271.0+	BUL-E0572:005-007	Sacrifice of child to remove barrenness; here: Firstborn child promised to earth-shrine if it cures barrenness of wife.
S0271.0+	BUL-E0761:002-003	Sacrifice of child to remove barrenness; here: Firstborn child promised to an earth-shrine (*teng*) if it cures barrenness of woman.
S0271.0+	BUL-E1267:002-003	Sacrifice of child to remove barrenness; here: Child promised to be sacrificed to earth-shrine which made childless couple fecund.
S0302.0+	BUL-E0761:006-	Children murdered; here: Mother decides to kill her daughter because she has promised to sacrifice her to an earth-shrine (*teng*).
S0302.0+	BUL-E1267:019-022	Children murdered; here: Father promises to sacrifice one of his children to an earth-shrine.
S0302.0+	BUL-E1435:006-	Children murdered; here: Parents decide to kill their daughter because she does not belong to their clan.
S0302.1+	BUL-E0008:001-	All new-born male children slaughtered; here: All new-born female children slaughtered.

S0302.1+	BUL-E0225:001-	All new-born male children slaughtered; here: All new-born female children slaughtered.
S0302.1+	BUL-E0292:002	All new-born male children slaughtered; here: All new-born female children slaughtered.
T0050.0+	BUL-E0514:002	Wooing; here: All men come to woo chief's beautiful daughter, but they fail.
T0050.0+	BUL-E0514:006	Wooing; here: God transforms into a leper in order to woo chief's daughter.
T0050.0+	BUL-E1328:003	Wooing; here: Hare woos chief's daughter.
T0052.4+	BUL-E0503:054-057	Dowry given at marriage of daughter; here: God gives many gifts to his daughter and her husband when they return to the young man's family.
T0090.0+	BUL-E0503:091	Love - miscellaneous motifs; here: A woman loves her husband more than the husband's parents do.
T0091.3.0+	BUL-E0182:030-038	Love of mortal and supernatural person; here: Three brothers marry women from the sky.
T0091.3.2+	BUL-E0503:008-	Love of Goddes for mortal; here: Half-woman, God's daughter, forces young man to marry her.
T0110.0+	BUL-E1328:004-006	Unusual marriage; here: Chief's daughter married to Hare.
T0111.0.1+	BUL-E0182:012-019	Marriage to wives from the sky who disappear; here: Women from the sky disappear into the sky after having cooked food for their husbands, three bachelors.
T0111.0.1+	BUL-E0426:024-	Marriage to supernatural wives who disappear; here: Three women come from the sky to cook food for three bachelors and disappear afterwards.
T0111.1.0+	BUL-E0514:015-	Marriage of a mortal and a God; here: Marriage of chief's daughter to God in the disguise of a leper.
T0111.1.2+	BUL-E0182:038	Man marries the daughter of a God; here: Three brothers marry three women from the sky.
T0111.1.2+	BUL-E0503:008-	Man marries the daughter of a god; here: Man marries a half-woman, God's daughter.
T0111.2+	BUL-E0182:011-038	Woman from sky-world marries mortal man; here: Three women from the sky marry three brothers on earth.
T0111.2+	BUL-E0426:022-	Woman from sky-world marries mortal man; here: Three women from the sky marry three brothers on earth.

T0111.2+	BUL-E1445:067-	**Woman from sky-world marries mortal man; here: Women from the sky (God) marry hunter.**
T0121.0+	BUL-E0503:008-	**Unequal marriage; here: Man marries a half-woman, God's daughter.**
T0131.1.3+	BUL-EO503:013-020	**Marriage against will of parents; here: Son marries half-woman, God's daughter, against will of his parents.**
T0136.4.2+	BUL-E0503:054-057	**Parting gifts after wedding; here: God gives many gifts to his daughter and her husband when they return to the young man's family.**
T0145.0.1+	BUL-E1445:067-	**Polygyny; here: Hunter marries women from the sky who prepare his food for him.**
T0145.2	BUL-E0259:001	**Second wife taken because first is barren.**
T0166.2+	BUL-E0674:008-	**Bridegroom must be taught sexual intercourse; here: Primeval human beings must be taught sexual intercourse by fowls.**
T0192.0+	BUL-E0503:008-027	**Marriage by force; here: Half woman, God's daughter, forces young man to marry her by demonstrating her power to kill him if he refuses.**
T0192.0+	BUL-E0514:021-023	**Marriage by force; here: Chief forces his daughter to marry leper, who succeeded in making her speak to him (breach of taboo).**
T0200.0+	BUL-E0182:039-	**Married life; here: Wives from the sky want to visit their parents; their husbands accompany them.**
T0200.0+	BUL-E0259:004	**Married life; here: Man has sexual intercourse with his barren wife who gives birth to six children after having visited earth-shrine.**
T0200.0+	BUL-E0572:002	**Married life; here: Husband consults earth-shrine because his wife is barren.**
T0200.0+	BUL-E1267:001-004	**Married life; here: Childless couple becomes fecund after promising one of the children to an earth-shrine.**
T0210.0+	BUL-E0674:001-034	**Husband and wife; here: Primeval husband and wife do not know how to beget children; they learn it from the fowl.**
T0210.0+	BUL-E0674:036	**Husband and wife; here: Wife shows husband how to perform sexual intercourse.**
T0210.1+	BUL-E0503:088-090	**Faithful wife; here: Wife, God's daughter, throws herself into the fire in order to revive her burnt husband.**

T0250.0+	BUL-E0514:024-045	Characteristics of wives and husbands; here: Wife maltreats husband, a leper (God) by shitting and pissing into his food and by smearing slimy soup on the compound wall.
T0280.0+	BUL-E0182:003-	Other aspects of married life; here: Women from the sky cook food for three bachelors while they are away at their bush field.
T0280.0+	BUL-E0426:012-	Other aspects of married life; here: Women from the sky cook food for three bachelors while they are away at their bush field.
T0280.0+	BUL-E0674:035-038	Other aspects of married life; here: Wife shows husband how to have sexual intercourse; she learnt it from the fowls.
T0294.0+	BUL-E0182:039-	Husband (wife) of supernatural being longs for old home and visits relatives; here: Wives from the sky want to visit their relatives.
T0400.0+	BUL-E0503:073-080	Illicit sexual relations; here: The former chief and all men of a village want to sleep with the new chief's wife (God's daughter).
T0411.1+	BUL-E0503:076	Lecherous father; here: Father desires to have sexual intercourse with his son's wife (God's daughter).
T0510.0+	BUL-E0259:004	Miraculous conception; here: Barren wife conceives and gives birth to six children after having visited earth- shrine.
T0510.0+	BUL-E0438:001-002	Miraculous conception; here: Ten women who are pregnant together, give birth to one son.
T0510.0+	BUL-E0572:001-007	Miraculous conception; here: Barren wife conceives and gives birth to children after having visited earth-shrine.
T0510.0+	BUL-E0761:002-004	Miraculous conception; here: Barren woman conceives and gives birth after having consulted an earth-shrine (*teng*).
T0510.0+	BUL-E1267:002-004	Miraculous conception; here: Power of an earth-shrine enables childless couple to beget children.
T0541.12+	BUL-E0438:001-002	Birth from nine mothers; here: Birth from ten mothers.
T0570.0+	BUL-E0438:001-002	Pregnancy; here: Ten women are pregnant at the same time and deliver one son together.
T0573.1+	BUL-E0674:044	Woman conceives and bears the same day; here: Woman conceives and bears after three days.
T0585.0+	BUL-E0438:002-006	Precocious infant; here: Ten women give birth to one son who grows quickly and names himself.

T0585.2.1+	**BUL-E0438:006**	**Child two months old speaks; here: Young child names himself Common-Son-Of-Ten-Women.**
T0589.1+	**BUL-E0438:002**	**Co-operative birth; here: Ten women deliver one son.**
T0596.0+	**BUL-E0438:006**	**Naming of children; here: Boy names himself: 'Common-Son-Of-Ten-Women'.**
T0610.0+	**BUL-E0292:003-**	**Nurture and growth of children; here: Mother hides her daughter and nurses her, although all girls are to be killed.**
T0615.0+	**BUL-E0438:003**	**Supernatural growth; here: Supernatural growth of Common-Son-Of-Ten-Women.**
T0645.2.1+	**BUL-E0008:001-**	**'Kill it if it is a girl'; here: Chief orders to kill all newborn girls and keep only boys alive.**
T0645.2.1+	**BUL-E0292:002-**	**'Kill it if it is a girl'; here: Rule: all newborn girls are to be killed.**
V0011.0+	**BUL-E0225:079-**	**Power to which sacrifice is made; here: All girls have to be sacrificed to an earth-shrine.**
V0011.0+	**BUL-E0259:003-**	**Power to which sacrifice is made; here: Sacrifice to earth-shrine.**
V0011.0+	**BUL-E0489:002-030**	**Power to which sacrifice is made; here: Human sacrifice (daughter) promised to the Earth (earth-shrine).**
V0011.0+	**BUL-E0572:005-007**	**Power to which sacrifice is made; here: Earth-shrine is promised human sacrifice (child) if it makes barren woman fecund.**
V0011.0+	**BUL-E0761:002-**	**Power to which sacrifice is made; here: Earth-shrine (*teng*) is promised human sacrifice (child) if it makes barren woman fecund.**
V0011.0+	**BUL-E1267:002-**	**Power to which sacrifice is made; here: Child promised as sacrifice to an earth-shrine.**
V0012.4.0+	**BUL-E0674:001-**	**Animals as sacrifice; here: A fowl is used in every religious ritual.**
V0012.4.06+	**BUL-E0259:139-146**	**Sheep (ram) as sacrifice; here: Ram sent by God to be sacrificed to an earth-shrine instead of firstborn child (girl).**
V0012.4.06+	**BUL-E0292:030-032**	**Sheep (ram) as sacrifice; here: Ram, coming down from the sky, is to be killed in a girl's stead.**
V0012.4.06+	**BUL-E0572:097-099**	**Sheep (ram) as sacrifice; here: Ram sent by God to be sacrificed to an earth-shrine instead of human being (girl).**

V0012.4.06+	BUL-E0761:080-082	Sheep (ram) as sacrifice; here: Sheep and other animals sent down by God to be sacrificed to an earth-shrine (*teng*) instead of human being (girl).
V0012.4.11+	BUL-E0674:001-	Bird as sacrifice; here: Fowl as a sacrifice in every ritual.
V0012.4.11+	BUL-E0761:080-082	Bird as sacrifice; here: Birds (fowls and guinea-fowls) and other animals are sent down by God to be sacrificed to an earth-shrine (*teng*) instead of human being (girl).
V0012.9+	BUL-E0225:095	Libations; here: Girl, condemned to be sacrificed to an earth-shrine, must brew millet beer, which is offered as a libation to the earth-shrine.
V0012.9+	BUL-E0259:006-	Libations; here: Girl, who is to be sacrificed to an earth-shrine, must brew millet beer which is offered as a sacrificial drink to the earth-shrine.
V0012.9+	BUL-E0572:018-036	Libations; here: Girl to be sacrificed to earth-shrine has to grind flour for millet beer, which is offered as libation to earth-shrine.
V0012.9+	BUL-E0761:006-	Libations; here: Girl to be sacrificed to an earth-shrine (*teng*) must brew millet beer, which is offered as libation to an earth-shrine (*teng*).
V0012.9+	BUL-E1267:011,017	Libations; here: Millet beer is brewed as libation to earth-shrine before sacrificing daughter to it.
V0013.0+	BUL-E1267:002-	Shrines; here: Shrine claims sacrifice of girl promised to it for giving childless couple fecundity.
V0017.0.1+	BUL-E0259:003-	Sacrifice to deity in order to obtain favours; here: Sacrifice of firstborn child (girl) to earth-shrine in order to make barren wife fecund.
V0017.0.1+	BUL-E0572:005-007	Sacrifice to deity in order to obtain favours; here: Sacrifice of firstborn child promised to earth-shrine in order to make barren wife fecund.
V0017.0.1+	BUL-E0761:003-	Sacrifice to deity in order to obtain favours; here: Sacrifice of firstborn child promised to an earth-shrine (*teng*) in order to make barren woman fecund.
V0017.0.1+	BUL-E1267:002-	Sacrifice to deity in order to obtain favours; here: Sacrifice of child promised to earth-shrine to obtain fecundity.
V0060.0+	BUL-E0514:032-	Funeral rites; here: Leper (God) goes to mourn at his wife's father's funeral.
V0113.0+	BUL-E0225:079-096	Shrines; here: Girl (chief's daughter) is to be sacrificed to an earth-shrine.

V0113.0+	BUL-E0259:002-	Shrines; here: Man takes his barren wife to earth-shrine which makes her fecund in exchange for her firstborn child.
V0113.0+	BUL-E0259:003-	Shrines; here: Earth-shrine is promised the sacrifice of firstborn child if it gives children to barren wife.
V0113.0+	BUL-E0489:002-	Shrines; here: Earth (earth-shrine) claims daughter as sacrifice to it if man's wife gives birth to many children;
V0113.0+	BUL-E0572:002	Shrines; here: Man consults earth-shrine in order to be granted children;
V0113.0+	BUL-E0572:005-006	Shrines; here: Earth-shrine claims sacrifice of first-born child (girl) for making barren wife fecund.
V0113.0+	BUL-E0761:002-003	Shrines; here: Barren woman consults an earth-shrine (*teng*) in order to give birth to children.
V0113.0+	BUL-E0761:003	Shrines; here: Firstborn child promised to an earth-shrine (*teng*) if it makes barren woman fecund.
V0201.0+	BUL-E0008:059	God; here: People in God's house are mixed (men and women).
V0201.0+	BUL-E0008:059	God; here: God sends woman from the sky to prevent sacrifice of girl.
V0201.0+	BUL-E0225:096	God; here: God sends ram in order to save girl from being sacrificed to an earth-shrine.
V0210.0+	BUL-E0259:138-	God; here: God sends ram and orders it to be sacrificed instead of a human being.
V0201.0+	BUL-E0292:030-031	God; here: Ram sent down from the sky (God) to prevent girl from being killed.
V0201.0+	BUL-E0402:002-	God; here: God lets Man die and return and Moon die and remain dead.
V0201.0+	BUL-E0426:012-	God; here: God (the sky) sends his daughters down to earth where they cook millet porridge for three bachelors.
V0201.0+	BUL-E0438:017-040	God; here: God sends a bull to take Common-Son-Of-Ten-Women's meat.
V0201.0+	BUL-E0438:049	God; here: God takes Common-Son-Of-Ten-Women, wrestling with his bull, into the sky.
V0201.0+	BUL-E0438:050	God; here: God has to judge the case between Common-Son-Of-Ten-Women and his bull.
V0201.0+	BUL-E0489:017-027	God; here: Brothers prophesy that God will save their sister in a wonderful way from being sacrificed.

V0201.0+	BUL-E0503:007-	God; here: God sends his daughter, disguised as a half-woman, to the earth in order to force a man to marry her.
V0201.0+	BUL-E0503:028-034	God; here: God lives in a house under the earth.
V0201.0+	BUL-E0503:054-057	God; here: God gives many gifts to his daughter and her husband when they return to the young man's family.
V0201.0+	BUL-E0514:006-	God; here: God transforms into a leper and marries chief's daughter.
V0201.0+	BUL-E0514:045	God; here: God resuscitates chief with a magic tail.
V0201.0+	BUL-E0514:046	God; here: God explains to chief that he has turned himself into a leper in order to force the chief's daughter to marry.
V0201.0+	BUL-E0572:097-099	God; here: God sends ram down from the sky to be sacrificed instead of a human being (girl).
V0201.0+	BUL-E0674:001-002	God; here: God creates man and wife and gives them a hen and a cock.
V0201.0+	BUL-E0761:080-	God; here: God sends down animals to be used as sacrifices instead of a human being (girl).
V0201.0+	BUL-E1328:032	God; here: God sends Hare a hoe, farm products and domestic animals.
V0201.0+	BUL-E1435:033-039	God; here: God sends supernatural being to save girl from being killed.
V0201.0+	BUL-E1698:001	God; here: God offers himself as food.
V0201.0+	BUL-E1698:001,006	God; here: God (Naawen), identified with the sky, ascends after an old woman broke a taboo.
V0201.0+	BUL-E1698:005	God; here: God makes it taboo to add a certain spice to the meat.
V0201.0+	BUL-E1856:001-	God; here: God and a river argue with one another over who is dependent on whom.
V0201.0+	BUL-E1856:033	God; here: No one can argue with the sky (God).
V0201.0+	BUL-E1856:039-040	God; here: God sends rain for a river which has dried up.
V0211.2.1.1+	BUL-E0514:006-	Christ disguised as leper; here: God disguised as leper marries chief's daughter.
V0232.3+	BUL-E1445:004-	Angels supply food to mortal; here: Women from the sky (God) descend to earth and prepare food for lone hunter.

W0126.0+	BUL-E0514:053-054	Disobedience; here: Magic tail loses its force when it is taken into a room against God's instructions.
W0141.0+	BUL-E0259:022-	Talkativeness; here: Girl is rebuked by her mother for being too talkative.
W0181.0+	BUL-E0503:073-080	Jealousy; here: Jealous former chief incites his people against boy who returned from God with God's daughter and many men, women and riches;
X0700.0+	BUL-E0674:008-	Humor concerning sex; here: Primeval man and woman do not know how to perform sex, they are taught how to do it by a cock.
Z0071.6+	BUL-E1435:008-010	Formulistic number: nine; here: Daughter condemned to be killed on the ninth day with nine sharpened knives.
Z0118.3+	BUL-E1856:001-	River personified; here: River argues with the sky (God) over who is dependent on whom.
Z0251.0+	BUL-E0438:001-	Boy hero; here: Common-Son-Of-Ten-Women defeats ogre Beard-Covers-River and later wrestles with God's bull.

VI. INDEX OF TALE TYPES ACCORDING TO AARNE-THOMPSON'S INDEX

AaTh 0100ff.+	**Wild Animals and Domestic Animals.**	BUL-E0182
AaTh 0150ff.+	**Man and Wild Animals.**	BUL-E0182 BUL-E1328
AaTh 0160B*+	**The Hare's Last Will.**	BUL-E1328
AaTh 0219*+	**Miscellaneous Tales of Domestic Animals.**	BULE-0182 BUL-E0426 BUL-E0674
AaTh 0300ff.+	**Supernatural Adversaries.**	BUL-E0438
AaTh 0334+	**Household of the Witch.**	BUL-E0426
AaTh 0335+	**Death's Messengers.**	BUL-E0402
AaTh 0400ff.+	**Supernatural or Enchanted Husband (Wife) or Other Relatives.**	BUL-E0182 BUL-E0426 BUL-E0503
AaTh 0450+	**Little Brother and Little Sister.**	BUL-E0489
AaTh 0500ff.+	**Supernatural Helpers.**	BUL-E0008 BUL-E0225 BUL-E0259 BUL-E0489 BUL-E0572 BUL-E0761 BUL-E0920 BUL-E1267 BUL-E1328 BUL-E1435 BUL-E1445
AaTh 0513+	**The Extraordinary Companions.**	BUL-E0438
AaTh 0530ff.+	**Animals as Helpers.**	BUL-E0008 BUL-E0225 BUL-E0292 BUL-E0674
AaTh 0545+	**The Cat as Helper.**	BUL-E0182 BUL-E0426
AaTh 0645+	**The Three Brothers.**	BUL-E0182

AaTh 0650A	Strong John.	BUL-E0438
AaTh 0650B	The Quest for a Strong Companion.	BUL-E0438
AaTh 0654+	The Three Brothers.	BUL-E0426
AaTh 0670+	The Animal Languages [...] The Advice of the Cock.	BUL-E0674
AaTh 0700ff.+	Other Tales of the Supernatural.	BUL-E0438
AaTh 0750A+	The Wishes.	BUL-E0489
AaTh 0750ff.+	God Repays and Punishes.	BUL-E0489 BUL-E1698 BUL-E1856
AaTh 0750ff.+	Religious Tales.	BUL-E0008 BUL-E0225 BUL-E0259 BUL-E0292 BUL-E0572 BUL-E0761 BUL-E0920 BUL-E1267 BUL-E1435
AaTh 0751A*+	A Man invites God to his house... [he] orders that a beggar, who has come to his door, be driven away... The beggar, it turns out, was God himself.	BUL-E0514
AaTh 0753A+	Unsuccessful Resuscitation.	BULE-0514
AaTh 0779+	Miscellaneous Divine Rewards and Punishments.	BUL-E0514
AaTh 0853+	The Hero Catches the Princess with her Own Words.	BULE-0514
AaTh 0900+	King Thrushbeard.	BUL-E0514
AaTh 0930ff.+	Tales of Fate.	BUL-E0259 BUL-E0292 BUL-E0572 BUL-E0761 BUL-E1267 BUL-E1435
AaTh 0934D	Nothing Happens without God.	BUL-E1856
AaTh 1070+	Wrestling Contest.	BUL-E0438

AaTh 1430ff.+	The Foolish Couple.	BUL-E0674
AaTh 1440ff.+	Stories about a Woman (Girl).	BUL-E0259 BUL-E0292 BUL-E0489 BUL-E0572 BUL-E0761 BUL-E0920 BUL-E1267 BUL-E1435
AaTh 1550ff.+	Stories about Married Couples.	BUL-E0674

VII. GLOSSARY OF WORDS IN BULI

biik, pl. *bisa*	n. 'child (male or female, related or unrelated, human or not), boy [...], descendant [...]' (Kröger BED), also 'son' or 'boy' in a wide sense of the word, i.e. any male person of a younger generation or any junior person to whom an elder may give orders. Thus a man of sixty will be a *biik*, a junior, 'son' or 'boy', to a man of eighty years of age.
bogluk, pl. *bogluta*	n. 'shrine or sacred object that receives sacrifices' (Kröger BED).
buuri, def. *buuni*, pl. *buura*, or (rare) *bue*	n. '1. kind, race, species, genus, type, sort [...] 2. lineage of varying span (from nuclear family up to the largest subdivisions of the Bulsa, e.g. *Atuga-bisa*), related group, family, people of one compound, people of one section or subsection, clan, village (*buuri* is esp. used, if the people of the lineage concerned do not form a local unit. Married women of another clan are not included [...]' (Kröger BED).
dabiak, pl. *dabaasa*	n. 'inner compound yard surrounded by living quarters, courtyard (cf. *nang-kpieng* n. cattle yard)' (Kröger BED).
dalong, pl. *dalongta*	n. 'outer room': 'room (*dok*) that forms a building unit with the adjacent *dayiik* (*dayiik* can be entered only through *dalong*; *dalong* can be used for staying there in daytime and for sleeping, *dayiik* only for sleeping).' (Kröger BED).
dayiik, pl. *dayiisa*	n. 'inner room': 'sleeping-room, bedroom, a room that forms a building unit with the adjacent *dalong* (*dayiik* can only be entered through the *dalong* and is esp. [built as] a sleeping-room and store [room] for very valuable objects and personal possession[s].' (Kröger BED).
dok, pl. *diina*	n. '1. room, hut, a round square house within the compound with either a flat roof (*gbong*) or a conical thatched roof [...] 2. set of rooms around an inner courtyard (*dabiak*) of a compound. compartment of a compound in charge of a woman who is called *dok-nyono* (owner of a compartment) [...] 3. Lineage segment of varying span [...], household, community [...]' (Kröger BED).
dung, pl. *dungsa*	n. 'four-legged, big animal; in a narrow, ritual sense only used for goat, sheep, cow and dog [...]' (Kröger BED), i.e. [domestic] animals, used in Bulsa economy and in sacrifices. - *Goai dungsa*, 'wild animals of the bush'; *yeri dungsa* 'domestic animals' (Kröger BED).
guuk, pl. *guuta*	n. 'ruin, ruined house, abandoned ancient settlement, (flat) hillock, where abandoned settlement formerly stood, rooms in a compound that have been destroyed by rain (compound still inhabited) [...] *guu(k)-yeri* [...] n., the house (not necessarily a ruin) where the ancestor of the inhabitants of several houses had lived, before various groups left that house to found their own houses.' (Kröger BED).

gbiim — n., onomatopoetic rendering of a sound of an unidentified bird, also called *gbiin*, pl. *gbiinsa* (cf. Kröger BED). This bird appears frequently in Bulsa tales as a messenger announcing some misfortune or unlucky accident which has happened or will happen.

jaab, pl. *nganta* — n. '1. thing [...], something, anything [...] 2. animal [...], beast, creature, figure (e.g. unrecognizable person), unidentified spirit or ghost (or used to avoid mentioning the name of a supernatural being), being (n.), person [...], somebody, someone, anybody, anyone [...]' (Kröger BED)

kaam, pl. *kaata* — n. A liquid spice prepared from the ashes of millet-stalks: 'Ashes of millet straw, water filtered through these ashes (used as an ingredient for soups)' (Kröger BED)

kikiruk, pl. *kikita* — n. 'fairy, ogre, monster (often harmful, can be born in a deformed or precocious child or in twins [...])' (Kröger BED) In the Bulsa tales, a *kikiruk* is usually a being of the bush or wildernis in contrast to the sphere inhabitated and cultivated by human beings.

kingkangi, pl. *kinganga* — n. 'inner wall of a compound, e.g. dividing cattle yard and set of rooms with their own yard. any other wall in the living quarters that can have a stepping ladder (*tiili*), also outer wall of living quarters (but not outer wall of cattle yard [...])' (Kröger BED).

kisi — v. '1. to be forbidden, to be taboo, to be avoided, to be improper; to forbid, to taboo, to avoid - *Ku a kisi kama*. It is taboo (forbidden) [...] 2. to hate [...] 3. to restrain (oneself) [...]' (Kröger BED).

kisuk, pl. *kisuta, kisita* — n. 'taboo, forbidden action, food or thing' (Kröger BED).

ko-biik, pl. *ko-bisa* — cmpd. n., lit. 'father's child', 'specific patrilineal raltive, descendant of another son of a common ancestor. If *ko-bisa* is contrasted with *ma-bisa*, *ko-bisa* refers to the more distant relationship or lineage segment, *ma-bisa* to the closer one.' (Kröger BED)

kum(u), kum(i) — v. '1. to mourn, to condole, to cry, to weep, to lament [...] *kum kuumu* to conduct a funeral (lit. to weep over a death. before the funeral you should not weep), to perform the funeral ceremonies [...] 2. [the verb is] used to describe the sounds and voices of several animals and lifeless things: to sound, to make a noise ... [e.g.] to twitter, chirp (birds) ...' (Kröger BED) The word *kum* also refers to the singing of funeral dirges as well as to the uttering of wailing sounds at a funeral ceremony, presribed by Bulsa custom.

kusung, pl. *kusungta* — n. 'shelter in front of the compound (open form usually rectangular, often covered with stalks of guinea corn, reception place for guests. favourite haunt of young and old men when they have finished work or in between times at work) [...]' (Kröger BED) - The *kusung* is also the place where the men gather for conversation.

nangkpieng, pl. *nangkpiengsa* — n. cattle yard, stockyard in the centre of a compund (*yeri*).

Naawen, or *Naawon* — n. < *nàab* chief, and *wen* sky, sun, god, the Sky-god, God, cf. *wen*.

saab, def. *saamu* — n. '[...] thick millet porridge, millet gruel' (Kröger BED); staple food of the Bulsa.

segri — v. 'to dedicate a child to a spirit who is henceforth the guardian spirit (*segi*) of the child (giving a name is included in a *segrika*) [...]' (Kröger BED).

segrika — v.n. 'ritual of acquiring a guardian spirit; naming ceremony' (Kröger BED). -

tanggbain, pl. *tanggbana* — n. < *teng*, 'earth' and *gbain*, 'skin'; 'earth-shrine; spirit of an earth-shrine, sacred place of the earth divinity, inhabited by an earth-spirit who receives regular sacrifices from the (human) owner of the *tanggbain*; it may be a sacred grove, tree, rock, hill, river, lake etc. [...]' (Kröger BED).

teng, pl. *tengsa* — n. '1. earth, ground, piece of land, plot, space [...] 2. earth, world [...] 3. Earth (a god or shrine [...]) [...] 4. country, land, area [...] 5. town, village, settlement [...]' (Kröger BED).

waaung, pl. *wiima* — n. 'monkey (several species of smaller long-tailed monkeys, e.g. Red Patas Monkey, Erythrocebus patas, not including bigger species such as baboon [...])' (Kröger BED).

wen, def. *weni*, pl. *wena* — n. The basic meanings of the word *wen* are: '1. sky, heaven [...] 2. sun [...] 3. weather, climate [...] season, period, time (of the year [...]) 5. God (the high God in Heaven ...).' But the word *wen* also means: '6. [the] religious concept denoting the 'alter ego' or 'personal god' of an individual (on the day of the *wen-piirika* the *wen* of a person descends from the sun and enters into a stone of *wen-bogluk* where it is henceforth worshipped as the *tuntueta-wen*, the saliva-*wen* of the living person; as this personal *wen* is also responsible for the person's destiny on earth, *wen* can also be translated by: destiny, fortune, luck...' (Kröger BED).

wen-piirika — comp. n. 'Ritual in which a divine power comes down from heaven (sun) [*wen*] to be henceforth worshipped in a shrine [*bogluk*]. (In some parts of the Bulsa area this ceremony is called *wen-seka* [<*se* v. to build, viz. the shrine or altar])' (Kröger BED).

VIII. BIBLIOGRAPHY

Titels marked with * contain Bulsa stories and/or other specimens of oral art of the Bulsa.

Aarne, Antti and **Thompson, Stith**
1961 The Types of the Folktale - A Classification and Bibliography. Second Revision. FFC No. 184. Helsinki: Suomalainen Tiedeakatemia. [Reprint 1981]

Agalic, James
1978* Story-Telling among the Bulsa of Northern Ghana. Zeitschrift für Ethnologie, vol. 103, p. 261-278.

1981 Sacrifice in Bulsa Traditional Religion (unpublished B.A. dissertation) Cape Coast, 97 p.

1983* Buli Yam Saka Wamagisima - Proverbs of the Bulsa. Institute of African Studies, University of Ghana [Legon, Accra], 40 p. (mimeographed manuscript).

Baumann, Hermann
1936 Schöpfung und Urzeit im Mythus afrikanischer Völker. Berlin: Dietrich Reimer.

Brüggemann, Anne
1986* Das Zwillingsmotiv in westafrikanischen Erzählungen der Bulsa, Mossi und Bambara. Kulturanthropologische Studien, vol. 13, Hohenschäftlarn bei München: Klaus Renner.

The **Concise Oxford Dictionary** of Current English
^{8}1990 Eighth Edition, edited by R. E. Allan. Oxford: Clarendon Press.

Haring, Lee
1982 Malagasy Tale Index, FFC 231, Helsinki: Suomalainen Tiedeakatemia.

Heermann, Ingrid
1981 Subsistenzwirtschaft und Marktwirtschaft im Wandel - Wirtschaftsethnologische Forschungen bei den Bulsa in Nord-Ghana. Kulturanthropologische Studien, vol. 2, Hohenschäftlarn bei München: Klaus Renner.

Kröger, Franz
1978 Übergangsriten im Wandel - Kindheit, Reife und Heirat bei den Bulsa in Nord-Ghana. Kulturanthropologische Studien, vol. 1, Hohenschäftlarn bei München: Klaus Renner.

1980 The Friend of the Family or the Pok Nong Relation of the Bulsa of Northern Ghana. In: Sociologus, vol. 30, p. 153-165.

1982 Ancestor Worship among the Bulsa of Northern Ghana - Religious, Social and Economic Aspects. Kulturanthropologische Studien, vol. 9, Hohenschäftlarn bei München: Klaus Renner.

1984 The notion of the moon in the calendar and religion of the Bulsa. In: Systèmes de Pensée, Cahier 7, p. 149-151.

1986 Der Ritualkalender der Bulsa (Nordghana). In: Anthropos, vol. 81, p. 671-681.

1987 Traditionelle und schulische Erziehung bei den Bulsa in Nordghana. In: Zeitschrift für Ethnologie, vol. 112, p. 269-283.

1988a Die Terrakottafunde des Koma-Gebietes (Nordghana). In: Paideuma, vol. 34, 1988, p. 129-142.

1992 Buli-English Dictionary - With an Introductory Grammar and an Index English-Buli. Münster: LIT-Verlag.

Schott, Rüdiger

1970* Aus Leben und Dichtung eines westafrikanischen Bauernvolkes - Ergebnisse völkerkundlicher Forschungen bei den Bulsa in Nord-Ghana 1966/67. Veröffentl.d.Arbeitsgemeinschaft für Forschung des Landes Nordrhein-Westfalen, Reihe Geisteswissenschaften, Heft 163, Köln und Opladen: Westdeutscher Verlag.

1973* *Kisuk*-Tiere der Bulsa - Zur Frage des 'Totemismus' in Nord-Ghana. In: Kölner Ethnologische Mitteilungen, vol. 5, p. 439-459.

1973/74* Haus- und Wildtiere in der Religion der Bulsa (Nord-Ghana). In: Paideuma - Mitteilungen zur Kulturkunde, vol. 19/20, p. 280-306.

1977* Sources for a History of the Bulsa in Northern Ghana. In: Paideuma, vol. 23, p. 141-168.

1978 Das Recht gegen das Gesetz: Traditionelle Vorstellungen und moderne Rechtsprechung bei den Bulsa in Nordghana. In: Recht und Gesellschaft - Festschrift für Helmut Schelsky zum 65. Geburtstag, hrsg. von Friedrich Kaulbach und Werner Krawietz, Berlin, p. 605-636.

1979 Mission und Entwicklung in Afrika - dargestellt am Beispiel der Bulsa in Nordghana. In: Weltmission in der Weltkrise..., ed. by Johannes Dörmann, St.Augustin, p. 63-80.

1980a Justice versus the Law: Traditional and Modern Jurisdiction among the Bulsa of Northern Ghana. In: Law and State - A Biannual Collection of Recent German Contributions to these Fields, vol. 21, Tübingen, p. 121-133.

1980b Le droit contre la loi: conceptions traditionelles et juridiction actuelle chez les Bulsa au Ghana du Nord. In: Gérard Conac (Ed.): Dynamiques et finalités des Droits africains. Recherches Panthéon-Sorbonne, Université de Paris I, Série Sciences Juridiques, Paris, p. 279-306.

1980c Triviales und Transzendentes: Einige Aspekte afrikanischer Rechtstraditionen unter besonderer Berücksichtigung der Bulsa in Nord-Ghana. In: Entstehung und Wandel rechtlicher Traditionen. Historische Anthropologie vol. 2, hrsg. von Wolfgang Fikentscher, Herbert Franke und Oskar Köhler, Freiburg/München, p. 265-301.

1980d Recht und Entwicklung in Afrika. In: Afrika zwischen Tradition und Fortschritt, hrsg. von Heinz Dietrich Ortlieb und Jürgen Zwernemann. Veröffentlichung des HWWA-Instituts für Wirtschaftsforschung. Hamburg, p. 69-88.

1980e* Vengeance and Violence among the Bulsa of Northern Ghana. In: La vengeance - Études d'ethnologie, d'histoire et de philosophie, vol. I: Vengeance et pouvoir dans quelques sociétés extra-occidentales, ed. by Raymond Verdier, Paris, p. 167-199.

1981a Märkte und Menschen in der Savanne - Entwicklungsprobleme in Nordghana. In: Leben am Rande der Sahara, hrsg. vom Bundesministerium für wirtschaftliche Zusammenarbeit in Verbindung mit dem Rautenstrauch-Joest Museum, Köln, p. 38-51.

1981b Law and Development in Africa. In: Law and State -A Biannual Collection of Recent German Contributions, vol. 24, Tübingen, p. 30-41.

1982a (mit Franz Kröger) Language and Culture of the Bulsa in Ghana. In: Recent German Research on Africa: Language and Culture, Part 1, German Africanistic Research, ed. by Bernd Heine. Edited by the Deutsche Forschungsgemeinschaft, Bonn/Tübingen, p. 76-79.

1982b* Der gegessene Gott - Mensch und Kosmos in afrikanischen Weltbildern. In: Die Entdeckung des Kosmos durch den Menschen, Studium Generale Wintersemester 1980/81, Schriftenreihe der Westfälischen Wilhelms-Universität, Heft 4, Münster, p. 89-135.

1982c Ehe und Familie in einer Gesellschaft westafrikanischer Bodenbauer (Bulsa in Nordghana). In: Ehe und Familie in verschiedenen Kulturen, Vortragsreihe 1981/82, hrsg. von Bernhard Mensen SVD, St.Augustin, p. 55-74.

1983* Glaube und Brauch der Schmiede bei den Bulsa in Nordghana. In: Hans-Peter Duerr (Ed.): Sehnsucht nach dem Ursprung - Zu Mircea Eliade. Frankfurt/M., p. 303-335.

1985 A Case of Living Law: Traditional and Modern Jurisdiction among the Bulsa in Northern Ghana. In: Quaderni Fiorentini per la storia del pensiero giuridico moderno, vol. 14, p. 149-172.

1986 Fetische Gur-sprachiger Völker (Tallensi, Bulsa, Lyela) in der westafrikanischen Savanne. In: Josef Franz Thiel (Ed.): Was sind Fetische? Roter Faden zur Ausstellung, vol. 9, Frankfurt/M., p. 171-230.

1987a Traditional Law and Religion among the Bulsa of Northern Ghana. In: Journal of African Law, vol. 31, p. 58-69.

1987b* Serment et voeux chez des ethnies voltaïques (Lyéla, Bulsa, Tallensi) en Afrique Occidentale. In: Droit et Cultures - Revue semestrielle d'anthropologie et d'histoire, vol. 14, p. 29-56.

1988a Traditional systems of social security and their present-day crisis in West Africa. In: F. von Benda-Beckmann et al. (Ed.): Between Kinship and the State - Social Security and Law in Developing Countries, Dordrecht (Holland) - Providence (Richmond, USA), p. 89-107.

1988b* Eidos und Ethos - Über einige Fragen der ethnographischen Inhaltsanalyse afrikanischer Erzählungen. In: Münchner Beiträge zur Völkerkunde, vol. 1 (Festschrift für László Vajda), München, p. 205-217.

1988c Die Ethnogenese von Völkern in Afrika. In: Rheinisch-Westfälische Akademie der Wissenschaften, Abhandlung 78, Studien zur Ethnogenese, vol. 2, Opladen, p. 7-42.

1988d* Les histoires des enfants terribles chez les Bulsa (Ghana du Nord) et les Mossi (Burkina Faso) comme sources ethnographiques. In: W. J. G. Möhlig, H. Jungraithmayr, J. F, Thiel (Ed.): Die Oralliteratur in Afrika als Quelle zur Erforschung der traditionellen Kulturen. Collectanea Instituti Anthropos, vol. 36, p. 125-138.

1989a Heil, Unheil und Verantwortung bei schriftlosen Völkern. In: Jahrbuch für Rechtssoziologie und Rechtstheorie, vol. XIV, p. 97-120.

1989b Bericht über laufende Forschungen zur Motivanalyse afrikanischer Erzählungen im Seminar für Völkerkunde der Universität Münster. In: Fabula - Zeitschrift für Erzählforschung, vol. 30, p. 83-95.

1989c* Gott in Erzählungen der Bulsa (Nord-Ghana). In: Paideuma, vol. 35, p. 257-272.

1990a* Afrikanische Erzählungen als religionsethnologische Quellen - dargestellt am Beispiel von Erzählungen der Bulsa in Nordghana. Rheinisch-Westfälische Akademie der Wissenschaften, Geisteswissenschaften, Vorträge G 305. Opladen: Westdeutscher Verlag, 74 p.

1990b Die Macht des Überlieferungswissens in schriftlosen Gesellschaften. In: Saeculum, vol. 41, Heft 3/4, p. 273-316.

1990c* Project of Comparative Analysis of Motifs and Themes in African Tales. In: Asian Folklore Studies, Nagoya, vol. XLIX-1, p. 140-142.

1990d* 'La femme enceinte éventrée' - Variabilité et contexte socio-culturel d'un type de conte ouest-africain. In: Veronika Görög (Ed.): D'un conte ... à l'autre - La variabilité dans la littérature orale, Paris, p. 327-339.

1990e Das Gesetz gegen die Religion? Recht und Religion im sozialen Wandel - dargestellt an Beispielen aus Westafrika. In: Ludwig Hagemann und Ernst Pulsfort (Ed.): 'Ihr alle aber seid Brüder' - Festschrift für A. Th. Khoury zum 60. Geburtstag, Würzburger Forschungen zur Missions- und Religionswissenschaft, Würzburg, p. 557-574.

1991 La loi contre la religion? Sur le rapport du droit et de la religion dans le changement social à partir d'exemples de l'Afrique de l'Ouest. In: Droit et Cultures - Revue semestrielle d'anthropologie et d'histoire, Paris, vol. 21, p. 16-31.

1992 Die soziale und religiöse Stellung des Bulsa-Schmiedes. In: Elisabeth Tietmeyer (Hrsg.): Zwei Eisen im Feuer - Schmieden im Kulturvergleich. Landschaftsverband Westfalen-Lippe, Westfälisches Museumsamt, Münster, p. 39-49.

Surgy, Albert de
1984 Origine et fonction humanisante de la mort selon les Mwaba (Togo du nord). Anthropos, vol. 79: 129-143.

Thompson, Stith
1955 Motif-Index of Folk-Literature. Revised and Enlarged Edition. 6 vol. Bloomington & Indianapolis: Indiana University Press.

Zwernemann, Jürgen
1961 Les notions du dieu-ciel chez quelques tribus voltaïques. In: Bulletin IFAN, série B, vol. 23, p. 243-272.

1968 Die Erde in Vorstellungswelt und Kultpraktiken der sudanischen Völker. Berlin: Dietrich Reimer.

1985 Erzählungen aus der westafrikanischen Savanne. Studien zur Kulturkunde, vol. 81. Stuttgart: Steiner Verlag.

FORSCHUNGEN ZU SPRACHEN UND KULTUREN AFRIKAS
RESEARCH ON AFRICAN LANGUAGES AND CULTURES
RECHERCHES SUR LES LANGUES ET CULTURES AFRICAINES

In dieser Reihe sollen Kulturen afrikanischer Völker durch Zeugnisse ihrer Sprachen wissenschaftlich dargestellt werden. Vereint und nicht getrennt werden daher die Linguistik und Ethnographie der Völker Afrikas in den "Forschungen zu Sprachen und Kulturen Afrikas" zu Wort kommen. Die Reihe soll vor allem der Veröffentlichung von mündlichen Überlieferungen afrikanischer Völker dienen - ihrer "oral history" ebenso wie ihren Erzählungen, Märchen, Sagen, Sprichwörtern und anderen Texten in afrikanischen Sprachen mit kommentierten Übersetzungen. Grundlage hierfür sind Wörterbücher, sofern sie über den lexikalischen Bestand der afrikanischen Sprachen hinaus auch die Kulturen der betreffenden Völker dokumentieren. Etwas vom Reichtum der Geisteswelt Afrikas soll mit den "Forschungen zu Sprachen und Kulturen Afrikas" sichtbar gemacht und festgehalten werden.

The present series is to represent the cultures of African peoples by publishing source materials in their own languages. The scientific disciplines of African linguistics and ethnography are to work together, and not separately in the series "Research on African Languages and Cultures". The series is meant, above all, to publish oral traditions of African peoples - their "oral history" as well as their stories and fairy tales, their legends and myths, their proverbs and other texts in African languages together with annotated translations. Dictionaries will also be published in this series, as far as they document not only African languages, but also the cultural heritage of the particular peoples. The series "Research in African Languages and Cultures" wants to show and to record some of the spiritual riches of Africa.

Dans cette nouvelle série, des peuples africains rendront témoignage de leurs civilisations par des textes publiés dans leurs propres langues. Les sciences de la linguistique et de l'ethnographie d'Afrique doivent surmonter leur isolement et collaborer étroitement dans la série "Recherches sur les langues et les cultures africaines". La série doit servir surtout à la publication des traditions orales populaires, c'est-à-dire de la "oral history" des peuples africains de même qu'à la publication de leurs contes, légendes, proverbes et d'autres textes dans les langues africains aves des traductions commentées. Des dictionnaires seront publiés également dans cette série pourvu qu'ils ne font pas seulement des inventaires léxiques, mais qu'ils documentent là-dessus aussi les civilisations reflétées dans les langues africaines. La série "Recherches sur les langues et les cultures africaines" a pour but de manifester et de documenter une partie de la grande richesse spirtuelle des peuples africains.

Bd./Vol. 1: **Franz Kröger: Buli-English Dictionary with an Introductory Grammar and an Index Buli-English. 1992. xvi + 572 Seiten/-pages, mit 164 Zeichnungen/with 164 drawings.**

Mit etwa 4.000 Stichwörtern wird der Wortschatz des Buli, einer bislang so gut wie unerforschten Gur-Sprache (westafrikanische Klassensprache) der Bulsa in Nordghana, erfaßt und ins Englische übersetzt. Zu jeder Bedeutungsvariante wird mindestens ein Beispielsatz mit englischer Übersetzung beigefügt. - *The vocabulary of Buli, a hitherto almost unexplored Gur language (West African class language) of the Bulsa in North Ghana, is detailed in about 4,000 headwords together with English translations. Every semantic variant is explained by at least one exemplary sentence in Buli and English.*

Bd./Vol. 2: **Rüdiger Schott: Bulsa Sunsuelima - Folktales of the Bulsa in Northern Ghana. Series S: Folktales of the Supernatural. Volume 1: Tales of the Sky-God (*Wen, Naawen*). Part I. 1993. xiv + 412 Seiten/pages.**

Der vorliegende Teilband mit 21 Erzählungen über den Himmelsgott *Naawen* leitet eine Reihe von Veröffentlichungen des reichen Erzählguts der Bulsa in Nordghana ein. Die Erzählungen werden in der Originalsprache Buli und in wörtlicher englischer Übersetzung wiedergegeben sowie mit ausführlichen Anmerkungen, Stichwort-, Motiv- und Typenverzeichnissen sowie einem Glossar versehen. - *The present part-volume, being the first in a series of publications of folktales of the Bulsa in North Ghana, contains 21 folktales dealing with the Sky-god Naawen. The stories are published in Buli, the original language, together with verbatim English translations; appendices contain detailed notes and annotations to each story, followed by indices of keywords, motifs and tale-types, a glossary and a bibliography.*

Bd./Vol. 3: **Ulrike Blanc: Lieder in Erzählungen der Bulsa (Nordghana) - Eine musikethnologische Untersuchung. [Songs in Folktales of the Bulsa (North Ghana). A study in the ethnology of music] ca. vi + 160 Seiten/pages. 1993 (in Vorbereitung/in preparation).**

Die meisten Erzählungen der Bulsa enthalten Lieder als wesentliche Bestandteile. In der vorliegenden Studie werden mehrere, zu zwei Erzähltypen gehörende Lieder transkribiert und auf ihre musikalischen und narrativen Strukturen hin untersucht. - *Most of the Bulsa folktales contain songs as their constituent elements. Numerous songs belonging to two tale-types have been transcribed and analysed with regard to their musical and narrative structures.*